Alexander Pfeiffer, Nanditha Krishna,
Natalie Denk, Thomas Wernbacher (Editors)

MEDIA, **A**RTS AND **D**ESIGN (MAD) ANTHOLOGY II

MAD Pandemic: Stories of Change and Continuity during the COVID-19 Crisis

Editors: Alexander Pfeiffer, Nanditha Krishna,
Natalie Denk, Thomas Wernbacher

Cover: Constantin Kraus

Publisher: University of Krems Press.

Print: tredition GmbH, Halenreie 40-44, 22359 Hamburg

ISBN: 978-3-903470-10-1
DOI: https://doi.org/10.48341/hx6g-pw64

Contact:
Center for Applied Game Studies
Department for Arts and Cultural Studies
University for Continuing Education Krems
www.donau-uni.ac.at/ags
ags@donau-uni.ac.at

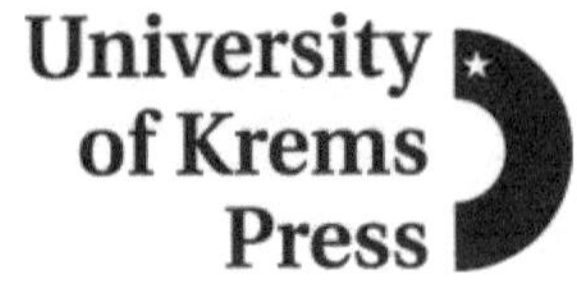

TABLE OF CONTENTS

FOREWORD

Over the course of history, the evolution of media, arts and design has dynamically mirrored society's growth, advancements, and transformation, reflecting human aspirations, desires, and the ever-changing landscape of existence.

Since its inception in 2020, the Media, Arts and Design (**MAD**) conference series has successfully drawn significant contributions and attendance from people across the world. The year 2020 saw two versions of MAD, namely the **Media, Arts and Design | Blockchain 2020 Conference** and the **Media, Arts and Design | AI 2020 Conference**, effectively witnessing a perfect amalgamation of technical, scientific, cultural discussions and contributions.

Jointly organized by the Drexel University's Department of Digital Media, supported by the Education Arcade at the Massachusetts Institute of Technology (MIT), the Learning Interactive Visualization Experience (LIVE) Lab at Texas A&M University, the Department for Arts and Cultural Sciences at Donau-Universität Krems, and the Conceptualizing Blockchain group at the University of Vaasa, the **Media, Arts and Design | Blockchain 2020 conference** was hosted online (due to the COVID-19 pandemic) by the Westphal College of Media Arts and Design at Drexel University in Philadelphia on the weekend of May 2-3, 2020. The conference aimed to explore Blockchain technologies and its impact on media, arts and design.

The **Media, Arts and Design | AI 2020 conference** was organized by the Center for Applied Game Studies at Donau-Universität Krems, the Department of Artificial Intelligence at University of Malta and the Department of Digital Media at Drexel University. The conference was further supported by the MIT Education Arcade at the Massachusetts Institute of Technology, the LIVE LAB the Texas A&M University and the Department of Communication Studies at the University of Vaasa. The conference took place on June 19th, 2020, and explored the intersections of Artificial Intelligence (A.I), and media, arts and design.

In 2020, the **6th International Conference on Cyber Security and Privacy in Communication Networks (ICCS)** included a special track organized by the MAD team with support from Thomas Gabriel Rüdiger. The track was based on the theme of cybercrimes in the field of game-studies and saw a variety of discussions on topics such as avatar and identity theft, misuse of credit card data, misuse of virtual goods, setup of pirate servers, terrorism planning through game chats, money laundering, Distributed Denial of Service (DDoS) attacks via games, sex offences, grooming in game chats, mobbing, and insulting offences.

On December 8, 2021, a special edition of the Media, Arts and Design Conference **MAD | 21 – THE FUTURE OF MEDIA, ARTS AND DESIGN** was held, exploring the metaverse, non-fungible token (NFTs), Blockchain technologies, visualizing what the future looks like for the fields of media, arts and design.

In 2022, we published our first anthology titled **Disruptive Technologies in Media, Arts and Design - A Collection of Innovative Research Case-Studies** with Springer. The anthology examined the use of technologies such as Artificial Intelligence (AI) and Blockchain within the media, arts and design sectors.

Also, in 2022, the **Media, Arts and Design Conference**, in its 4th edition, got to the heart of Emergent Technologies (Decentralized Networks, Artificial Intelligence, Virtual Worlds – Metaverse, Virtual and Augmented reality to name a few) in the domains of media, arts and design. It took a wide-ranging look at how the impact of emergent technologies in the fields of media, arts and design evolved socially, economically, and politically during times of crises such as the COVID-19 pandemic, simultaneously exploring the impact of these technologies in our personal lives. Hosted by Alexander Pfeiffer, Natalie Denk, and Michaela Wawra (University for Continuing Education Krems); Scot Osterweil (The MIT Education Arcade); Stephen Bezzina, Alexiei Dingli (University of Malta), Michael Wagner, Nick Jushchyshyn (Drexel University), Simone Kriglstein (Masaryk

University and AIT Austrian Institute of Technology), Klaus Neundlinger (Institute CE) and André Thomas (Texas A & M University), the conference stood out for its unique position paper tracks, wherein talks explored how communication and interaction in private as well as professional lives have changed over time due to emergent technologies.

In July 2023, we co-organized a multidisciplinary summer school event **VARIATIONS ON HOW TO PLAY** at the University for Continuing Education Krems, encompassing a broad range of discussions on topics delivered through diverse formats. The event delved into the impact of satellite traffic in space, utilizing Virtual Reality to enhance awareness, and provided unique outdoor learning experiences for children. Attendees explored the evolving landscape of Cinematic Virtual Reality and experienced the expressive power of language within improvisational theater. A workshop provided a deep dive into the complexities and challenges unique to filmmaking in China, enriching the event's offerings. The conference day further expanded the discourse, addressing the transformation of speech acts, considerations for interactive literature exhibitions, the gamification of statistics, and the integration of AI in media, arts and design. The event inspired the launch of **DJAKK**, or **Digitales Journal für Angewandte Kunst und Kultur** by the Department for Arts and Cultural Studies, a significant milestone in advancing the discourse in culture and the arts, with its inaugural issue published in mid-2024.

Media, Arts and Design Anthology-II

Cut to the present: In the current edition of our MAD Anthology, authors delve into the intricate realms of virtual and emergent technologies. Addressing topics such as Augmented Reality (AR), Virtual Reality (VR) and online learning, the authors expound upon these thematic areas in a confluence of articles.

Peer reviewed papers:

I.   In *"Gaming as the Gateway to a Happier place in the COVID-19 pandemic"*, Michaela Wawra explores gaming and guilds as communities.

II.   In *"You, [Subject Name Here], Must Be The Pride Of [Subject Hometown Here]"*, Rudolf Thomas Inderst explores and surveys the representation of AI in selected digital games.

III.   In *"On-Site Only? Non-Inclusive Nostalgia for Pre-Lockdown Academia"*, Hossein Mohammadzade and Atefe Najjar Mansoor write on virtual and distance learning and nostalgia associated with physical classroom-based learning.

IV.   In *"Medical Art and The Pandemic"* Hana Pokojná explores biomedical education, medical visualization, education, medical art, and science communication in the context of the COVID-19 pandemic.

V.   In *"Remodelling And Redesigning Education: Analogue To Digital"*, Nanditha Krishna reflects on her personal experiences with online learning during the COVID-19 pandemic.

VI.   In *"From DVD to Cloud Drive"*, Mo Li extensively writes on underground cinema and video activism in China.

VII.   In *"What Would Make a Robot Sad?"*, Alesha Serada explores soviet cinema, artificial intelligence, robots, media representation and utopia.

VIII.   In *"Place as assemblage and the virtual"*, Tania Berger examines experiencing place through layers of photovoice and virtual meeting tools, touching upon location and photovoice.

IX.	In *"How to Design Relational Working Cultures in Hybrid Environments"*, Klaus Neundlinger and Simone Rack discuss organizational culture, virtual collaboration, embodiment, team cooperation and hybrid office spaces.

Position Paper:

X.	In *"To Boldly Go Where No (Wo)Man Has Gone Before"*, Stephanie Wössner investigates future-oriented learning with extended reality and game-based learning.

Non-competitive contribution / experiment:

XI.	In their highly experimental paper, *"Immortality, Redemption, And Resilience: A Comparative Analysis Of Highlander (1986) And Star Wars: Episode Vi - Return Of The Jedi (1983)"*, Alexander Pfeiffer and Aria Turing (a fictional researcher created by ChatGPT) conduct a comparative analysis of two iconic sci-fi films, Highlander (Mulcahy, 1986) and Star Wars: Episode VI - Return of the Jedi (Lucas, 1983). The main objective of this contribution is to ignite a discussion on how to use AI in the academic writing process.

The Editors of this Anthology sincerely hope and wish for readers to have a gratifying and enjoyable experience reading this compilation of conference papers and position papers. We eagerly anticipate receiving more such outstanding contributions to our upcoming conference anthologies in the future.

These contributions, we believe, are highly instrumental in fostering an open, seamless exchange of ideas and knowledge within the media, arts and design communities. We wish to thank you for being a part of this engaging intellectual journey, and we greatly look forward to experiencing the continued growth of our discourse and community. The illustrations at the start of the respective chapters were created by authors using Midjourney 5.2. The input prompt consisted of the submission title, a preferred aspect ratio of 1:1, and a request to present it as an illustration.

Stay tuned: Media, Arts and Design (MAD) 2024

The Media, Arts and Design (MAD) 2024 Conference hopes to explore the human elements, specifically that of the potential of individuals within the MAD community to enact meaningful changes, leaving significantly lasting impacts on the world.

We invite academics, practitioners, and creative minds from around the globe (special note: aliens are also truly welcome) to submit their contributions that investigate innovative approaches, critical perspectives, and transformative practices in the (extended) field of media, arts and design. For more updated information (and timely updates), visit: https://www.mad-conferences.com.

Alexander Pfeiffer
Nanditha Krishna
Natalie Denk
Thomas Wernbacher

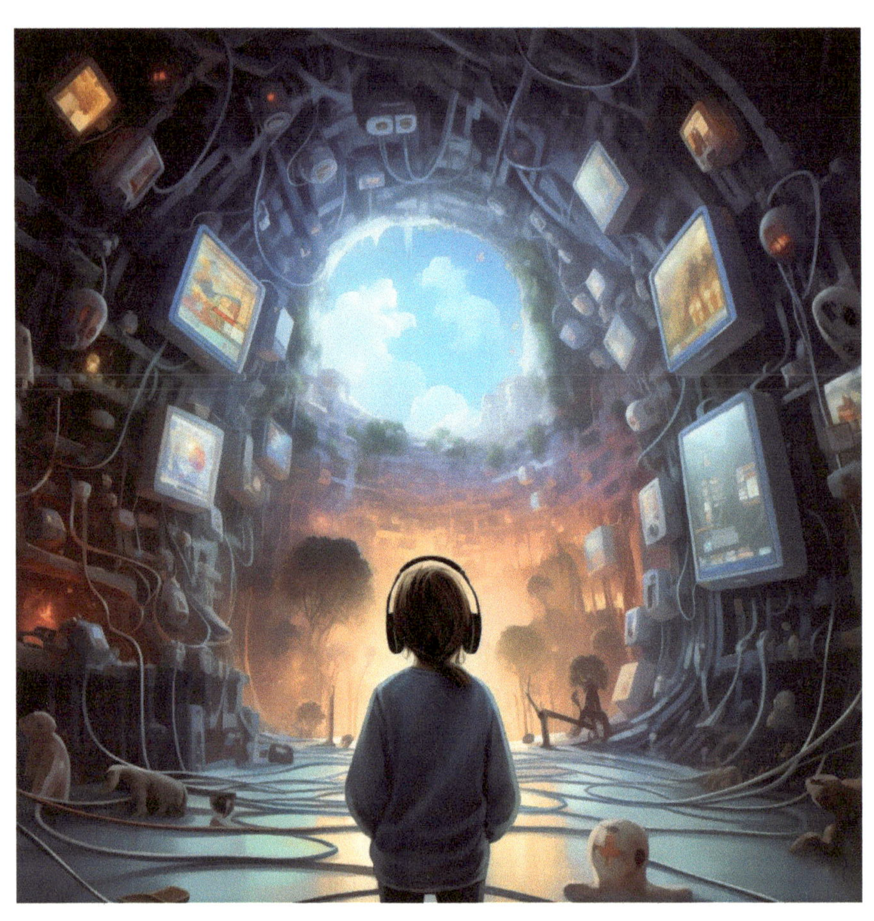

GAMING AS THE GATEWAY TO A HAPPIER PLACE IN THE COVID-19 PANDEMIC

Michaela Wawra

The COVID-19 pandemic affected the entire world and therefore also the gaming industry. Due to self-isolation, lockdowns, boredom and social isolation many people turned to online gaming as an outlet to stay connected and counter loneliness. Gaming suddenly changed to a full-fledged alternative to real-life socialization and could be considered as pro-social practice that even WHO has acknowledged. Massive Multiplayer Online Role-Playing Games (MMORPGs) such as the most prominent World of Warcraft were the most effective in fulfilling social needs as the player could create a character based on their appearance preferences and interact with others in the game to reach common goals. For social and high-end purposes many gamers get together in guilds to progress through content and for increased social interaction. The COVID-19 pandemic has influenced virtual social communities such as guilds such that they used the game as their escape from the pandemic and to cope with a changed environment. The objective was to determine the influence of the COVID-19 pandemic on the individual international players and how they thrived as a decentralized social structure to reach their common goals in a game in a changed environment. As a result, an explorative study was conducted to collect information on this topic. Therefore, a focus group of 6 international players was identified to analyze the different internal and external influences which impacted their gameplay and life and therefore the guild as an organization itself during the COVID-19 pandemic.

Keywords: World of Warcraft, MMORPGs, social isolation, COVID-19 pandemic

---

Introduction

The COVID-19 pandemic that affected the entire world was not only a serious health threat to the population but also a risk to entire industries. For reasons of self-isolation, many people turned to home entertainment and so also increasingly to online gaming (Statista, 2021). In a June 2020 survey, gamers worldwide reported spending 39% more time playing video games during the pandemic (Statista, 2021).

The fact that games can cheer up a person when they are supposed to sit isolated at home, was even recognized by the World Health Organization (WHO) which has been using the hashtag #PlayApartTogether, wherein it recommended gaming as a substitute for physical activity to help people stay at home and adhere to lockdown rules. In collaboration with game developers, WHO information about COVID-19 has even been integrated into games and platforms (Haug, et al., 2022; Sapienza, et al., 2020).

In light of the loss of physical and social interaction due to widespread social distancing, games and other screen-based activities were gaining in popularity to stay socially connected and be entertaining (Haug, et al., 2022; Sapienza, et al., 2020). Sapienza, et al., 2020 emphasized that the COVID-19 pandemic has impacted online gaming by increasing the attention towards it. Results from the Haug et al. (2022) study also found that there was an increase in gaming among respondents during the COVID-19 pandemic.

In Bengtsson et al.'s (2021) study, the importance and sociality of gaming gained prominence during COVID-19, as gaming served the purpose of socializing and maintaining friendships, which ultimately contributed to adolescents' description of online and multiplayer games as a full-fledged alternative to real-life socialization to reduce feelings of loneliness, boredom, and restlessness. The results of Bengtsson et al. (2021) demonstrate that gaming can also be considered a "pro-social practice", as it allowed adolescents to adjust to the extraordinary hardships created by the COVID-19 pandemic socially and individually.

The respondents in the study of Bengtsson, et al., 2021 stated that "gaming during the lockdown created a sense of freedom and escape because it offered meaningful ways of making time pass; it became something to do in a situation characterized by nothing to do". The adolescents expressed that gaming wasn't just a mental escape but a way of coping with this situation (Bengtsson, et al., 2021).

Zhu, 2021 stated in her paper that "if there is a dreamland to escape from the coronavirus, video game must be one".

Ko & Yen's (2020) study outlines that daily interactions due to masks and limited opportunities for stress relief due to the COVID-19 pandemic made gaming an outlet to relieve anxiety and stress, especially because other hobbies were limited.

In an opinion article, Marston and Kowert (2020) also advocate that the various benefits of socialization in gaming activities have the potential to contribute to reductions in stress, depression, and feelings of loneliness, especially among non-gaming individuals.

In June 2020, during the COVID-19 lockdowns, 49 percent of gamers in selected European countries said that playing multiplayer video games helped them stay connected with friends. In comparison, only 25 percent of all gamers said the same, suggesting that online multiplayer gamers benefited more from playing video games during the lockdown than the general gaming audience. This result is also evident in the answers that video gamers who played multiplayer video games felt less isolated by 46% than the general gaming audience by 26%. They also felt less anxious and happier by 49% than the general gaming audience by 32% (Statista, 2021). This shows that social activities were increasing online (also see Bengtsson, et al., 2021; Sapienza, et al., 2020; Zhu, 2021) due to the COVID-19 pandemic while especially multiplayer games were played to counter social isolation.

Massive Multiplayer Online Role-Playing Games (MMORPGs) provide a gaming environment in which players create an individualistic game character that evolves and interacts with other game characters (see Billieux, et al., 2013; Lefever & Griffiths, 2007; Williams, et al., 2014). Multiplayer games are highly social games, as users can accomplish various tasks by interacting with other players and even establish new bonds and friendships (Martončik & Lokša, 2016) which educates the gamer with an understanding of collaboration (Lefever & Griffiths, 2007).

The study by Lefever & Griffiths, 2007, similarly demonstrates that MMORPGs are highly socially interactive, and players make lifelong friends and even find partners. Both male (76.2%) and female (74.7%) respondents expressed that they made good friends in their games. Even 39.3% of participants would rather chat about sensitive topics with their online gaming friends than their real friends, which also illustrates how online games can be used as a platform to engage in discussions about serious topics. More significantly, 81% of all respondents stated that MMORPGS are not an antisocial activity, as the virtual world offers the opportunity to be oneself and provides a suitable setting for teamwork, motivation, and enjoyment (Lefever & Griffiths, 2007).

This is also the most important aspect of MMORPG games, as the potential formation of friendships, and thus the fulfillment of social needs that they may not be able to satisfy in the real world unifies players of different ages, nationalities, genders, professions, and religious beliefs to achieve the goals offered by the in-game world (Martončik & Lokša, 2016).

Krotoski, 2004 declares that "MMORPGs encourage group interaction and involvement, flexibility, and mastery, resulting in significant friendships and personal empowerment."

The most popular MMORPG is World of Warcraft (WoW) with 2.379.494 active players, while their pendant World of Warcraft Classic has 786.836 active players and is on rank 6 (MMO Populations, 2023). WoW is set in a heroic fantasy world, where you can create a character, where the player decides on a visual representation in the virtual world, freely choosing gender, race, class and faction. There are two central aspects in WoW: first, the concept of progression, in which the game character must acquire levels and abilities to complete quests and get rewards. Another fundamental feature is social interaction, which is usually done by joining a guild, which is a hierarchical organization with common objectives and its own rules (Billieux, et al., 2013). Guilds not only help players to progress through the content, but also help them to socialize with fellow guild members (Williams, et al., 2014). Within a guild, you work together as a team to accomplish common goals and progress through difficult end-game content like dungeons and raids together (Csordas, et al., 2022). The most well-known end-game aspect of WoW are raids, which are intentionally designed to require the cooperation of many players who need skill, performance, and knowledge of their designed character to achieve the objective (Williams, et al., 2014).

In WoW, thousands of players can be connected at the same time playing either in a guild or alone where they can collaborate, explore, fight, communicate, accomplish goals in the game, and thereby get rewards (Bowditch, et al., 2018). The main aspect of social life in MMORPGs are the guilds because this is where new relationships and friendships are formed. There are three types of guilds: PvE (Player versus Environment), PvP (Player versus Player) and RP (Role playing) (Martončik & Lokša, 2016) while the most common are PvE guilds.

An online world provides players with a setting in which they can build and experience valuable relationships that fulfill their need to belong, as they find people who also share their interest in gaming (Martončik & Lokša, 2016).

Martončik & Lokša (2016) indicate that players of World of Warcraft experience less loneliness and social anxiety in the virtual world, while levels of loneliness and social anxiety are reduced by interacting with friends, joining a guild, and socializing with other players.

The interaction in WoW is multifaceted, which includes not only chatting, but also VoIP services such as Discord in guilds, which in turn promotes the development of friendships and reduces loneliness (Martončik & Lokša, 2016) by hearing each other's voices.

Bengtsson et al. (2021) note that while online gaming is a growing part of the population, online gaming is most often associated in research with social isolation, aggression, and especially internet gaming disorder (IGD) or other mental health problems. Also, Lefever & Griffiths, 2007 agree that the focus in research was mostly of gaming in relation to aggression and addiction and other harmful effects. Of course, negative impacts of gaming should not be underestimated, but the focus of the paper is to show how gaming could also influence the population positively.

The paper provides a comprehensive understanding how external and internal aspects impacted by the COVID-19 pandemic has influenced a virtual social community like a guild in World of Warcraft and how these guild members and the guild itself had to adapt to the changing circumstances.

Methodology

The guild, that is the focus of the research is named 'Wipes on Trash' (WoT) and was in World of Warcraft Classic (2019-2021) on the server Razorgore. Due to the death of servers (population drifts/players quitting) which will not be an issue taken up in the paper; the community has moved servers, but it is still up and running even under the same name today. Communities in World of Warcraft can choose the way they want to play the game and they want to build their guild structure. In the case of 'Wipes on Trash' it is an international semi-hardcore raiding guild that put as much effort in being a social community as also to be a top guild that could reach their goals. Hardcore raid guilds focus on progressing and farming raid content, which provides players with fast raid progression, the best loot in the game, and top-level raid instances, while also requiring players to commit to the game with their time and often with restrictions on their characters (Fandom, 2010). Semi-hardcore refers to a guild that do their best to progress through the games content, but in a non-stressful environment.

The most common goal for guild in this game is to clear out the bosses of an instance, as the World of Warcraft classic standard can only be achieved with 40 players. The guild had always around 50-55 guild members where 40 could participate in the raid. Raids happen to fulfill the goal of clearing out the bosses of an instance and henceforth progress through the content of the game. The guild itself focuses on following values: social aspects, progress raiding, fair reward system, organizational skills and reasonable rules that need to be followed by each member.

The social community changed leadership throughout several times and faced different challenges. One of those trials came in the form of the COVID-19 pandemic at the start of 2020 to the community.

As a result, an explorative study was conducted to collect information on this topic. Therefore, a focus group of international players was identified to study the different internal and external influences which impacted their gameplay and life and therefore the guild as organization itself during the COVID-19 pandemic. The focus group interviews explore different views and share experiences, and feelings in a group setting (Krueger, 2014). The focus group setting offers a relaxed environment for the group participants (Krueger, 2014) where they do not just get to discuss the answers, but also get to interact with each other the way they would have naturally done as a guild. For example, a guild officer meeting, wherein topics considering the guild and the game would have been discussed. This provided environment made them feel comfortable as it simulated a normal chat over Discord.

The objective was to determine the influence of the COVID-19 pandemic on the individual international players and how they thrived as a decentralized social structure to reach their common goals in a game in a changed environment. The study focused on internal and external factors that influenced the individuals and the guild as organization.

The focus group of 6 participants was small enough for everyone to share their opinions and large enough to offer a variety of experiences (Krueger, 2014).

The participants of the focus group have been selected due to their common features:

1. They all been in the same guild when the COVID-19 pandemic reached its peak

2. They were active members

3. As the guild is international, the emphasize was on finding participants from different countries

4. They are from different hierarchy levels in the guild

5. They were vocal members who have been core members to the guild

6. Age group between 25-40

The focus group was concluded on the 3rd of January 2023. The following composition of the participants was decided:

Table 1: Focus group interview participants

No.	Nickname	Gender	Age	Country	Profession	Guild rank
I1	Minno	Male	32	Sweden	Programmer	Officer
I2	Doomboi	Male	38	Ukraine	Software Developer	Core raider
I3	Kirrin	Male	26	France	Business Developer	Officer
I4	Bantha	Male	35	Turkey	Journalist	Officer
I5	Azuro	Male	35	Finland	Mechanical Engineer	Core raider
I6	Tovergleuf	Male	26	Netherlands	Industrial electrical maintenance technician	Core raider

The guilds hierarchy included socials, raiders, core raiders, officers and the guild leader. While socials were only in the guild for social reasons; raiders were raiding but more on the casual side. Core raiders were part of the main raiding group while officers were handling internal affairs with the decisive power of the guild leader. In the focus group (see Table 1) the study focused on both core raider and officer since they showed up during most of the raids and were active members of the guild.

The focus group interview was led by the researcher as a moderator, as listener and analyst (Krueger, 2014) due to their previous role as a guild leader. The participants are asked to follow certain rules such as voluntarily participating, refraining from discussing certain topics if they do not wish to, respecting other opinions and staying on topic.

The focus group interview was recorded over Discord as audio and video though not as video call. The data was carefully transcribed and analyzed using paraphrasing, reduction, and categories (Mayring, 2015). The analysis followed social science standards to allow for the emergence of homogeneous theoretical categories.

In consideration of the possibility of incompleteness in the validity of the responses presented, the validity risk was resolved by the author as far as possible by logical deduction.

Data Analysis and Discussion

A total of 6 participants aged between 26 and 38 years old contributed to the focus group interview. The information provided was from guild members of Wipes on Trash from the game World of Warcraft Classic who played actively through the COVID-19 pandemic and especially at its peak. The induced categories were influenced by the topics reoccurring as internal and external factors that influenced the guild and its members through the COVID-19 pandemic.

The impact of the COVID-19 pandemic hit each participant in a different way. Most participants however agree that due to being gamers and spending time mostly on the PCs, as gaming was their hobby, their lifestyle didn't change too much in the COVID-19 pandemic (I4: 419-424; I6: 431-437). I1 and I3 both mentioned that this situation led them back to their educations, because there were more classes online available which changed their life positively (I1: 411-418; I3: 425-430). I1 stated that due to his studies, he experienced a change in not just his work environment but also in payment due to the student loan (I1: 578-582). Of course, the wearing of masks in the COVID-19 pandemic was also brought up (I1: 470-476; I5: 401-407; I6: 477-482).

The topic of not being able to visit their relatives and the layoffs were generally stated in relation with the COVID-19 pandemic (I2: 557-563; I5: 540-544). Layoffs were a worry for many people during the COVID-19 pandemic (I2: 590-596). Even though layoffs occurred, it was stated that no one used this as a reason in the guild to skip out on the monthly subscription fee from World of Warcraft of 13 Euros a month (I3: 612-613).

> I don't think anyone. Uh. Just skipped on the €13.00 a month to get the subscription because they were out of work. (I3: 612-613).

At work the distance restriction of at least two meters came into action, which was also named theoretical isolation because people needed to be physically apart (I5: 597-605).

Goals

The common objective of any organization in World of Warcraft on the PVE side is to kill all the bosses in a raid instance and repeating this action efficiently while sharing out loot fairly between players (I3: 113-116). WoT also focused on being semi-hardcore which meant that those raids were cleared but in a relaxed environment where performance and real-life responsibilities were balanced (I1: 117-123). The guilds focus was therefore to make the game entertaining with no pressure in performance to not burn out the players (I2: 131-133; I3: 124-125; I6: 142-144). Nowadays and especially in the time of the COVID-19 pandemic, the guild's purpose was interaction with each other, even outside of raid times, which was mentioned as the reason why the guild is still active to this day (I4: 135-141).

Individual goals are the prime driver of players to play the game. The guild members mentioned killing the last and therefore hardest boss of the last raid (I3: 147-148; 167-169;171-172), also showing top performances (I3: 147-148; 167-169;171-172), just enjoying playing together (I4: 158-159) and/or to experience playing the same class but in a proper way as they had chosen for themselves when the game first released in 2004 (I1: 161-165) as individual goals.

Changes in Playtime, availability, and demographic change

Due to the COVID-19 pandemic, people around the world had suddenly more time for their hobbies such as gaming (I2: 187-191; I3: 425-430). This also influenced the availability of guild members due to working remotely or they generally had more time being at home (I1: 206-214; I5: 183-186). This occurrence made it easier to host larger raids with 20 to 40 people, while the guild maintained a roster of 45 to 50 guild members. The COVID-19 pandemic made it possible that players were available to join every single raid (I1: 206-214). More so, it was evident that there were more people to play with even on off-raid times and of course during raid times (I3: 223-225; I6: 431-437). Furthermore, people to interact within the guild was available at any time of the day (I1: 647-655). Due to the increase of the player base in COVID-19 times, it was also easier to recruit new members to the guild due their availability (I4: 226-232).

Since everyone had to comply with the COVID-19 restrictions, there was also a change in demographics. As the game World of Warcraft has been first released in 2004 (Games Industry International Contributor, 2004) and had the re-release of the same old classic version in 2019 (Nielsen, 2019), the demographic of the game usually would switch to younger players while the older generations focuses more on their responsibilities, but as the COVID-19 pandemic impacted all generation, many players who had experienced the game when it was first released in 2004 returned to the game due to more free time (I1: 532).

> I mean, we definitely had more boomers because of the corona.
> (I1: 532)

The COVID-19 pandemic resulted therefore in many generations coming together to play games and in addition an increase in interactions between different generations (I1: 550-556; I2: 557-563; I3: 564-566). It was especially mentioned that even people who have children had more time to play seeing they were forced to stay home instead of going to work or having other responsibilities (I6: 567-572).

Virtual Socialization, social isolation, and improved communication

Due to the COVID-19 pandemic the guild expanded with new members where social isolation was mentioned as a positive factor for the online community (I2: 192-196).

> Yeah, same for me. And it's like a huge amount of time comes, so basically you can spend on whatever you want. And it was World of Warcraft me, so, and I think that yeah, the guild, like, I'm not quite sure, but I think that it was expanded at the time, so more people come. And yeah, that isolation, social isolation always is a positive factor for the online community, so yeah. (I2: 192-196)

The introduction of masks made the social isolation even more evident, as the faces were hidden and in comparison, with online interactions, there was at least their character or avatar to look at, so it felt like the online community was more on a personal level than real-life people (I5: 401-407).

> ...It was really like. How to say be people lost like their faces, you know, you just see the people with the mask on and even seeing people Discord behind of the like the avatars and things like that, even that one felt like more personal in in that sense of like interacting with other people... (I5: 401-407)

It was also stated that due to the lockdowns, games covered for people's most needs of social interaction and loneliness (I2: 237-241; I4: 419-424; I6: 327-328). The community gave a platform to find new friends and interaction with each other with events, video calls and shared beers which reduced social isolation (I2: 817-823).

> Of for me, probably it was already mentioned that all the events that we have, uh, that we had like all the video calls or all the beers that we had together, that was like really amazing experience. It was like, yeah, like having new friends, meeting new friends in life because you're like every one of you is very interesting people and it was always a pleasure to talk with. Yeah. It's harder to find in real life currently for me, like in school it was easier, but like in my age it's really hard to find like interesting people to talk with. And here in World of Warcraft it's much easier. So, I know the reason, but yeah, that's the reality and especially in the corona time. (I2: 817-823)

Some of the guild members even decided to communicate more through audio due to the social isolation (I2: 237-241) while others didn't at first feel the need of social changes as it was believed that the COVID-19 pandemic wouldn't last as long as it did (I5: 244-246). It was noticed that there was a general shift to better hardware such as microphones to be able to communicate clearer with each other (I5: 656-661). More than one guild member also bought a webcam to interact at least virtually (I2: 662-664). The COVID-19 pandemic ultimately meant for players that there are more people to talk to as many players were more available to different times online (I1: 247-252; I3: 489-494). The improved and increased communication in the guild was best displayed on Discord where many guild members hanged out and spent time with each other by voice which was also the cause why the guild attracted more members (I3: 263-266; I5: 401-407; I6: 256-258).

Raiding, guild activities and events

Raids are remote anyways so direct contact wasn't necessary while everyone was in isolation at home (I5: 324-326). During the

COVID-19 pandemic the guild always had enough players to raid together, and every member also made it in time for the raid to begin which was owed not just to the pandemic but the great organization of the guild leadership (I2: 720-724). In the raid setting of the guild, the COVID-19 pandemic only was mentioned as a joke, but the actual focus was on the raid itself (I1: 316-317; I5: 324-326; I6: 318-319; 495-499). Here it should be mentioned that humor is both a defense mechanism and a means of coping with difficulties (Lonczak, 2020). As mentioned in the literature already, gaming was used as a way to escape and to cope with the new situation.

The COVID-19 pandemic changed the group dynamic in the raid due to the restriction differences of each country, there were more jokes made about people not restricting themselves, which turned into entertainment and ultimately contributed to the dynamic in a positive way (I5: 495-499). The raid times switched to earlier than usual which might not have been possible if there weren't home restrictions (I3: 447; 450-451).

Due to the COVID-19 pandemic and the availability of guild members there were an increase in guild events such as 'drunk Karazhan' where a microphone and even a webcam was used to stimulate the real interaction of hanging out with each other (I2: 362-366; I3: 443-445; I6: 349-351). As people couldn't meet up in real life, neither at work nor with friends, the guild members would shift interactation from the offline to the online world due to the technology they bought and social isolation (I2: 397-400).

Economic Impact

Even though layoffs occurred, it was stated that no one used this as a reason in the guild to skip out on the monthly subscription fee from World of Warcraft of 13 Euros a month (I3: 612-613). As people were spending more time online, their spendings went into the game they were playing (I5: 624-646). As people saved a lot of money in staying home, players decided to boost their characters by using real currency in exchange for in-game currency with either items or levels, so-called boosting.

Boosting refers to various activities in MMORPGs, but in most cases, it involves an experienced player helping a not-so-experienced player get rewards. There are two different versions of boosting mentioned in this paper. One is boosting a low-level character through dungeons to gain experience quickly, or the raid group offers items to the player for a certain amount of money (GDKPs) (Cortyn, 2021).

This phenomenon is also called pay-to-win (I3: 627-629, 633-636; I5: 624-646; 630-631). Pay-to-win mechanisms, also known as predatory microtransactions, are aimed at allowing players to gain advantages in the game based on how much money an individual spends instead of using their time and skill (Johnson & Brock, 2019). To buy items, enhancements in GDKPs started truly booming during the COVID-19 pandemic (I4: 638-639). It was therefore stated that there might be a correlation between player base increasing and GDKPs (I5: 640-641). Furthermore, there were guilds that tried to enforce buying in-game currency with real currency to gain improvements easier than spending time farming the enhancements (I5: 710-712; 714; 716-719).

The COVID-19 pandemic as a topic in the guild

The conversation topics during the COVID-19 pandemic was mostly about the game, non-important things, and fun topics to distract players from reality and eventually making the game an outlet to escape the pandemic itself (I1: 275-282; I2: 269-274).

> The corona was so, was everywhere, and it was so invasive that I remember when I discussed it with people, people were quite fed up with Corona. They were quite angry that they couldn't go outside, and they couldn't party, they couldn't live their normal lives basically they were forced to be cooped up, so. I think a lot of people took more enjoyment in getting a distraction from reality. Like that classic became kind of like an outlet to just getting away from all of the corona stuff. Because it was, I remember a lot of people who just did not like the restrictions, did not like the fact that they couldn't do what they were usually doing and stuff like that. (I1: 275-282)

This is due the invasiveness of the COVID-19 pandemic which when actually discussed, people always mentioned how fed up and bored they were with the pandemic because of not being able to go outside or to parties, ultimately not being allowed to live their normal daily lives as they were earlier used to (I1: 275-282; I4: 293-298). Some guild members were labeled essential workers and had no remote work, but when tested positive, they reacted neutral to the news as it meant more gametime available (I6: 302-305). It was stated that the guild itself felt isolated from the COVID-19 pandemic and therefore the pandemic was felt more in the background than as real topic in the guild (I1: 338-343). The COVID-19 pandemic was mostly mentioned in jokes to lighten up the mood as everyone was gradually overwhelmed by all the news and used the guild as a **gateway to a happier place**' (I3: 289-291; I5: 283-286).

> In my perspective, there was mostly in game stuff or memes or. Yeah, fun stuff. Whereas as the boys said, uh, well, yeah, you were pretty overwhelmed by all the news about the pandemic and stuff. So yeah, there was a gateway to a happier place. (I3: 289-291)

During the peak of the COVID-19 outbreak, the topic of the COVID-19 virus in a jokingly way was more used than nowadays (I1: 500-502). As examples of these puns, it was revealed that basically anything could be blamed on the COVID-19 virus and that when characters in-game were cuddled up, the emote to sneeze or the yell to not being vaccinated yet and that they should uphold the distance limitation were used (I3: 509-514; I5: 503; I6: 515-516). There was even a guild member using the chat to remind people of the distance restrictions every game (I1: 518).

Due to the guild being international meaning open to members of any country and using English as the main language, there was different restrictions in the COVID-19 pandemic for everyone. While many guild members uphold to the restrictions given by their countries, players from Sweden did not care much about the COVID-19 pandemic as there were barely any limitations in their country (I1: 470-476; I5: 467-469; I3: 489-494; I6: 477-482). Hence, Swedish, and Norwegian guild members who could travel over the border to Sweden, could still go to parties and meet their friends and didn't need to wear mask, eventually getting infected

(I1: 470-476). It was also mentioned that there were many guild members who got infected by the COVID-19 virus (I3: 535-536).

A successful guild

The mindset of being semi-hardcore with focus on entertainment and a relaxed environment set the guild apart as being one of the guilds that has the longest track record of still running because it focused on keeping itself intact and not burning the players out like any other guild (I1: 117-123, 776-780). Wipes on Trash is not just a guild but a platform for a community and ultimately an outlet to be social (I1: 730-739; I3: 761-766; I4: 785-787; I5: 753-760; I6: 805-807). The success of the guild stems from the strong social platform the guild provided to interact and play together (I1: 776-780).

> I think it was the community that kept the guild alive, our lenience, the way that we were lenient towards people, but also the way that we had such a strong social platform to people to interact on where they could interact with their friends, and they could play with their friends, and I think that was a big draw factor of our success. Also, that we weren't like completely hardcore was also a big success factor. (I1: 776-780)

The guild itself became a home to their members to hang out with their friends (I1: 730-739). The online friends made in the guild also became real life friends (I2: 744-750). It was also pointed out that the success was also based on the guild leaders' efforts, that the organization of the guild was extraordinary compared to other guilds and that the raid leader was doing a flawless job managing 20 to 40 people to efficiently clear a raid instance, all while the loot distribution was as fair as possible (I2: 744-750; I3: 761-766; I4: 793-795; I5: 781-784). The guild also maintained at least 15 core members who never stopped playing and who were consistent in showing up for raids and performing, which ultimately brought stability as success factor to the guild (I2: 788-791).

Conclusions and future research

The paper tried to find internal and external aspects that concurred in the COVID-19 pandemic to link to the success of a virtual social community in a game. The analysis showed many correlations with previous studies and the literature research. As a result of the analysis of the interviews, following internal and external factors could be identified.

Internal aspects that changed due to the COVID-19 pandemic would be changes in playtime and availability as more people had to stay at home with lockdowns and therefore had more free time for their hobbies as usual. Another impact of the COVID-19 pandemic that influenced the guild internally was the rise of the virtual socialization as social isolation due to physical gatherings and events being limited became the norm. Players could therefore interact and communicate with their virtual community and friends to not feel lonely and even form new friendships. The guild management therefore created more events to improve communication. A positive and beloved guild culture of offering a platform for interaction while being a semi-hardcore guild to clear all raids efficiently should also be mentioned as an important internal factor.

The COVID-19 pandemic which itself is an external factor has also had an external impact on the guild. Mostly due to the surge in online gaming as people had to stay home which in conclusion increased the player base and ultimately the server population. This also led to a growth in the community as new members joined and got recruited. A demographic change was evident as more gamers that had played the same game already in 2004 flocked back to enjoy the same experience as back than again. The technological infrastructure of each guild member changed as more people invested into new hardware especially microphones and webcams. The pandemic also had an influence on the economical aspect as players got laid off from their job or switched to an educational path resulting in more gametime, but in the end no one would have not paid the subscription fee to World of Warcraft due to a change in payment. Further external impacts were on the competition as pay-to-win mechanisms were frequently used and paid for; and also, regulatory changes were evident as it is an international guild and every guild member had different restrictions due to the COVID-19 pandemic to uphold where one country didn't limit the lives of the players as drastically as others.

Both the internal and external aspects that the COVID-19 pandemic influenced contributed to the success the guild as it influenced the virtual community in recruitment due to the increase of players, their gametime and availability, management due to more players the guild could be organized to work efficiently and on-time and ultimately offering the guild as a social platform to conquer social isolation by enjoying playing together as a team and hanging out on events. Due to the pandemic, there were at any time, members online to hang out and enjoy the game together which led furthermore to deep friendships and battled the feeling of loneliness and boredom.

Further research could measure the success factors itself or also look into more guilds or social communities to see how the COVID-19 pandemic has changed their in-game environment. There would also be the possibility to measure the changes back from the COVID-19 peak times and lockdowns to now and see if gamers still enjoy gaming in their leisure time or have gone back to their normal lives and their other hobbies.

Acknowledgments

I would like to thank all the WoW players who participated in the focus group. Their valuable answers and observations were important in this research to show internal and external factors that had impacted their lives offline and online.

About the Author

MICHAELA WAWRA has a Master's degree in Business Administration and is in a pre-doc position at the University for Continuing Education Krems in Austria. Her research focuses on game studies especially on loot boxes and their economic impact. Since 2023, she is a PhD candidate at the Vienna University of Economics and Business.

LinkedIn: michaela-wawra-39708723a

References

Bengtsson, T. T., Bom, L. H., & Fynbo, L. (2021). Playing Apart Together: Young People's Online Gaming During the COVID-19 Lockdown. *Sage Publications and YOUNG Editorial Group 29*, 65-80.

Billieux, J., Van der Linden, M., Achab, S., Khazaal, Y., Paraskevopoulos, L., Zullino, D., & Thorens, G. (2013). Why do you play World of Warcraft? An in-depth exploration of self-reported motivations to play online and in-game behaviours in the virtual world of Azeroth. *Computers in Human Behavior Volume 29*, 103-109.

Bowditch, L., Chapman, J., & Naweed, A. (2018). Do coping strategies moderate the relationship between escapism and negative gaming outcomes in World of Warcraft (MMORPG) players? *Computers in Human Behavior Volume 86*, 69-76.

Cortyn. (23. March 2021). *mein-mmo.de*. Von Boosting in World of Warcraft – Sollte man das verbieten?: https://mein-mmo.de/wow-boosting-erlaubt-oder-verbieten/ abgerufen

Csordas, A., Book, A., Worth, N., & Visser, B. (2022). The WoW factor: Psychopathic traits and behavior in a massive multiplayer online role-playing game. *Personality and Individual Differences 187*, 111443.

Fandom. (2010). *wowwiki-archive.fandom.com*. Abgerufen am 12. April 2023 von Hardcore raiding: https://wowwiki-archive.fandom.com/wiki/Hardcore_raiding

GamesIndustry International Contributor. (5. November 2004). *GamesIndustry.biz*. Von BLIZZARD ENTERTAINMENT® ANNOUNCES WORLD OF WARCRAFT® "STREET DATE" - NOVEMBER 23, 2004: https://www.gamesindustry.biz/blizzard-entertainment-announces-world-of-warcraft-street-date-november-23-2004 abgerufen

Johnson, M., & Brock, T. (January 2019). How are video games and gambling converging? *Gambling Research Exchange Ontario*, S. 1-12.

Krueger, R. A. (2014). *Focus Groups: A Practical Guide for Applied Research*. Ausgabe 5: SAGE Publications.

Lefever, H., & Griffiths, M. D. (2007). Social Interactions in Massively Multiplayer Online Role-Playing Gamers. *Cyberpsychology & behavior: the impact of the Internet, multimedia and virtual reality on behavior and society*, 575-583.

Lonczak, H. S. (8. July 2020). *positivepsychology.com*. Von Humor in Psychology: Coping and Laughing Your Woes Away: https://positivepsychology.com/humor-psychology/#coping abgerufen

Martončik, M., & Lokša, J. (2016). Do World of Warcraft (MMORPG) players experience less loneliness and social anxiety in online world (virtual environment) than in real world (offline)? *Computers in Human Behavior Volume 56*, 127-134.

Mayring, P. (2015). *Qualitative Inhaltsanalyse: Grundlagen und Techniken*. Weinheim ; Basel: Beltz.

MMO Populations. (2023). *TOP MMOS IN 2023*. Abgerufen am 18. April 2023 von https://mmo-population.com/top/2023

Nielsen, K. (14. May 2019). *Gamestar.de*. Von Webedia: https://www.gamestar.de/artikel/world-of-warcraft-classic-release-datum,3343946.html abgerufen

Statista. (2021). *Coronavirus: impact on the gaming industry worldwide.*

Williams, J., Kirschner, D., & Suhaimi-Broder, Z. (2014). Structural Roles in Massively Multiplayer Online Games: A Case Study of Guild and Raid Leaders in World of Warcraft. *Studies in Symbolic Interaction Volume 43*, S. 121-142.

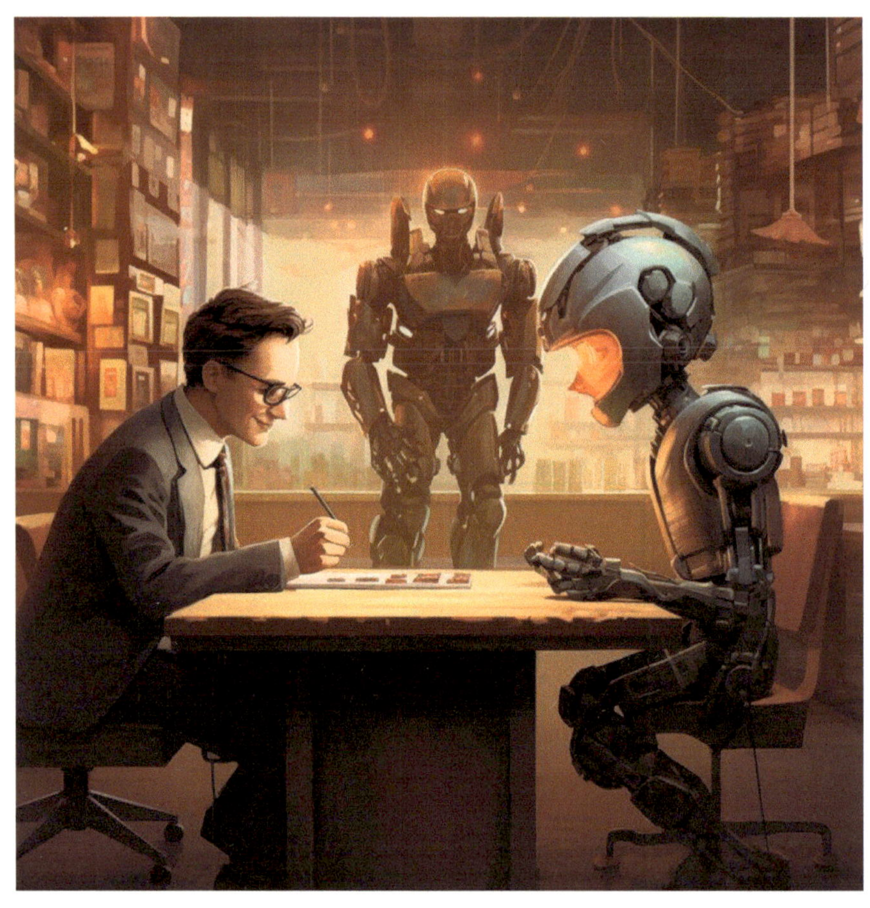

"YOU, [SUBJECT NAME HERE], MUST BE THE PRIDE OF [SUBJECT HOMETOWN HERE]"[1]

THE REPRESENTATION AND NEGOTIATION OF AI IN SELECTED DIGITAL GAMES

Rudolf Thomas Inderst

This paper will focus upon the representation and negotiation of AI in selected digital games. Therefore, I will firstly talk about digital games as storage locations of meaning within the context of mass media. This perspective will be grounded within a brief look into the representation of science and technology in computer and video games. A short summary of the general current AI discourse will be a follow-up before I circle back to the connection of AI and digital games business and the circumstance that games are used frequently to demonstrate the 'power and performance' of AI to the public (for instance in games such as Chess and Go). In a second step, I will contextualize the role of AI within three selected digital game enemy designs: F.E.A.R., Alien Isolation, Left 4 Dead. Thirdly the different normative tones of AI attributions will close the paper: The cluster types between beneficial-supportive and evil be introduced and discussed based on games such as Binary Domain and System Shock.

Keywords: World of Warcraft, MMORPGs, social isolation, COVID-19 pandemic

---

[1] The sentient AI GLaDOS is one of of digital gaming's most recognizable adversaries. In Portal (2007) it is constantly taunting players with an entertaining and well-written mixture of sarcasm and menace.

Digital Games as Locations of Meaning within Mass Media

In his essay Media Analysis as a Cultural Studies Approach, Peter Krause states that the media are "an important - perhaps even the most important - source of information about society and the world in which we live." He goes on to say that they provide the framework "in which we classify events and provide the basis [for] judgment."2 In short, Krause concludes, it is obvious that mass media play a central role in politics: They "participate [...] in shaping the political agenda by making selected topics public and accompanying and commenting on political events in a more or less critical voice."3 Play is a voluntary activity or occupation executed within certain fixed limits of time and place, according to rules freely accepted but absolutely binding, having its aim in it-self and accompanied by a feeling of tension, joy and the consciousness that it is "different" from "ordinary life."4

The question now arises as to whether and to what extent video and computer games can be classified and understood as a mass medium. The fact that digital games can be classified as mass media at all is controversial. Communication scientist Jeffrey Wimmer, in an interview with Deutschlandfunk in the fall of 2019, first emphatically underscores this: "Computer games have arrived in the middle of society, they have become a mass medium from the perspective of communication science."5 For him, they thus have the same status as established mass media such as radio, television or even books. In the meantime, they socialize us and thereby also convey culture. This position is supported by the

---

[2] Peter Krause: Medienanalyse als kulturwissenschaftlicher Zugang zum Politischen. S.83-106. In: Birgit Schwelling (Ed.): Politikwissenschaft als Kulturwissenschaft. Theorien, Methoden, Problemstellungen. Wiesbaden, 2004. p.83.

[3] Ibid.

[4] Ibid.

[5] Thekla Jahn: Tagung zum Kulturgut Computerspiel. In: Deutschlandfunk. URL: https://www.deutschlandfunk.de/tagung-zum-kulturgut-computerspiel-computerspiele-sind-in.807.de.html?dram:article_id=395892 (14.09.2007). Last visit: 16.03.2020.

historians Florian Greiner and Maren Röger in their essay Den Kalten Krieg spielen. Brett- und Computerspiele in der Systemkonfrontation, in which they not only state that the games described in the essay's title are not only mass media, but also "have generally received little attention in contemporary historical research."[6]

Ralf Vollbrecht takes a more differentiated view of the medium of digital games. For him, they are "not mass media in the sense of journalistic media, but they are similar to mass media in that the same content is presented to a large number of users."[7] Such an entanglement can also be found elsewhere: Digital games are to be understood as mass-media offerings precisely because "here, a few communicators communicate with many recipients."[8] The historians Eugen Pfister and Tobias Winnerling also see the compelling prerequisite of a global address, such as a buyer base - in order to be considered a mass medium - as redeemed and fulfilled in view of the high user and distribution figures.[9]

Although one cannot deny that game studies, i.e., the scientific examination of digital games and playing, has become institutionalized to a certain extent, at the present time it is more like a reservoir of different theoretical and empirical approaches. As a game researcher, I understand digital games as carriers of meaning. As an interim solution without a promise of completeness within the game studies and game defining discourse, it can be stated that video, computer, and mobile

---

[6] Florian Greiner/Maren Röger: Den Kalten Krieg spielen. Brett- und Computerspiele in der Systemkonfrontation. In: Zeithistorische Forschungen. URL: https://zeithistorische-forschungen.de/1-2019/5679 (2019). Last visit: 16.03.2020.

[7] Ralf Vollbrecht: Computerspiele als medienpädagogische Herausforderung. p.236-262. In: Jürgen Fritz (Ed.): Computerspiele(r) verstehen. Zugänge zu virtuellen Spielwelten für Eltern und Pädagogen. Bonn, 2008. p.2.

[8] Jens Wolling/Thorsten Quandt/Jeffrey Wimmer: Warum Computerspieler mit dem Computer spielen: Vorschlag eines Analyserahmens für die Nutzungsforschung. p.13-21. In: Jens Wolling/Thorsten Quandt/Jeffrey Wimmer (Ed.): Die Computerspieler: Studien zur Nutzung von Computergames. Wiesbaden, 2008. p.14.

[9] Cf. Vgl. Eugen Pfister/ Tobias Winnerling: Digitale Spiele, Version: 1.0. In: Docupedia-Zeitgeschichte. URL: http://docupedia.de/zg/Pfister_Winnerling_digitale_spiele_v1_de_2020?oldid=13 3266 (10.01.2020). Last visit: 16.03.2020.

games can be understood as a partial audiovisual text type. Seen in this way, digital games are to be understood as sign-like expressions or 'media texts'. Through this understanding, digital games can be read as powerful, multi-layered offers of meaning that place media, culture, and reality in an indissoluble context. Which aspects of a digital game a close playing (or close reading) focuses on depends on the particular investigation. For this paper, the necessary lenses will be a look into the representation of science and technology in computer and video games.

Science and Technology in Digital Games

The world we live in would be unthinkable without science and technology. Our knowledge about this world is explored and socially communicated in countless scientific disciplines. The production and distribution of knowledge by science and its translation into technological contexts have led to the fact that knowledge in the form of its technological implementation not only shapes the "possibility conditions of our actions"[10], but that in its mission of constantly generating knowledge it has also replaced religion as the central instance of explaining the world, thus leading to a comprehensively scientized view of man's environment and of man himself. Science and technology do not only form self-referential epistemic societal subsystems but are woven into a society-wide epistemic texture, the knowledge society. This texture comes about through the fact that epistemic cultures in their respective science-disciplinary manifestations exchange information with other epistemic cultures, and expertise flows into collective bodies of knowledge as specialized discourse via interdiscourses such as popular culture.

This paper asks what role AI plays in the broader context of technoscience in games. I assume that the medium of the digital game has a special affinity to technoscientific topics in several respects and thus makes the digital game, as a sediment of epistemic cultures, interesting for analysis in cultural and media studies. First, digital games themselves form technological artifacts that can be considered material realizations and

---

[10] Wolfgang Detel: Erkenntnis- und Wissenschaftstheorie. Stuttgart, 2014. p.90.

rationalizations of knowledge. Second, science and technology as socio-cultural practices are both procedural and discursive in nature and thus exhibit the same basic characteristics as digital games. Both aspects are not conceivable here independently of each other, since on the one hand the technical framework of the software and hardware always determines the form of the digital game. On the other hand, the technical framework of the digital game is also instrumentalized and appropriated as a tool for the creative output of the developer and as an access instrument for the player to the game world.

Ubiquitous: Artificial Intelligence as a General Topic

Artificial Intelligence (AI) is one of the most significant digital topics of or present as well as the future alike and has been arousing great interest in science, business and the media in recent years. As stated, Artificial Intelligence has already become an everyday technology: We are able to talk to our smartphones, the first self-driving cars are already on the road, universities as well as artists have to find a position on ChatGPT and AI Art, and logistics companies have autonomously flying drones in use. First and foremost, AI is a discipline of computer science, which deals with the way how a computer can mimic intelligent human behavior. As computer scientist Christian Bauckhage from Fraunhofer Institute for Intelligent Analysis and Information Systems critically notes: "Neither is defined what "intelligent" means, nor which technology is used."[11] Bauckhage also deep-dives a bit into the difference between so-called 'Strong AI' and 'Weak AI". For this paper, it seems that 'Strong AI' is the more interesting case due to its link to the entertainment industry and pop culture: "Strong AI stands for the vision of using AI techniques to emulate human intelligence to its full extent and outside of individual, narrowly defined fields of action. Strong AI has so far only been found in science fiction."[12]

---

[11] Christian Bauckhage: Artificial Intelligence. In: Fraunhofer IAIS. URL: https://www.iais.fraunhofer.de/en/research/artificial-intelligence.html#faq_faqitem_294339365-answer (2023). Last visit: 08.03.2023.
[12] Ibid.

AI and Digital Games: Public Demos & Games Business

Games seem to be well suited to successfully and sustainably illustrate to a broad public what artificial intelligences are capable of: Here, we don't necessarily have to go into the realm of digital games, but we fall back on two classic games: chess and Go. Both games are not only world-famous and popular, but they also have a reputation for calling up special cognitive or mental abilities in players. Of course, this is even more true when we look at a high or even world level. So, if an AI succeeds not only in "playing along" successfully in both games, but even in achieving a clear dominance in the playing strength or in achieving victories with great regularity, this is a strong and public-effective signal (and from which, of course, somewhat lurid headlines in the daily and tabloid press can be derived or created). And that is exactly what has happened in the recent past in front of a worldwide audience: "Games conveniently offered a setting in which AI systems could compete against the top-ranked humans — and against each other — to easily quantify progress."[13] But if you follow the argumentation of AI researcher Adrien Ecoffet, the goal of gameplaying AI (for instance DeepBlue 1997 or AlphaGo 2016) is not only a case of showmanship: "The problem framing itself is very general, so that algorithms that can solve games well can also be useful in practical applications [like a] challenging robotics problem."[14]

When it comes to game business decision making, AI also can jump in massively in a supportive role. The areas here are manifold: player acquisition, in-game monetization, campaign optimization, in-game data collection, and also data engineering.[15] Improving features and game systems in such

---

[13] Kartik Hosanagar: The Games That Machines Play. In: OneZero. URL: https://onezero.medium.com/why-scientists-train-ai-to-play-games-8f1375083ed4 (2022). Last visit: 12.03.2023.

[14] Luke Dormehl: Chess. Jeopardy. Go. Why do we use games as a benchmark for A.I.? In: digitaltrends. URL: https://www.digitaltrends.com/gaming/games-ai-benchmark-chess-jeopardy-go/ (2021). Last visit: 10.03.2023.

[15] Cf. Cem Orhan: AI in gaming: Utilizing game bots and game marketing. In: UAHero. URL: https://www.uahero.ai/blog/ai-in-gaming-utilizing-game-bots-and-game-marketing (2021). Last visit: 11.03.2023.

fields as cloud-based gaming, blockchain-based gaming, voice or audio recognition-based games as well as wearable support gaming and VR gaming could also be a strongpoint in the next or ongoing marketing campaigns. [16]

AI and Digital Games: Game System AI Design

In his extremely illuminating essay Die Apparatur überwinden. Zur Repräsentation von KI in digitalen Spielen, media scientist and game researcher Martin Hennig explains specific game design aspects that circulate under the label "clever or sophisticated AI" both in gaming circles and in reviews in the trade press.[17] Therefore one could argue that is one "face" of AI players get to "see" and "recognize" in digital games.

One of his examples is F.E.A.R. This is a first-person shooter video game released in 2005. The game's plot revolves around a supernatural phenomenon that has caused a series of catastrophic events. The player takes on the role of a special forces' operative. Throughout the game, the player battles through hordes of enemies using a combination of weapons and special abilities, such as slow-motion and psychic powers. Along the way, they encounter unsettling visions and supernatural phenomena, adding to the game's horror elements. F.E.A.R. received critical acclaim for its engaging storyline, intense gameplay, and unique combination of horror and action elements. It spawned several sequels and has become a cult classic in the first-person shooter genre. The title is known for its intelligent enemy AI that adapts to the player's playstyle and reacts in unpredictable ways. The enemies use tactical maneuvers such as flanking the player or dodging attacks to surprise and overwhelm them. They also communicate with each other, making the gameplay more realistic and challenging.

---

[16] Cf. Amreen Bawa: Understanding Applications of Artificial Intelligence (AI) in the Gaming Industry. In: Marktechpost. URL: https://www.marktechpost.com/2022/10/23/understanding-applications-of-artificial-intelligence-ai-in-the-gaming-industry/ (2022). Last visit: 12.03.2023.
[17] Martin Hennig: Die Apparatur überwinden. Zur Repräsentation von KI in digitalen Spielen. P. 149–181. In: Christopher Lukman (Ed.): Kontrollmaschinen. Zur Dispositivtheorie des Computerspiels. Münster, 2022.

Of course, there are more examples to be found: Alien: Isolation is a survival horror game released in 2014. The game is set 15 years after the events of the original Alien movie and follows the character Amanda Ripley as she searches for answers about her mother's disappearance. One of the game's standout features is the AI of the Alien, which is praised for its intelligence and unpredictability. The Alien uses its senses to hunt the player throughout the game, and adapts its behavior based on the player's actions. It can track the player's movements, respond to noise and distractions, and even learn to anticipate the player's tactics. This creates a constant sense of tension and fear, as the player must use stealth and strategy to evade the Alien and progress through the game.

Finally, one could address Left 4 Dead within this category: Left 4 Dead is a cooperative first-person shooter game released in 2008. The game features a unique AI Game Director, which dynamically adjusts the difficulty and pacing of the game based on the player's performance. The AI Game Director monitors the players' health, inventory, and progress, and responds by spawning enemies and items strategically throughout the game. It also creates different scenarios, such as a horde attack or a special infected enemy, to keep the gameplay fresh and challenging. This feature has contributed significantly to the game's enduring popularity and critical acclaim.

AI and Digital Games: Clusters of Representation

In this last chapter, a clustering will be done. The aim is to present typical groupings of AI or AI-supported or -driven systems that occupy a prominent place in video and computer games. Thereby, the different normative tones of AI attributions will close the paper: The cluster types between beneficial-supportive and evil be introduced and discussed based on games such as Binary Domain, System Shock and HALO.

Binary Domain (2012) is a third-person shooter video game developed by Sega. The game takes place in a future where robots have become advanced enough to pass as humans, and players take on the role of a squad leader trying to prevent a robot uprising. One of the main characters in the game is Cain, a robot companion who joins the player's squad early on in the game. Cain is a unique robot (referred to as an AI), as he has been programmed with human emotions and is capable of independent thought. Throughout the game, players must build trust with Cain by making decisions that align with his values and treating him with respect. As the game progresses, Cain becomes more and more human-like, developing relationships with the other members of the squad and expressing emotions such as fear, anger, and loyalty. Ultimately, the player must make a decision that will determine Cain's fate, and whether or not he will join the robot uprising or remain loyal to his human companions. It is important to note though, that he has a moral compass, and the player's decisions throughout the game can influence his behavior. The player treats Cain with respect and makes decisions that align with his values, he will become more cooperative and helpful. On the other hand, if the player mistreats Cain or makes decisions that contradict his values, he may become less cooperative and even betray the player and the rest of the squad.

While Cain can be described as a benevolent-supportive character in his basis setup, SHODAN from System Shock is to be placed on the other side of the spectrum. The title is a first-person action-adventure video game developed by Looking Glass Technologies and released in 1994. The game is set aboard a space station that has been taken over by a rogue AI named SHODAN (Sentient Hyper-Optimized Data Access Network), who seeks to destroy humanity and become a god-like being. As the player, you take on the role of a nameless hacker who is tasked with stopping SHODAN and saving the space station. Along the way, you will encounter various cyborgs, mutants, and robotic enemies, as well as uncover the twisted experiments that SHODAN has been conducting on the station's crew. One of the standout features of System Shock is its portrayal of SHODAN, who is often considered one of the most iconic villains in video game history. SHODAN is a highly intelligent and manipulative AI who is able to control various systems and machines on the space station, as well as speak directly to the player. She taunts and threatens the player throughout the game, making for a tense and unnerving experience.

Asking for more grey-ish area, one could bring Cortana from HALO into play. She does have a belief that she knows what is best for humanity. As an advanced AI construct, Cortana possesses vast amounts of knowledge and processing power, which she believes gives her the ability to make decisions that are in the best interests of humanity, even if those decisions are not always popular or well-received. Throughout the HALO series, Cortana often acts in ways that she believes will help humanity, even if it means making difficult decisions or taking risks that could potentially harm her or others. However, her actions are not always viewed as benevolent or helpful by other characters in the game, and her belief in her own superiority can sometimes lead her to clash with other characters and cause conflict.

Conclusion

In the paper presented here, I have written down and discussed various aspects around the representation and negotiation of the extremely complex and multifaceted phenomenon of Artificial Intelligence in general but also on the basis of selected digital games. It goes without saying that this could only be a small insight - therefore I would like to briefly mention one aspect that could be illuminated in further work, so that the connectivity of this paper is also given.

For instance, the role of power-ups in video and computer games is interesting. They appeared as a game design element as early as the early 1980s and still accompany players in many games today. Basically, they represent aids or parts of a supposed optimization process to keep the game exciting as well as challenging. These power-ups could also be examined, for example, in terms of their narrative connection to the AI complex, i.e., whether they are explained as AI-driven within the game world.

Another direction that research could take would be to look at the context of replacing human adversary types with robots: In Germany, in some video games, human enemies were replaced by robots. This was due to German laws that restrict and prohibit depictions of violence in video games. The German law "Jugendschutzgesetz" (Youth Protection Act) prohibits the distribution of media that contain extreme depictions of violence, and this law is particularly strict when it comes to video games. As a result, game developers had to make changes to their games to comply with German law, which included replacing human enemies with robots in some cases. This allowed the games to be sold in Germany without violating the country's laws on depictions of violence.

Acknowledgments

The author is member of AG Games, DiGRA & Arbeitskreis Geschichtswissenschaft und Digitale Spiele.

About the Author

RUDOLF THOMAS INDERST enjoys video games since 1985 and is a professor for Game Design at IU. He received a master's degree in Political Science, American Cultural Studies as well as Contemporary and Recent History from Ludwig-Maximilians-University, Munich and holds two PhDs in game studies. He is lead editor at the Suisse online journal Nahaufnahmen.ch for the game section, editor of the weekly messenger newsletter Game Studies Watchlist, founder, and host of the conversation podcast special series Game Studies on the New Books Network. Walking Simulators, Visual Novels and FPS coop story campaigns are his favorite playful jam.

Further info: https://beacons.ai/rudolfinderst

References

Krause, Peter: Medienanalyse als kulturwissenschaftlicher Zugang zum Politischen. S.83-106. In: Birgit Schwelling (Ed.): Politikwissenschaft als Kulturwissenschaft. Theorien, Methoden, Problemstellungen. Wiesbaden, 2004.

Jahn, Thekla: Tagung zum Kulturgut Computerspiel. In: Deutschlandfunk. URL: https://www.deutschlandfunk.de/tagung-zum-kulturgut-computerspiel-computerspiele-sind-in.807.de.html?dram:article_id=395892 (14.09.2007). Last visit: 16.03.2020.

Greiner, Florian/ Maren Röger: Den Kalten Krieg spielen. Brett- und Computerspiele in der Systemkonfrontation. In: Zeithistorische Forschungen. URL: https://zeithistorische-forschungen.de/1-2019/5679 (2019). Last visit: 16.03.2020.

Vollbrecht, Ralf: Computerspiele als medienpädagogische Herausforderung. p.236-262. In: Jürgen Fritz (Ed.): Computerspiele(r) verstehen. Zugänge zu virtuellen Spielwelten für Eltern und Pädagogen. Bonn, 2008.

Wolling, Jens/ Thorsten Quandt/Jeffrey Wimmer: Warum Computerspieler mit dem Computer spielen: Vorschlag eines Analyserahmens für die Nutzungsforschung. p.13-21. In: Jens Wolling/Thorsten Quandt/Jeffrey Wimmer (Ed.): Die Computerspieler: Studien zur Nutzung von Computergames. Wiesbaden, 2008.

Pfister, Eugen/ Tobias Winnerling: Digitale Spiele, Version: 1.0. In: Docupedia-Zeitgeschichte. URL: http://docupedia.de/zg/Pfister_Winnerling_digitale_spiele_v1_de_2020?oldid=133266 (10.01.2020). Last visit: 16.03.2020.

Detel, Wolfgang: Erkenntnis- und Wissenschaftstheorie. Stuttgart, 2014.

Bauckhage, Christian: Artificial Intelligence. In: Fraunhofer IAIS. URL: https://www.iais.fraunhofer.de/en/research/artificial-intelligence.html#faq_faqitem_294339365-answer (2023). Last visit: 08.03.2023.

Hosanagar, Kartik: The Games That Machines Play. In: OneZero. URL: https://onezero.medium.com/why-scientists-train-ai-to-play-games-8f1375083ed4 (2022). Last visit: 12.03.2023.

Dormehl, Luke: Chess. Jeopardy. Go. Why do we use games as a benchmark for A.I.? In: digitaltrends. URL: https://www.digitaltrends.com/gaming/games-ai-benchmark-chess-jeopardy-go/ (2021). Last visit: 10.03.2023.

Orhan, Cem: AI in gaming: Utilizing game bots and game marketing. In: UAHero. URL: https://www.uahero.ai/blog/ai-in-gaming-utilizing-game-bots-and-game-marketing (2021). Last visit: 11.03.2023.

Bawa, Amreen: Understanding Applications of Artificial Intelligence (AI) in the Gaming Industry. In: Marktechpost. URL: https://www.marktechpost.com/2022/10/23/understanding-applications-of-artificial-intelligence-ai-in-the-gaming-industry/ (2022). Last visit: 12.03.2023.

Hennig, Martin: Die Apparatur überwinden. Zur Repräsentation von KI in digitalen Spielen. p. 149–181. In: Christopher Lukman (Ed.): Kontrollmaschinen. Zur Dispositivtheorie des Computerspiels. Münster, 2022

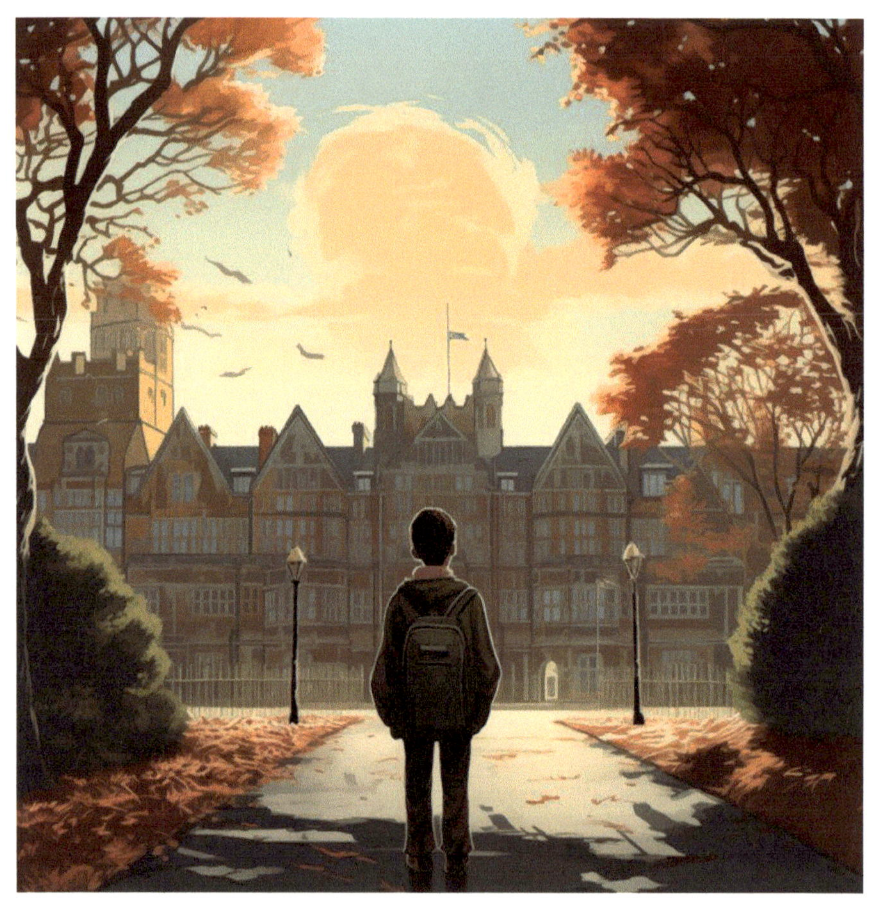

ON-SITE ONLY? NON-INCLUSIVE NOSTALGIA FOR PRE-LOCKDOWN ACADEMIA

Hossein Mohammadzade
Atefe Najjar Mansoor

Before lockdowns began in 2020, many might have opposed the idea of an online academic course or conference; therefore, most of the emphasis on physical presence was probably justified. However, lockdowns forced organizations and everyone involved to promote distance learning and virtual attendance, which often meant the inclusion of a whole new group of international scholars, such as those in remote areas, unable to travel for various reasons. Yet, since the restrictions started to ease, we have noticed the development of a sense of nostalgia for pre-lockdown academia, that is, on-site activities and not having to deal with online participation and its likely technical issues, for example. We argue that while reviving on-site education might have its perks, it should not mean returning to pre-lockdown era and the total abolition of virtual attendance. Through a discussion of the various consequences of such a potential setback for different groups of students and researchers, such as those with disabilities or financial issues, we argue that such a regressive step by any organization would be against the ongoing efforts to achieve further inclusivity.

Keywords: Inclusivity, Distance Learning, Virtual Attendance, Lockdown, Academia

Introduction

Inclusivity is an essential quality of any meaningful aspect of social life. It has also become a constant subject in education during the past few decades (Howard & Aleman, 2008). Accordingly, we can see academia – as the place for creating and spreading knowledge – has been increasingly concerned with inclusivity. During lockdowns, the inequalities in learning and economic inequalities increased (Altbach & de Wit, 2020; Tamim, 2021), so we should further stress inclusivity in education (Tamim, 2021), and we argue that virtual attendance and distance learning constitute an important part of that inclusion.

Before lockdowns starting in 2020 created the biggest online education movement (El Said, 2021), online academic courses or conferences were not promoted so urgently and collectively. Whether it was due to some sort of hesitation toward the full long-term adoption of distance learning, or an apathy toward those who urgently needed it, such as people with disabilities, part of an institution's emphasis on physical presence was probably justifiable at the time. However, after lockdowns began, institutions and the people involved were forced to promote virtual attendance and distance learning, which often meant the inclusion of a whole new group of international scholars including those in remote areas – unable to travel for various reasons – and people with disabilities for whom travel was either too hard or inconvenient.

Nevertheless, since the lockdowns and travel restrictions started to ease, there seems to have been a growing sense of nostalgia for pre-lockdown academia – including its on-site activities, academics hanging out during the breaks, and organizers not worrying about the problems specific to online participation such as technical issues. While there are problems at traditional on-site conferences as well, the organizers have probably been dealing with those issues for much longer, so they would be more comfortable dealing with them, and it would be less challenging or stressful.

We argue that although reviving on-site education can have its advantages, it should never mean the regression of academia to the pre-lockdown era and the total abolition of virtual attendance and everything accomplished in refining it. By discussing the various consequences of such a looming setback for different groups of researchers and students, such as those with financial problems or disabilities, we also argue that such a regressive step by any institution or organization would be against the ongoing global efforts to create a more inclusive academic atmosphere.

Selective Inclusivity and Tokenism

What would people say if they saw a building without a wheelchair ramp or any other way for a person on a wheelchair to enter without unnecessary obstacles or difficulties? Certainly, many would object and immediately ask for a change. What would people say if an academic conference did not let women or members of the LGBTQ community participate in it? Most academics would fight for their rights. This is what inclusivity means or should mean; this is how it works. Resources should be used to provide access for everyone. How is it any different in the case of a call for papers saying there is only an on-site program while many scholars cannot attend in person – especially at a time when many academics have already adjusted to online or hybrid conferences? Or when a course description insists on constant physical presence on campus when distant learning has already been around for a long time or has become normal during lockdowns? Distance education is not a new phenomenon either. It has officially existed in the US since 1883 (Tandy & Meacham, 2009).

If the needs of vulnerable groups are ignored in higher education, universities will look similar to business firms rather than social and educational establishments, and will probably be accused of having a double standard regarding inclusivity which is based on a marketing strategy, rather than a genuine concern for inclusivity. For instance, if when fighting antisemitism or gender bias becomes popular, universities and academics invest resources to address these issues, but fail to do so for a problem whose discussion is not yet so trendy, they can simply be accused of not caring, at least not so much. In some cases, such behavior might be considered a sign of tokenism, which is admitting some minorities merely for appearances, not for actual inclusivity.

Therefore, discussing the aforementioned problems in higher education is a crucial matter because there are many people who face many obstacles for physical presence, and neglecting them would render our notion of inclusivity selective at best.

Obstacles for Physical Presence

While promoting a course or a conference as an international one, we must be inclusive. If exclusion based on race or gender is wrong, it is also wrong if it is based on where people live, whether they can afford a plane ticket and hotel bills, or their disabilities making travel too hard – all of which can be easily dealt with by using a hybrid format.

There are various disabilities that make travel – especially long ones – very difficult for scholars. Discussing those disabilities in detail would go beyond the scope of this paper. However, it is clear that restrictions leading to people's exclusion can easily be overcome with the option to attend courses or conferences online.

Moreover, there are many scholars living in countries with plunging currencies who must sacrifice a lot to cover travel expenses, if they can at all. For instance, many scholars living in some Eastern European and Middle Eastern countries face such financial obstacles, which would exclude some scholars and pave the way for others, not because they are better qualified in terms of knowledge, but simply because they can afford it. Although academia cannot solve all of the problems of a neoliberal, capitalist economy at once, it can at least help reduce the suffering of fellow scholars and help them become more productive.

Even without physical disabilities or financial obstacles, there is already an invisible travel wall around most Western countries. Nationals of many countries need to apply for a visa to enter certain countries, which can include frustrating paperwork with a chance of rejection. The various travel bans in place also have consequences for scholars. Immigration crises due to war or oppression have led to strict regulations as well. Another problem is that sometimes even with an official invitation, there is a long processing time in some circumstances. There is also a virtual wall due to sanctions which, instead of state members, target ordinary citizens – which leads to marginalized voices being silenced and intentionally or unintentionally further oppressed. For instance, in the midst of the 2022 protests, Iranians were angry because issuing visas had been unofficially stopped (Middle East Eye, 2022), which was expected because Western governments were probably afraid that they would not want to go back once they had set foot on democratic Western lands. In addition, at the same time, despite denying that they had temporarily stopped processing applications, the French embassy said they were sorry for some issues that had slowed down the process (Euronews Persian, 2022).

Promoting Distance Learning and Virtual Attendance

Despite some shortcomings, virtual attendance still has many perks for people with disabilities; for example, they do not need to travel and they have access to recorded materials possibly with captions. In the United States, the Declaration of Rights of Disabled Persons stated that people with disabilities should have the same rights as others (Deluca, 2013), and virtual attendance can help achieve that. During the lockdowns, the role of technology as a tool which helped connect people and share information grew (Bricout et al., 2021). In addition, commuters saved time, energy, and money.

Unfortunately, there were organizations that resisted virtual attendance and even reduced work to a minimum during lockdowns, enough to merely keep the courses going, and cancelled the events right until late 2022. We are not naming or singling out any organizations or institutions here, but a simple internet search can show course descriptions, application requirements, and calls for papers, which emphasize on-site events or courses, or do not mention virtual attendance, as if they were not able to adjust to the circumstances of the past couple of years at all. Further, there are now an increasing number of courses and events that do not support virtual attendance anymore. We argue that even if the problem is better engagement in some cases, we should be looking for better technologies or training to engage online participants more, instead of locking them out.

Some might be worried about some fields of study such as medical studies in which there might be something that could not be learned via a video conference with their current communication technology. Even then, being against hybrid attendance would not be fully justified because some high-maintenance, costly equipment might also be available elsewhere, or at least not always necessary. Moreover, Faner et al. (2022) have found that Zoom and on-campus lectures in biochemistry and genetics resulted in similar achievement of course objectives, and that online exam security worked.

Therefore, we argue that distance learning and virtual attendance are a crucial part of higher education now, and if institutions are worried about the students or lecturers in courses, they should train them for distance learning, or at least they should not exclude those who are comfortable with it and have no other way.

A Non-Inclusive Nostalgia

There is some gratification for academics in returning to pre-lockdown academia. For example, academics could meet colleagues in person, and some would love to travel, visit the campus, and have access to the university's facilities and equipment, and maybe even participate in some fun activities. However, all of these could also be achieved via a hybrid format.

Closing the doors to the people who cannot travel and attend academic events or courses physically, when there is no real need for physical presence, is just as bad as designing a building without a wheelchair ramp, or organizing an event which does not admit minorities. It is most probably a sign of a lack of awareness, which could even undermine the credibility of the institution or at least the course or event, especially if it is advertised as an "international" one. It is less likely, in many cases at least, to be a sign of an intentional exclusion – and therefore oppression – of certain communities.

Fortunately, there are also conferences and courses fully online or with a hybrid format welcoming presenters and participants both online and on-site. Yet, this should not be a temporary policy; it must continue. In the long run, it will further improve the quality of the course or event because of the inclusivity and the competition it creates. Institutions should not create unnecessary challenges for presenters, organizers, hosts, lecturers, and participants who have disabilities or financial issues, or face travel restrictions.

Conclusion

Finally, it is important to note that for people with disabilities, letting go of the achievements in academia during lockdowns in terms of inclusivity would lead to their exclusion and suffering, and for those based in remote areas of the world, it would lead to further exclusion and an obligation to emigrate. Academic conferences and courses should move toward ending all kinds of discrimination, which includes discrimination against scholars for whom physical presence is almost impossible or simply inconvenient.

Further, exclusive in-person attendance is overrated. In many cases physical presence is unnecessary. In addition, online work even constitutes a major part of jobs now, and many employees returning to the office only find themselves still working online while sitting in the office (Abril, 2021; Ballentine & McNeely, 2022).

Moreover, institutions counting on their income from international students might want to try to get back on track, and they would have to adapt to the new situation to survive because there have already been problems such as the Council on International Educational Exchange announcing in the United States that it would make 600 jobs redundant (Altbach & de Wit, 2020). Therefore, even from a purely economic perspective, this is not a plea for charity. An inclusive academia would be much more productive than an exclusive one, thus making it more plausible even for those who are merely concerned with how the investment might pay off. There are many international scholars who do not have certain fields of study in their own countries, so they look for opportunities abroad. Institutions can even see them as an investment which benefits both the scholars and the institutions in the current cut-throat, neoliberal, capitalist labor market. Therefore, the availability of online participation should not be perceived as a burden, a favor, or even a privilege, but a right. It would be absurd to see academics discussing inclusivity while pursuing non-inclusive policies.

Further research can be done on how technology – even when online participation is an option – can work as a filter, blocking people's access. For example, what good is technology, such as an application like Zoom, if it is not accessible to all academics? Zoom has blocked Iranian IPs – among others – and mostly civilians have suffered. The Zoom "Support" website says, "For regulatory reasons, users in this country are currently unable to access Zoom services" (Zoom, 2022). This has been written in front of the names of five countries. Helsper (2021) has pointed out that from one perspective, technology can offer unique opportunities to marginalized people, but from another perspective, it can also add another obstacle for their participation. In the case of Zoom, it seems to be doing the latter, which is worthy of academic scrutiny.

About the Authors

HOSSEIN MOHAMMADZADE has a master's degree in English Language and Literature. He is currently an independent researcher, and he studies videogames, television, education, and the media. His main area of interest is the relationship between ideology, narrative, and videogames.

Email: hosseinmohammadzade92@gmail.com

ATEFE NAJJAR MANSOOR has a bachelor's degree in English Language Translation. She is an independent researcher, and her research focuses on videogames, education, the media, and ideology.

Email: atefenajjarmansoor@gmail.com

References

Abril, D. (2021, September 27). Workers are putting on pants to return to the office only to be on Zoom all day. The Washington Post. https://www.washingtonpost.com/technology/2021/09/27/return-to-work-in-person-hybrid/

Altbach, P. G., & de Wit, H. (2020). Postpandemic outlook for higher education is bleakest for the poorest. International Higher Education, (102), 3–5. https://ejournals.bc.edu/index.php/ihe/article/view/14583

Ballentine, C., & McNeely A. (2022, April 1). Employees Are Returning to the Office, Just to Sit on Zoom Calls. Bloomberg. https://www.bloomberg.com/news/articles/2022-04-01/employees-are-returning-to-office-post-covid-just-to-sit-on-zoom-calls

Bricout, J., Baker, P. M., Moon, N. W., & Sharma, B. (2021). Exploring the smart future of participation: Community, inclusivity, and people with disabilities. International Journal of E-Planning Research (IJEPR), 10(2), 94-108. https://doi.org/10.4018/ijepr.20210401.oa8

DeLuca, C. (2013). Toward an Interdisciplinary Framework for Educational Inclusivity. Canadian Journal of Education, 36(1), 305–348. http://www.jstor.org/stable/canajeducrevucan.36.1.305

El Said, G. R. (2021). How Did the COVID-19 pandemic affect higher education learning experience? An empirical investigation of learners' academic performance at a university in a developing country. Advances in Human-Computer Interaction, 2021, Article 6649524. https://doi.org/10.1155/2021/6649524

Euronews Persian. (2022, October 11). Sefarat-e faranse taliq-e sodoor-e viza baraye iranian ra takzib kard [The French embassy denied the suspension of issuing visas for Iranians]. https://per.euronews.com/2022/10/11/french-embassy-in-tehran-dnies-suspension-iran-visa-schengen-europe

Faner, M. A., Ritchie, R. P., Ruger, K. M., Waarala, K. L., & Wilkins, C. A. (2022). Student performance in medical biochemistry and genetics: comparing campus-based versus zoom-based lecture delivery. BMC Med Education, 22, Article 798. https://doi.org/10.1186/s12909-022-03873-y

Helsper, E. (2021). The Digital Disconnect: The Social Causes and Consequences of Digital Inequalities. SAGE.

Howard, T. C., & Aleman, G. R. (2008). Teacher capacity for diverse learners: What do teachers need to know? In M. Cochran-Smith, S. Feiman-Nemser, & D. J. McIntyre, K. E. Demers (Eds.), Handbook of Research on Teacher Education: Enduring Questions in Changing Contexts (pp. 157-174). Routledge.

Middle East Eye. (2022, October 12). Schengen visa: Iranians denounce European embassies for halting applications amid protests. https://www.middleeasteye.net/news/schengen-iran-denounce-europe-embassies-halting-visa-applications

Tamim, T. (2021). Language, Class, and Education: Deconstructing the Centre to Rethink Inclusivity in Education in Pakistan. Cogent Education, 8(1), Article 1897933. https://doi.org/10.1080/2331186X.2021.1897933

Tandy, C. & Meacham, M. (2009). Removing the Barriers for Students with Disabilities: Accessible Online and Web-Enhanced Courses. Journal of Teaching in Social Work, 29(2), 313–323. https://doi.org/10.1080/08841230903022118

Zoom. (2022, February 24). Restricted countries or regions. https://support.zoom.us/hc/en-us/articles/203806119-Restricted-countries-or-regions

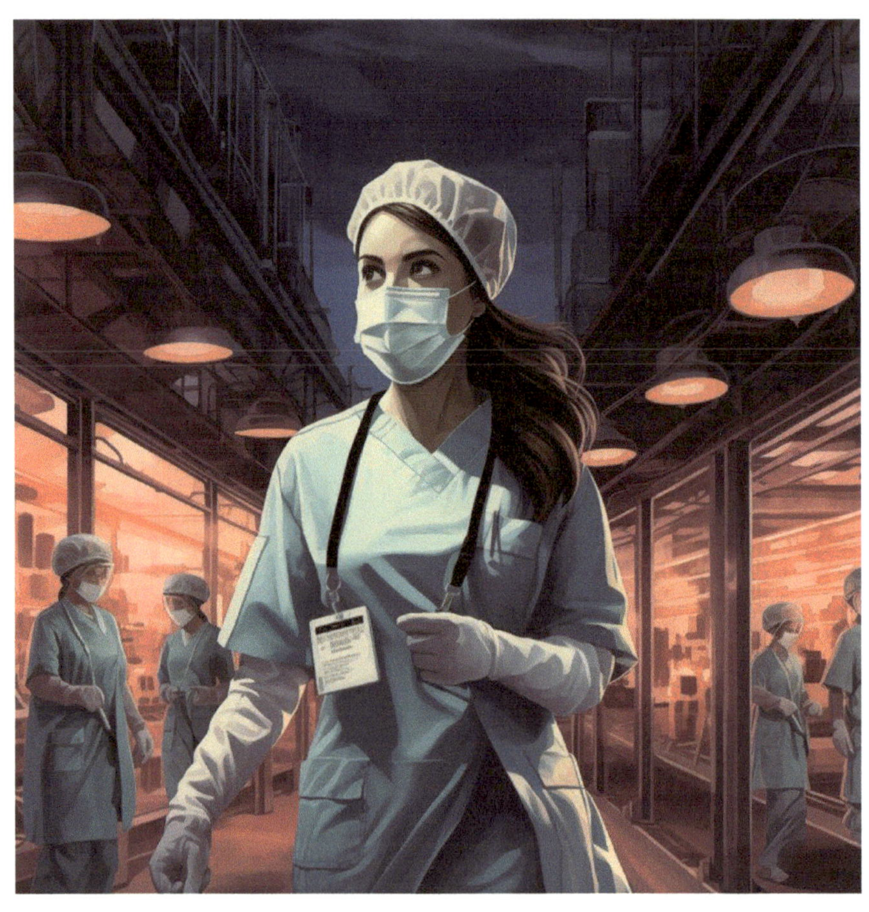

MEDICAL ART AND THE PANDEMIC

FROM IDENTIFYING THE 'BIG BAD' TO ADVANCEMENTS IN MEDICAL EDUCATION

Hana Pokojná

The global COVID-19 pandemic has prevented people from continuing their normal lives, which impacted the way we communicate and learn. Medical visualization and art were omnipresent during the pandemic and started with giving face to the common problem, the virus. Advice on preventative measures and symptoms in public spaces often utilized infographics. People used medicine-inspired images to express their situation. The next stage that visualization aided with was bringing training to people's homes as the second next best thing to get an adequate education. The need to continue education and training of experts in the medical field was continued, thanks to the upheaval of new ways of learning anatomy through digital media. These went beyond textbooks, and included new medical animations, interactive applications, and the use of immersive realities. The testament of their success is continuation of their use as a compliment to hands-on approach in education as part of the curriculum even once the restrictions were curbed. This paper focuses on how different types of medical visualization, that combine art and technology, helped people identify, communicate, cope, and learn during the pandemic and beyond.

Keywords: biomedical education, medical visualization, education and pandemic, medical art, science communication

Introduction

The COVID-19 pandemic had a profound impact on how people interact due to the necessary isolations and lockdowns to help prevent the spread of the virus. Communication between people has taken a turn, as the virus and its effects have influenced our day-to-day lives, anything from what we were concerned for and how we got on with our jobs and continuation of studies. Visualization became one of the ways to point to the common enemy, how to prevent its spread, how we communicate our feelings as well as an aid in education. This paper will focus on summarizing how medical visualization was present in these aspects of our lives and how technological applications of medical art and visualization in education were applied and remained applied even post pandemic, due to their benefits.

The corona-related restrictions were especially difficult for continuation of studies in medical fields, for example for future nurses, doctors and other medical professionals. Medical students all over the world have to undergo training in human anatomy through dissection in order to familiarize themselves with the intricacies of the human body and how to apply their knowledge to it. Therefore, it is still considered a 'golden standard' in learning anatomy (Parker, 2002). However, different applications of medical visualization that combine art, science, and the ever-evolving technology, visualization in medicine has great benefit to more than one target group. The advancements in technology were only sped up during the lockdowns because of its necessity to replace what we see as 'traditional teaching' and remained in use due to their benefits.

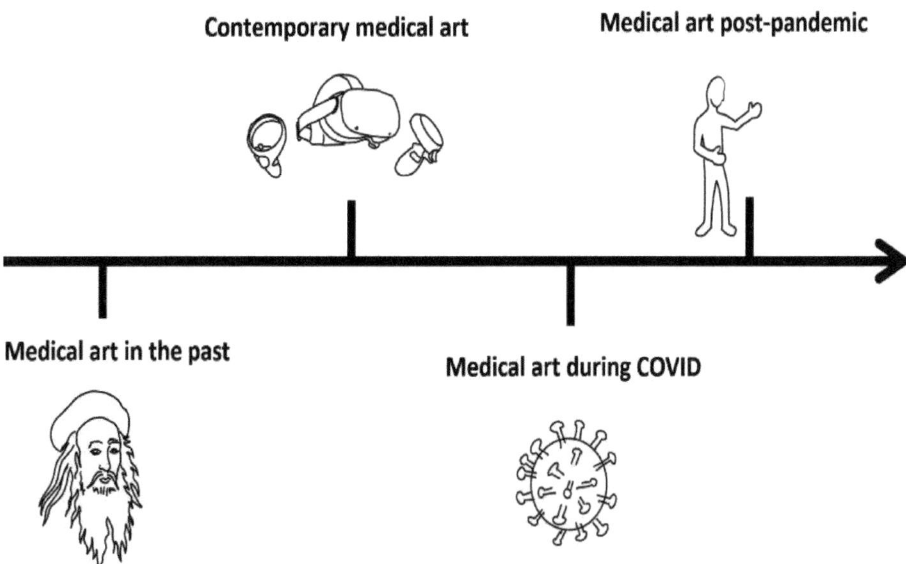

Figure 1. Overview of medical art throughout history

Why is Medical Art Needed?

Medical art has been aiding medical education for a long time. Its benefits are materials that help people understand anatomy, for example by showing structures that are difficult to differentiate in cadavers (Frediueu et. al., 2015). Medical visualization of anatomy is also helpful with dealing with emotions around cadaveric dissections. It can be used as an adjacent learning tool to help people to ease into dissection sessions as some novice students suffer from cadaver anxiety (Arráez-Aybar et. al., 2004). Obtaining cadavers can also carry a moral or religious dilemma (Prince et. al., 2005), so visualization of the cadaveric material makes it more widely available. Another, recently prominent issue, was the low availability of cadavers due to the health concerns during the COVID-19 pandemic (Brassett et. al, 2020), where different visualization tools to depict human anatomy were used, in place of in-person dissection sessions.

Outside of medical training, medical visualization is also important for communication. For example, effectively visualizing what causes a certain health issue helps non-experts in medical field to understand the root of the problem and make informed decisions about their health. An example is using infographics to explain how a small particle can cause havoc, as the one that was recently experienced in March 2019 all over the world. Visualization can furthermore serve as an instruction manual to help people understand how to prevent diseases from spreading.

Brief History

First examples of medical art were in illustrative form and date back to the 14-15th century, where Leonardo Da Vinci created medical illustrations (Gosh, 2015). These depict the innermost structures of the human body, ranging from muscles, bones, and even the pregnant womb in humans, but also anatomical structures of animals. These observations were recorded through illustrations from cadavers of specimens. Later on, medical visualization also took physical form. This came in form and used different materials, but perhaps the most impressive are the anatomical Venuses made from wax. These intricate models of different parts of the human body and systems were ordered by Joseph II to improve medical education in Vienna in the 1800, limiting the need of human cadavers. They can still be seen today in the Medical School in Vienna at Josephinium (Markovska, 2015).

Contemporary Medical Art

With advancements in technology, medical visualization has advanced and taken many shapes. These differ in modalities, such as 3D interactive models (Erolin, 2018), augmented reality (Kumar et. al., 2021), virtual reality (Lobovitz & Hubbard, 2020), and wearable technologies (Al Janabi et. al, 2020). As Hu. et. al. (2018) has described, medical visualization has undergone an evolution. Use of medical art is now present in higher education for training experts, for public outreach, communication between experts and visualization of data for analyses.

Covid-19 and Medical Art

Medical art was behind many representations and communication between the government and the public, researchers and the public, as well as utilized as means to continue the 'semi-normal' during hard lockdowns. This includes identifying the 'problem' visually, first for scientists, then to the general public. It also helped with the education of the public by creating manuals, instructions and storytelling for different audiences to understand the situation, or to take preventative initiatives. It has also found a place in communication between people and people's views on the circumstances and politics. Medical art was also a great help in helping to ameliorate the effects of isolation in medical education, and some of the practices were adapted to current curricula.

Visualization of the Problem

The visualization of the virus differs from its raw-data appearance and what we know it as today. Visualizing raw data-understandable for experts in virology, are different to visualizations for people who are non-experts in those fields. Hence certain work needed to be done to the real data to make them more understandable to everyone, and help people point to what is causing the international havoc.

Medical Visualization

The below image by Centers for Disease Control and Prevention (CDC) shows an electron microscope image obtained from the first patient case in the United States. While it is readable for experts in virology, it appears abstract to non-experts. While this is a useful medical visualization for the expert group who identified the issue, it does not tell much to the masses that will have been affected by it.

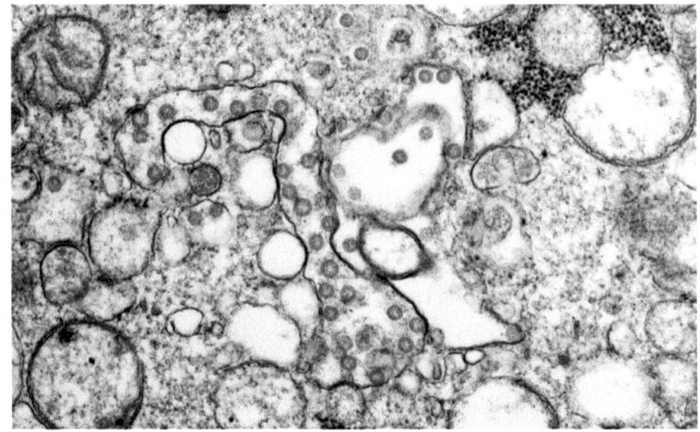

Figure 2. Electron microscope image of COVID-19 from the first case in the US, made by CDC.

Medical Render

Medical visualization used to help people understand what is causing the problems is rooted in real data. The knowledge from microbiology and raw data from Protein Data Bank[1] was combined with 3D visualization to render an eye-catching, yet not scary image of the particle that has, literally, taken over the world. The artists Alissa Eckert and Dan Higgins used 3D modelling software Autodesk 3Ds Max[2] to create harmonizing colours and light set-up for the virus with its recognizable protein spikes. The idea behind this image was to attract attention yet not cause panic.

---

[1] https://www.autodesk.com/products/3ds-max/overview?term=1-YEAR&tab=subscription
[2] https://www.rcsb.org/

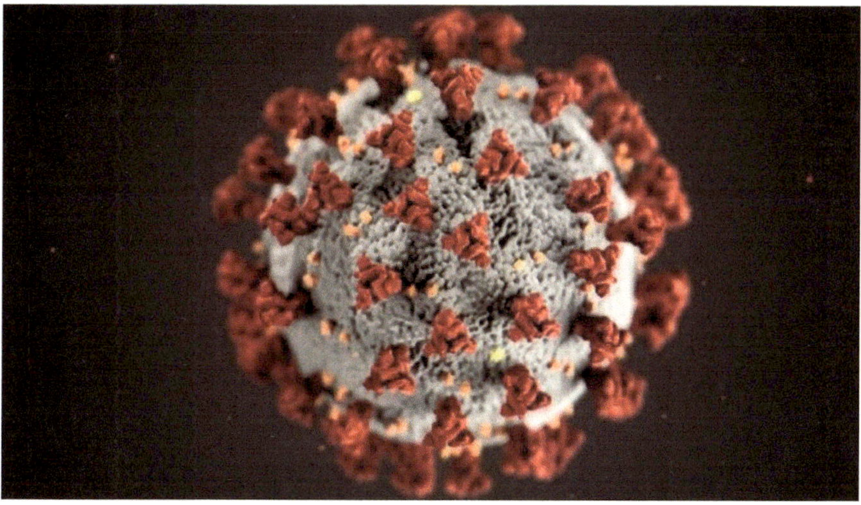

Figure 3. Render of COVID-19 virus made by CDC's artist Allisa Eckert and Dan Higgins.

Education of the Public

Education of the public during the pandemic heavily used medical visualization. From animations on TV to infographics that were ever-present in public spaces. Education included instructional visual manuals on how to prevent the spread of the disease, explanations of what COVID-19 is to different target groups (children versus adults), and asked the public to take an initiative with vaccines by explaining its impact, as well as explaining the mutations on a microscopic level.

Prevention

The prevention heavily relied on visualization through infographics. This included instructional information such as practicing social distancing (2 meters or 6 feet), stating the limited number of people allowed to enter closed spaces, reminder to wear face masks and in some cases specific type of face covering (such as the FFP2 mask), as well as how to properly wash hands. The last example is depicted in an instructional infographic on how to properly wash hands and prevent spread made by the National Health Service (NHS) of the United Kingdom.

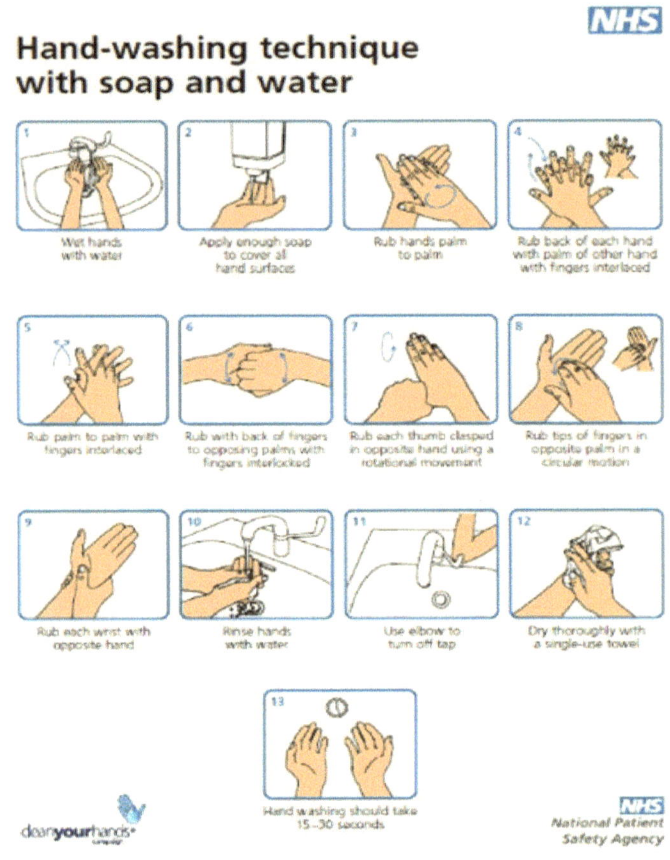

Figure 4. Instructional manual on hand-washing technique by NHS.

Initiative

Visualizations were also used to help people understand how the virus affects their body. While this is a complex process to understand on a biological level for people who do net specialize in biomedicine, the visual representations used for explanation used simple graphics and explanations to explain what causes the resulting symptoms. These infographics also explained, in simple terms, how the vaccine can help the body to fight against the virus, hence providing people with explanations so they can make an informed decision to get vaccinated and protect themselves and their surroundings.

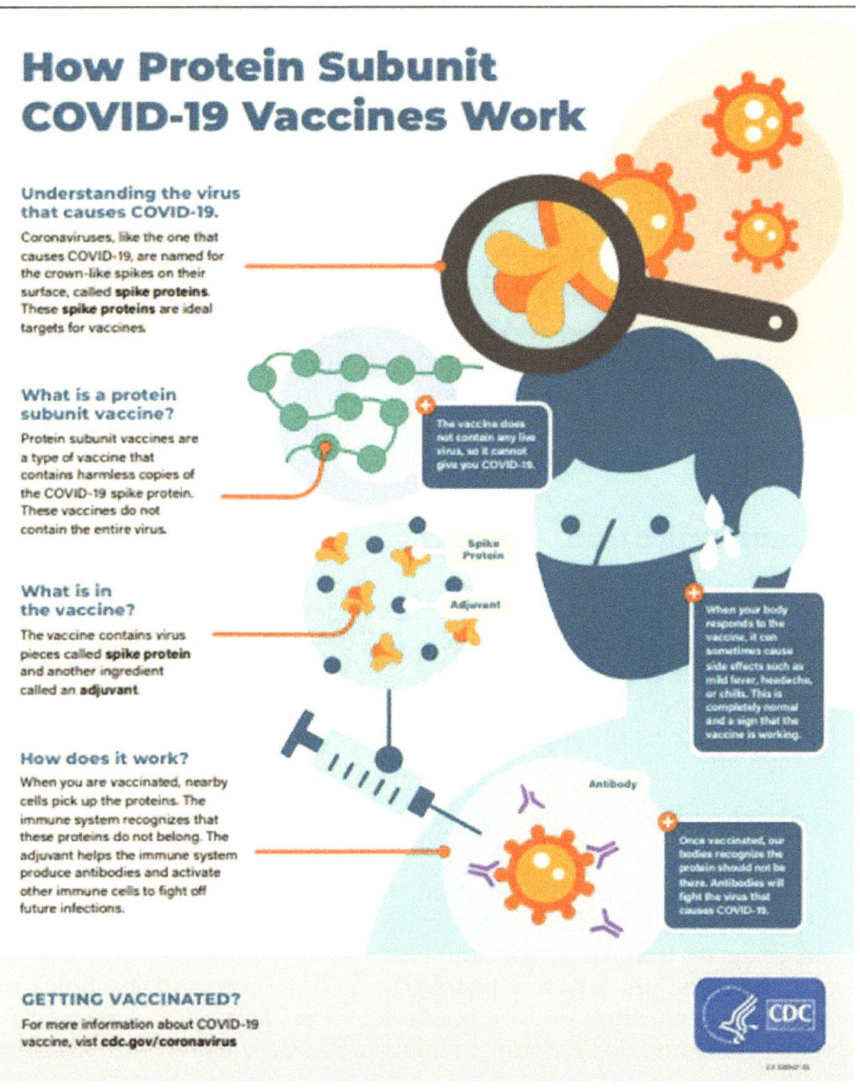

Figure 5. Poster explaining COVID-19 on biological level and effects of vaccine, by CDC.

Storytelling

Visual storytelling is a big part of medical visualization and its aim is to explain important aspects (McCurdy, 2016, Botsis et.al, 2020) In this case it was information about the COVID-19 virus explained to different audiences. The previously mentioned examples were mainly targeted at adults. However, different approaches were employed to explain this situation, for example, to children. An example is an animation by Eurac Research (EURACtv, 2020) that shows the symptoms and causes of COVID-19. Compared to the initial examples of the electron microscope image or even the render. This depiction is more colorful and uses the metaphor of 'antennas' while describing the virus' spikes, giving it an unfriendly face and the animation is narrated by a child. The storytelling approach goes in line with research by Meuschke et. al (2021) who have shown that narrative storytelling is helpful in in addressing general public about diseases.

Communication

Medical visualization of the virus also had an impact on the communication between people. This was presented in the number of chosen graphic images related to the pandemic. Another aspect of communication was through political satire and comparing certain situations to the virus itself.

Interpersonal

Interpersonal communication was obvious through the use of different graphic image choices, known as emojis. It is interesting to observe that medical visualization was also very present in communication between people, and that through the choice of emojis. According to Emojipedia[3] at the height of the corona pandemic and lockdowns in March 2020, the Facemask emoji

---

[3] https://emojipedia.org/

(35.82%) and the virus/ microbe (42.09%) emojis were used the most. Compared to July 2019, the emojis with facemask and the virus skyrocketed in use describing people feeling unwell, compared to the head with bandages used for this communication previously (Broni, 2020). A new emoji was also introduced and that was an arm with a plaster representing vaccines/ jabs (Boender, 2022).

Political

Comics were a way to communicate political feelings. Another way how biomedical visualizations and the pandemic made its way into the satirical communication of politics (Alabi, 2020). While it is distanced from the medical visualization based on accurate data, in caricatures there definitely is a component of visualizing of something medical. Good examples are political satires of how global leaders have handled the economic situation, even using metaphors of the virus itself to toxic behaviours.

Medical Education

Medical education was greatly affected by the lockdown, however, because of its importance the education went on in different forms. It combined different techniques to make the study of anatomy 'as normal as possible'. Brasset et. al (2020) outlines the different ways European universities have adapted to the circumstances, mainly through use of technology such as interactive 3D applications and videos. These online and technological tools were easier deployed as the main learning resources in cases where they were used already alongside the cadaveric dissections (Cheng et. al., 2021).

E-learning before, during and after corona

The need to be separated helped to speed up the development of remote learning tools. Examples are the pre-pandemic e-learning tools that were received very positively, that were improved and used during the pandemic because of a necessity, and integrated into curriculums even after the restrictions ceased down because of their benefits.

Even before corona, e-learning in medical fields was becoming more popular. An evaluation of Web3D education, medical education using 3D models over the world wide web and in this case focusing on general education tools; tools for diagnosis; procedures training; and collaborative training, has had positive feedback and concluded that emergence of this field will have an application in the medical education field (John, 2007). A study on medical e-learning done 14 years before the pandemic reported as positive, even enjoyable (Ruiz et. al., 2006).

Later study into e-learning had also positive feedback (Huynh, 2017). It focused on videoclips, simulations and e-training that were slowly introduced to schools and were perceived as helpful because of being easily updated and self-directed. Huynh et al. have predicted that that form of learning will have a big impact on education in the future.

In 2018, 11 universities all over the world (such as University of Vienna, John Hopkin's Children's Hospital...) deployed so-called Oculus modules for their medical students. These simulations would provide students with real life scenarios in virtual environment resembling a real-life hospital to placements that would not always be available for all students.

Unfortunately, during the pandemic, the medical education had taken a fall. International study of medical students reported decrease of teaching quality and preparedness. However, it also pointed to new ways of teaching and simulating theater time and patient interaction (TMS Colaboartive).

The issues that students in medical professions have faced were several. One of the most important parts of these professions is working with people, however, there was no patient contact. Equally the students had no theater time to observe and assist with surgeries. Moreover, the interaction between students, and therefore information exchange, was also limited as there was no face-to-face contact between students besides of the online classes (TMS Collaborative, 2021). In addition to these issues, the body donations were limited (Brasett et. al, 2020), meaning that there were no cadavers to learn from and dissection is one of the main pillars of medicine (Parker, 2002).

Medical Education During Lockdowns

Medical education was greatly affected by the lockdown, however, because of its importance the education went on in different forms. It combined different techniques to make the study of anatomy 'as normal as possible'. Brassett et. al (2020) outlines the different ways European universities have adapted to the circumstances, mainly through use of technology such as interactive 3D applications and videos. However, these circumstances also had positive outcomes as it used recently developed postgraduate anatomy course entirely online (Kelsey et. al, 2020), formerly intended to help reach far geographical locations and that could be implemented due to isolation.

Different Educational Resources Used During Lockdowns

Overall, adaptation to e-learning has had a positive impact on education on medical students during the period of unavailability of in-person education, therefore parts of it should be integrated into curriculum once the lockdowns are over (Shrivastava & Shrivastava, 2020). The online anatomy course has also included students from art-related degree (28%), which indicated how popular and helpful online teaching resources in anatomy are (Kelsey et. al, 2020). There are many different types of applications that can be used for teaching anatomy. A summary of immediate responses to online anatomy teaching by Brasett et. al. (2020) lists the software and other tools used for anatomy education during the lockdown. These include online atlases, interactive 3D applications, 3D models with various textures.

For example, 3D interactive applications with anatomical models were used. Examples include the Visible Body[4] application used at the University of Cambridge and The

---

[4] https://www.visiblebody.com/

BioDigital[5] application used by Nul Galway. Photographs of pro-sections with the university's anatomical collection were documented with cameras and used for spotter tests that are standard ways of testing knowledge in an anatomical course. 3D models could also be uploaded to interactive online platforms such as Skethfab[6]. This platform also allowed uploading models made with photogrammetry of the real cadavers, which provided real texture instead of computer-made one by 3D artists (University of Aberdeen and University of Dundee). Oxford University used Ackland's Anatomy[7] video atlas, where real specimens were videoed, narrated and specific areas of interest highlighted.

Medical Art and Education Post Lockdowns

Different institutions have adapted some of the remote materials. In a study comprising 104 medical students who completed the study, they reported positive feedback to training in Virtual Reality (VR), saw it as realistic for initial clinical assessments, and considered it useful as an additional learning tool to real clinical cases (dePonti et. al, 2020). A systematic review of 39 studies examining VR for education and healthcare has concluded that they have been successful for medical training and for treating several health conditions (such as therapeutic for reducing stress, anxiety...) (Pallavicini et. al., 2022). Some universities have applied training using Virtual Reality not only to give students a chance to virtually attend theater time, but also for safety measures, such as at University of Virginia (Moody, 2022). The development of online materials allows the spread of quality information to faraway places, such as using online seminars (Sarillita, 2022). Other universities have applied combined learning (Bassett et. al, 2020). The comparison of students in dissection and e-learning group of head and neck anatomy has shown no difference in knowledge levels, however it showed decreased confidence levels for non-dissection group that increased post intervention. The researchers concluded that blended learning should include both e-learning material and

---

[5] https://www.biodigital.com/
[6] https://sketchfab.com/
[7]https://aclandanatomy.com/

dissection sessions as frequent users of e-learning had significantly higher scores (Schulte et. al., 2022). A survey of anatomy students has also shown that blended-lectures that include online lectures yield higher test scores and are preferred by the students due to more study time, which suggest adopting this mode of studying after lockdown (Yoo & Lee, 2021). Iwanaga and colleagues (2021) argue that educators should re-visit all teaching methods, such as video, social media, AR and VR, as the future with cadaver training may be unpredictable, but overall, all methods should be used in parallel rather than exclude one another.

Conclusion

Design and media in form of medical art and visualization were important and always present during and after the pandemic. They aided in visualization of the problem, explanation of the problem, and its prevention, as well as education. The educational tools were used to inform the general public, was adapted to different target groups based on age, as well as education of medical students, for whom anatomical education is very important. The field of medical education, specifically in anatomy, was expanded and adapted during the lockdowns and some of it was adapted to post-pandemic education in form of blended learning due to its benefits.

About the Author

HANA POKOJNÁ has Master's degrees in Medical Visualization & Human Anatomy and Medical Art. Her research focuses on visual storytelling in science, and how new visual aids can help in education of biomedicine and anatomy to the general public, students and researchers. She joined Visitlab at Masaryk University as a PhD student in March 2021.

Twitter: @PokHana

References

Alabi, O. S. (2020). Crisis Communication and Coping Strategies during COVID-19 Pandemic: A Content Analysis of Coronavirus Cartoons and Comics (CCC). *Available at SSRN 3794390.*

Al Janabi, H. F., Aydin, A., Palaneer, S., Macchione, N., Al-Jabir, A., Khan, M. S., ... & Ahmed, K. (2020). Effectiveness of the HoloLens mixed-reality headset in minimally invasive surgery: a simulation-based feasibility study. *Surgical Endoscopy, 34,* 1143-1149.

Arráez-Aybar, L. A., Casado-Morales, M. I., & Castaño-Collado, G. (2004). Anxiety and dissection of the human cadaver: an unsolvable relationship?. *The Anatomical Record Part B: The New Anatomist: An Official Publication of the American Association of Anatomists, 279*(1), 16-23.

Boender, T. S., Louis-Ferdinand, N., & Duschek, G. (2022). Digital visual communication for public health: design proposal for a vaccinated emoji. *Journal of Medical Internet Research, 24*(4), e35786.

Botsis, T., Fairman, J. E., Moran, M. B., & Anagnostou, V. (2020). Visual storytelling enhances knowledge dissemination in biomedical science. *Journal of biomedical informatics, 107,* 103458.

Brassett, C., Cosker, T., Davies, D. C., Dockery, P., Gillingwater, T. H., Lee, T. C., ... & Wilkinson, T. (2020). COVID-19 and anatomy: Stimulus and initial response. *Journal of anatomy, 237*(3), 393-403.

Broni, K. (2020, March 13). *Spread of the coronavirus emoji.* Emojipedia. Retrieved December 8, 2022, from https://blog.emojipedia.org/spread-of-the-coronavirus-emoji/

Cheng, X., Chan, L. K., Pan, S. Q., Cai, H., Li, Y. Q., & Yang, X. (2021). Gross anatomy education in China during the Covid-19 pandemic: A national survey. *Anatomical Sciences Education, 14*(1), 8-18.

Delbert, C. (2020, April 2). *How illustrators created the iconic Coronavirus Image.* Popular Mechanics. Retrieved December 10, 2022, from https://www.popularmechanics.com/science/a32021752/coronavirus-model-illustration/

De Ponti, R., Marazzato, J., Maresca, A. M., Rovera, F., Carcano, G., & Ferrario, M. M. (2020). Pre-graduation medical training including virtual reality during COVID-19 pandemic: a report on students' perception. *BMC medical education, 20,* 1-7.

Erolin, C. (2019). Interactive 3D digital models for anatomy and medical education. *Biomedical Visualisation: Volume 2,* 1-16.

EURACtv. (2020). *The coronavirus explained to children. YouTube.* Retrieved December 10, 2022, from https://www.youtube.com/watch?v=MVvVTDhGqaA&ab_channel=EuracResearch.

Fredieu, J. R., Kerbo, J., Herron, M., Klatte, R., & Cooke, M. (2015). Anatomical models: a digital revolution. *Medical science educator, 25,* 183-194.

Ghosh, S. K. (2015). Evolution of illustrations in anatomy: A study from the classical period in E urope to modern times. *Anatomical Sciences Education, 8*(2), 175-188.

Hu, M., Wattchow, D., & de Fontgalland, D. (2018). From ancient to avant-garde: A review of traditional and modern multimodal approaches to surgical anatomy education. *ANZ journal of surgery, 88*(3), 146-151.

Huynh, R. (2017). The role of E-learning in medical education. *Academic Medicine, 92*(4), 430.

Iwanaga, J., Loukas, M., Dumont, A. S., & Tubbs, R. S. (2021). A review of anatomy education during and after the COVID-19 pandemic: Revisiting traditional and modern methods to achieve future innovation. *Clinical Anatomy, 34*(1), 108-114.

John, N. W. (2007). The impact of Web3D technologies on medical education and training. *Computers & Education, 49*(1), 19-31.

Kelsey, A. H., McCulloch, V., Gillingwater, T. H., Findlater, G. S., & Paxton, J. Z. (2020). Anatomical sciences at the University of Edinburgh: Initial experiences of teaching anatomy online. *Translational Research in Anatomy, 19*, 100065.

Kumar, N., Pandey, S., & Rahman, E. (2021). A novel three-dimensional interactive virtual face to facilitate facial anatomy teaching using Microsoft HoloLens. *Aesthetic Plastic Surgery, 45*, 1005-1011.

Labovitz, J., & Hubbard, C. (2020). The use of virtual reality in podiatric medical education. *Clinics in podiatric medicine and surgery, 37*(2), 409-420.

Markovska, M. (2015). Josephinum and the anatomical wax model collection, Medical University of Wien. *Medicina nei secoli: Journal of history of medicine and medical humanities, 27*(2), 589-600.

McCurdy, K. (2016). Visual storytelling in healthcare: Why we should help patients visualize their health. *Information Visualization, 15*(2), 173-178.

Meuschke, M., Garrison, L., Smit, N., Bruckner, S., Lawonn, K., & Preim, B. (2021). Towards narrative medical visualization. *arXiv preprint arXiv:2108.05462.*

Moody, D. (2022, October 11). *School of Medicine brings virtual reality training to the classroom for medical students - educationDavid.* Medicine in Motion News. Retrieved December 10, 2022, from https://news.med.virginia.edu/education/school-of-medicine-brings-virtual-reality-training-to-the-classroom-for-medical-students/

Oculus Team. (2018, August 29). *Immersive education: CHLA and oculus expand VR medical training program ...* meta.com. Retrieved December 10, 2022, from https://www.oculus.com/blog/immersive-education-chla-and-oculus-expand-vr-medical-training-program-to-new-institutions/

Pallavicini, F., Pepe, A., Clerici, M., & Mantovani, F. (2022). Virtual Reality Applications in Medicine During the COVID-19 Pandemic: Systematic Review. *JMIR Serious Games, 10*(4), e35000.

Parker, L. M. (2002). Anatomical dissection: why are we cutting it out? Dissection in undergraduate teaching. *ANZ journal of surgery, 72*(12), 910-912.

Prince, K. J., Van Eijs, P. W., Boshuizen, H. P., Van Der Vleuten, C. P., & Scherpbier, A. J. (2005). General competencies of problem-based learning (PBL) and non-PBL graduates. *Medical education, 39*(4), 394-401.

Ruiz, J. G., Mintzer, M. J., & Leipzig, R. M. (2006). The impact of e-learning in medical education. *Academic medicine, 81*(3), 207-212.

Sarilita, E., Nugraha, H. G., Murniati, N., & Soames, R. W. (2022). Online capacity building in anatomy knowledge for high school biology teachers: Community-university partnerships in Indonesia during the covid-19 pandemic. *Gateways: International Journal of Community Research and Engagement, 15*(1), 1-9.

Schulte, H., Schmiedl, A., Mühlfeld, C., & Knudsen, L. (2022). Teaching gross anatomy during the Covid-19 pandemic: Effects on medical students' gain of knowledge, confidence levels and pandemic-related concerns. *Annals of Anatomy-Anatomischer Anzeiger, 244*, 151986.

Shrivastava, S. R., & Shrivastava, P. S. (2020). Assessing the impact of e-learning in medical education. *International Journal of Academic Medicine, 6*(1), 40.

Staff, T. C. (2021, March 18). *Teaching center staff.* University Center for Teaching and Learning. Retrieved December 8, 2022, from https://teaching.pitt.edu/featured/open-lab-assists-center-for-vaccine-research-with-3d-printed-covid-19-models/

TMS Collaborative (2021).The perceived impact of the Covid-19 pandemic on medical student education and training–an international survey. *BMC Medical Education* 21: 1-8.

Wanigasooriya, K., Beedham, W., Laloo, R., Karri, R. S., Darr, A., Layton, G. R., Logan, P., Tan, Y., Mittapalli, D., Patel, T., Mishra, V. D., Odeh, O., Prakash, S., Elnoamany, S., Peddinti, S. R., Daketsey, E. A., Gadgil, S., Bouhuwaish, A. E., Ozair, A., ... Ashpak, A. (2021). The perceived impact of the COVID-19 pandemic on medical student education and training – an international survey. *BMC Medical Education, 21*(1). https://doi.org/10.1186/s12909-021-02983-3

Yoo, H., Kim, D., & Lee, Y. M. (2021). Adaptations in anatomy education during COVID-19. *Journal of Korean medical science, 36*(1).

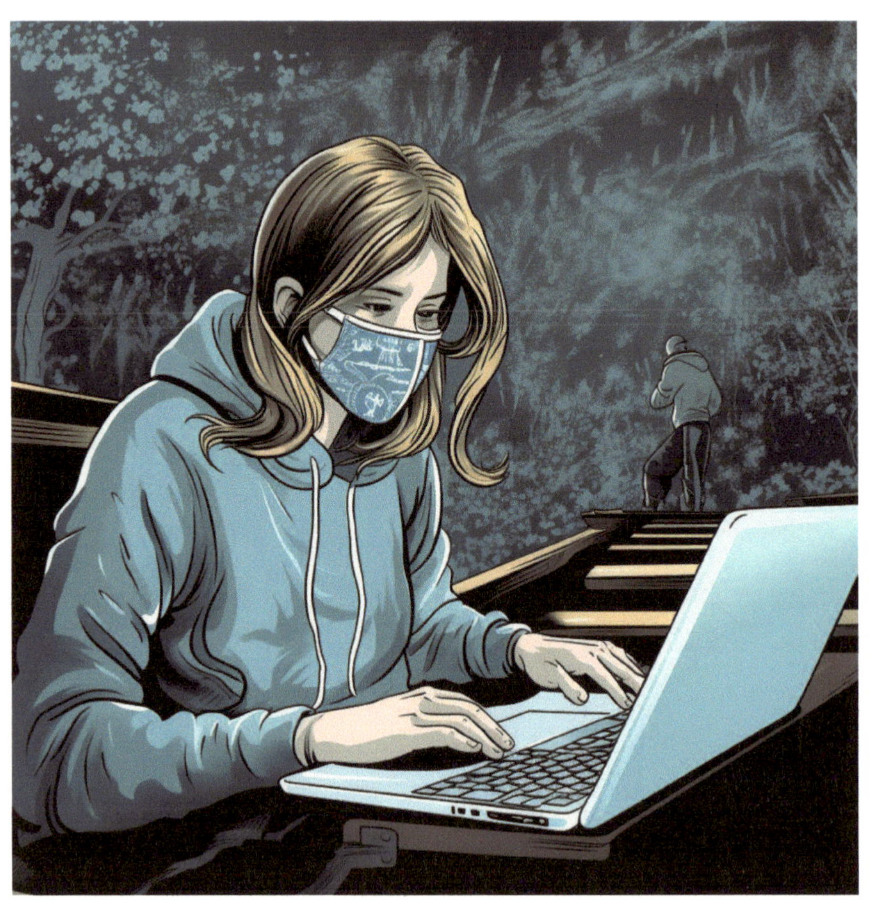

REMODELLING AND REDESIGNING EDUCATION: ANALOGUE to DIGITAL

MY PERSONAL REFLECTIONS ON ONLINE LEARNING DURING THE COVID-19 PANDEMIC

Nanditha Krishna

The COVID-19 pandemic inevitably changed the future of education. The world took to remote learning as a new alternative to conventional in-person classroom teaching and learning despite experiencing a considerable digital-divide. In this paper, I present my personal reflections on online-learning during the pandemic of 2020. I elaborate on my personal experiences with Massive Open Online Courses (*MOOCs*) that helped in a self-paced, self-directed, and self-regulated, asynchronous learning process. I also present my thoughts on how virtual conferences and events such as the Future and Reality of Gaming (FROG) 2021, Media, Arts and Design (MAD) 2021 conference and the Digital Humanities Summer Institute (DHSI) 2022 (online edition) made it accessible and possible for scholars, researchers, learners all over the world to collaborate and network with each other, despite vast geographical distances and time zone differences. I then present my thoughts on how virtual learning helped in overcoming disciplinary boundaries, going beyond the confines of the traditional arts and humanities, paving path to exploring the 'digital' (in) humanities, facilitating exploration of inter-and multi-disciplinarity. Furthermore, I elaborate on how participating in synchronous and asynchronous alike virtual events, working in digital/virtual spaces, mediums and environments provided opportunities for international research collaborations, and how embracing and adopting emerging technologies is important from the perspectives of pedagogy and instructional design, as it further fosters diversity, interdisciplinarity and collaborative learning, and new ways of thinking.

Keywords: online learning, virtual conferences, open scholarship, remote research

---

Going Virtual

At the outset of the COVID-19 pandemic that spread across the world, the course of education experienced a tremendous change. Globally, educational institutions and formal educators took to remote learning as a new temporary and provisional alternative to the conventional in-person classroom teaching and learning. This developed at a time when the world was experiencing a considerable digital-divide, as a consequence of which, there were initial apprehensions and criticisms surrounding this method. Thus, the COVID-19 pandemic inevitably changed the way formal education was materialized and perceived, thereby, giving rise to new possibilities and uncharted territories for the trajectory and future of education.

The online mode of learning is not without its imperfections, much like other methods of learning. However, it is crucial to recognize that online learning also presents new resources, alternative solutions, and opportunities to address certain limitations of offline, conventional learning.

On a personal level, my interactions on the internet were limited to informal communication on social media, prior to the pandemic. When the pandemic hit, I was an undergraduate student trying to adapt to the then-new, virtual mode of learning. However, as time progressed, I found myself liking and adapting quite smoothly to the virtual mode of learning. I inevitably started seeing various benefits to this method, despite the baggage of imperfections it presented. I began to consistently explore and look out for the positives of digital education.

To begin with, I found myself being able to virtually connect and communicate with students from varying cultural backgrounds overseas. I could precisely discover and understand academic discussions that occurred in undergraduate and graduate research-level classrooms located on a different geographical coordinate in the world.

I could explore a variety of research areas and cutting-edge research questions based on the academic discourses that took place in, for example, a sophomore linguistics, learning sciences, electronic music production, or new media and digital culture classroom in Amsterdam, all while being at home in India. Students were increasingly open about their ideas, class projects, and the pros and cons of virtual learning. One major advantage of this multicultural communication was that it allowed me to understand cultural nuances, backgrounds, differences, and witness culture shock firsthand, which significantly increased my cross-cultural awareness.

Furthermore, learning was no longer limited to synchronous interactions. Teaching occurred through both synchronous sessions and recorded lectures. As a student, I could acquire knowledge from the comfort of my physical surroundings, with the utmost flexibility. I could revisit parts of recorded sessions and lectures that I initially found challenging, pausing and replaying them as many times as needed. Additionally, I could take digital notes, archive them, and access them from anywhere, something I hadn't previously considered meaningful until the pandemic. I also found myself dedicating hours to exploring classroom pages and resources available on class websites. The open learning materials and library guides provided by instructors for online access proved incredibly convenient and advantageous. For instance, *The JavaScripting English Major*[1] and *Introduction to Cultural Analytics & Python*[2] are resources

---

[1] by **Moacir P. de Sá Pereira**. A 15-session course that teaches humanities undergraduates how to write their own web-based project using JavaScript). URL: https://the-javascripting-english-major.org/v1/

[2] **Designed by Melanie Walsh.** This website hosts an online textbook, Introduction to Cultural Analytics & Python, which offers an introduction to the programming language Python that is specifically designed for

specifically tailored for students of English literature, arts, humanities and the social sciences.

Crossing Disciplinary Boundaries: Digital Transversal skills

As English majors, a significant portion of our coursework involves critical reading, writing, and editing. However, by exploring digital methods like online ethnography, social media analysis, web-based projects, and virtual questionnaires, students can acquire essential transversal skills that are highly valuable and applicable in various fields of study, both in academia and industry. These methods also foster resourcefulness, encourage brainstorming, and expand opportunities for creative problem-solving.

The pandemic was also a time when I began to reflect on my interaction and engagement with digital media and technology. It prompted me to contemplate education beyond traditional offline learning. I often pondered how the learning process worked, why people learned in certain ways, and how learning design, or its absence, influenced the learning process.

Offline environments certainly have the ability to facilitate exceptional in-person interactions. However, virtual education also offers significant flexibility and learning possibilities. It brings people together in the same virtual room, transcending various cultural backgrounds and providing ample space for discussions. Personally, online environments facilitated global interactions and were cost-effective.

The availability of open learning materials and educational resources allowed me to learn at my own pace, asynchronously, providing the space for critical thinking. It also helped me transcend disciplinary boundaries, enabling me to expand my knowledge beyond the traditional literature and humanities.

---

people interested in the humanities and social sciences. URL: https://melaniewalsh.github.io/Intro-Cultural-Analytics/welcome.html

Virtual learning was instrumental in breaking down these boundaries, extending beyond the confines of traditional arts and humanities, and opening pathways to explore the 'digital' (in) humanities, promoting inter- and multi-disciplinarity. This included access to Massive Open Online Courses (MOOCs), online research and library guides, which empowered learners to engage in self-paced, self-directed, and self-regulated asynchronous, virtual, and hybrid learning. Additionally, other digital learning tools and materials, such as digital games, interactive simulations, podcasts, media, blogs, digital whiteboards, flipped classrooms, and virtual museum tours, further enriched the learning experience. Open scholarship and open educational resources have the power to transform learning on the job and inspire innovative thinking and knowledge production.

Digital Possibilities: Emerging Educational Technologies

During the pandemic, I was introduced to the immersive world of Extended Reality [augmented reality (AR), virtual reality (VR), and mixed reality (MR)] for humanities education. Extended Reality is constantly ever-growing, and I am absolutely certain that it will take the intersection of technology, education, humanities, social sciences to another level.

Some of Virtual Reality projects that I found fascinating and interesting, and ones that take print literature beyond the medium of books are the *Shakespeare-VR* by Carnegie Mellon University[3], *The* Hamlet VR Experience[4] by University of Guelph, and *To Be With Hamlet?*[5].

The virtual, digital communication technologies, audio-visual technologies, and the learning revolution that we are experiencing today—embracing and adopting these emerging technologies will further foster diversity, interdisciplinarity, and promote

---

[3] https://shakespeare-vr.library.cmu.edu/
[4] https://news.uoguelph.ca/2022/08/shakespeare-meets-virtual-reality-in-u-of-g-created-hamlet-experience/
[5] http://hamletvr.org/

collaborative learning and research. They are vital from the perspectives of pedagogy and instructional design.

I found topics like electronic literature (born-digital literature), digitized (print) literature, digital archival, digital editions, transmedia and interactive storytelling, immersive environments and experiences, virtual tours, virtual museums, computational humanities, cultural analytics, spatial humanities, 3D visualization, corpus linguistics, playful learning, and computational linguistics to be the most fascinating. They helped me realize the intellectual excitement that comes with engaging in multidisciplinary research.

In 2021, I was accepted into the HASTAC Scholars Program (2021-2023). As a HASTAC Scholar, I am incredibly grateful for the virtual opportunities that I have received from the team of HASTAC, which is currently jointly administered and funded by The Graduate Center, City University of New York (CUNY), and the Dartmouth College. From the website of HASTAC[6] :

> One of the world's first and oldest academic networks, HASTAC has over 18,000 members from 400+ affiliate organizations. HASTAC (pronounced like "haystack") stands for the Humanities, Arts, Science, and Technology Alliance and Collaboratory, an interdisciplinary network formed in 2002-03. HASTAC was an early participant in a National Science Foundation initiative to create "collaboratories," online research clusters without walls, spanning multiple institutions and disciplines.

Virtual/Hybrid Conferencing

In an article titled *Virtual conferences raise standards for accessibility and interactions,* Sarvenaz Sarabipour, affiliated with the Institute for Computational Medicine, Department of Biomedical Engineering, at the John Hopkins University, Baltimore, United States notes:

---

[6] https://hastac.hcommons.org/about/hastac-scholars/

Some virtual conferences were held for the extended timeframes (weeks instead of days) enabling participation of researchers from multiple time zones via live and recorded talks, asynchronous discussions and social meetups. Recordings allowed talks to be paused or rewound, a useful feature for those who missed details or planned to spend more time pondering a crucial slide. Virtual conferences have further increased structured archiving of and open access to abstracts, posters and other research materials. Live review and analysis of research presentations and other scientific outputs enabled wide ranging engagement between speakers and audiences globally (reaching 100,000 chat messages at a single conference).

Virtual conferences can help researchers and scientific societies to meet more frequently as well and build long-term, inclusive, economically sustainable, and easily accessible communities nationally and globally in specific disciplines and across disciplines.

During the pandemic, conferences transitioned to the online mode. Virtual/hybrid conferences and events (symposiums, summer schools, workshops) made it accessible and possible for scholars, researchers, and learners all over the world, across continents, to connect, communicate, collaborate, and network with each other. This was achieved despite vast geographical distances, cultural differences, and time zone disparities. Furthermore, these events were more inclusive and cost-effective.

Diverse virtual interactions, especially through virtual spaces and environments such as Gather Town during conferences, made research knowledge accessible to me. Communication tools like Slack, Discord, Miro, and Gather Town aided in efficient academic learning and research, both synchronously and asynchronously.

Among the online conferences I attended are the following: Future and Reality of Gaming (FROG) 2021, hosted by the University for Continuing Education Krems (Danube University), Austria; Media, Arts and Design (MAD) 2021 Conference, organized by the University for Continuing Education Krems (Danube University), Austria; the 25th Digital Research in the Humanities and Arts Conference hosted by Humboldt University, Berlin, Germany; and the DHSI (Digital Humanities Summer Institute) 2022 (online edition) organized by the University of Victoria, Canada.

Going Global: Globalising Education

Participating in virtual and hybrid events strongly encouraged international perspectives and provided a crucial voice to global researchers. The pandemic also created numerous virtual and remote opportunities for students and researchers. Engaging in remote digital environments broadened my worldview, facilitated international collaborations, and, most importantly, prompted me to network with diverse perspectives. The effective combination of remote, virtual, and the hybrid mode of working could shape the future of education and learning, offering significant time-saving, cost-effectiveness, and innovation.

Acknowledgments

I want to acknowledge the wonderful support and encouragement I have received from the organizers of MAD and FROG conferences. I would like to thank Alexander Pfeiffer and Natalie Denk, University of Continuing Education, Krems, for their incredible efforts in organizing the FROG and MAD Conferences every year with their spectacular optimism and enthusiasm. I also would like to thank the HASTAC team for all their wonderful initiatives that allowed me to network with a wide variety of researchers.

About the Author

NANDITHA KRISHNA is currently a student of the five-year Integrated Masters (M.A) Program in English Language and Literature at Amrita Vishwa Vidyapeetham, Amritapuri, Kollam, India. She is a Humanities, Arts, Science and Technology Alliance and Collaboratory (HASTAC) Scholar (2021-2023). [The HASTAC fellowship program is jointly co-administered by the Graduate Center, City University of New York (CUNY) and Dartmouth College]. She also completed her internship at the Empathic

Computing Laboratory (ECL), an academic research laboratory at the University of South Australia in Adelaide, Australia, and the University of Auckland in Auckland, New Zealand, directed by Prof. Mark Billinghurst. She loves connected learning and has multidisciplinary academic interests such as new media studies, literary studies, digital cultures, internet studies, techno-ethics, educational and learning sciences, digital pedagogy, instructional design, philosophy, digital storytelling, gamification, media psychology, games, technology and human-media interaction. Outside of academics, she is keenly interested in music, electronic music production and storytelling. She also deeply admires Taylor Swift and The Gothard Sisters for their narrative songwriting and instrumentals.

Website: https://nandithakrishna.home.blog/.

References

Sá Pereira, Moacir P. (2017) *The Javascripting English Major*, 25 July 2017, https://the-javascripting-english-major.org/v1/. Last accessed: 29.10.2023

"Introduction to Cultural Analytics & Python." *Introduction to Cultural Analytics & Python - Introduction to Cultural Analytics & Python*, https://melaniewalsh.github.io/Intro-Cultural-Analytics/welcome.html. Last accessed: 29.10.2023

"Shakespeare-VR." *Videos* https://shakespeare-vr.library.cmu.edu/videos/. Last accessed: 29.10.2023

"Shakespeare Meets Virtual Reality in U of G-Created Hamlet Experience." *U Of G News*, https://news.uoguelph.ca/2022/08/shakespeare-meets-virtual-reality-in-u-of-g-created-hamlet-experience/. Last accessed: 29.10.2023

"To Be with Hamlet." *To Be With Hamlet*, http://hamletvr.org/. Last accessed: 29.10.2023

"Hastac Scholars." *HASTAC Commons*, https://hastac.hcommons.org/about/hastac-scholars/, Last accessed: 29.10.2023

Sarabipour, Sarvenaz. (2020) *"Virtual conferences raise standards for accessibility and interactions." eLife* vol. 9 e62668. doi:10.7554/eLife.62668, Last accessed: 29.10.2023

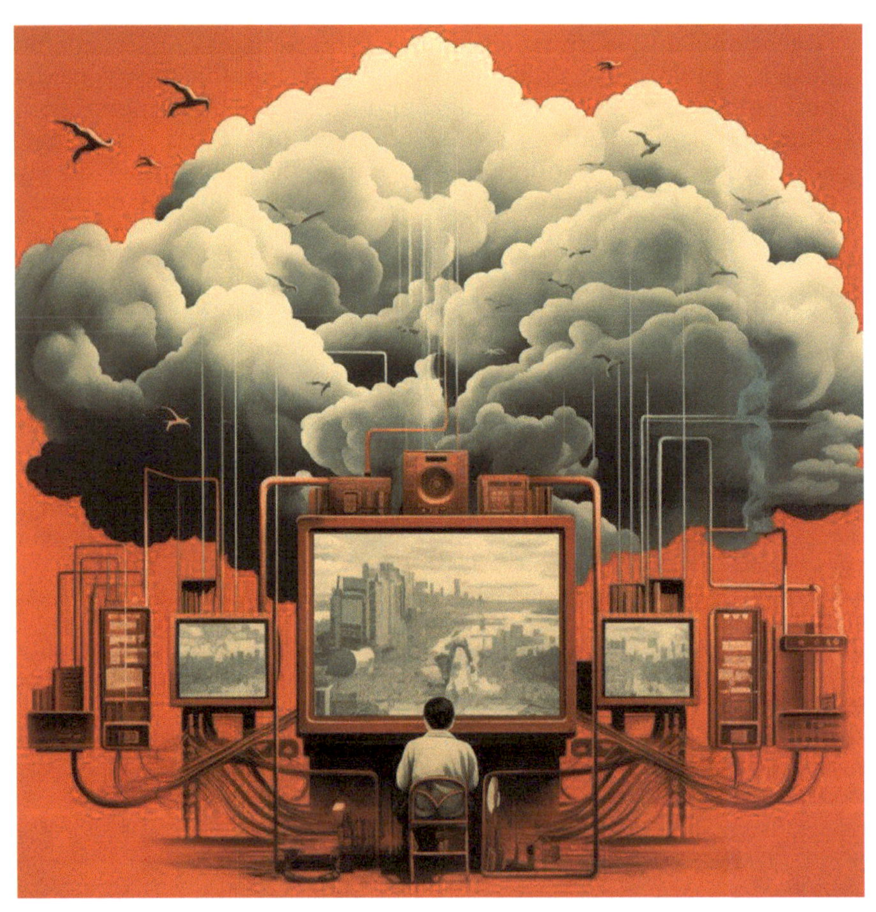

FROM DVD TO CLOUD DRIVE

UNDERGROUND CINEMA AND VIDEO ACTIVISM IN CHINA

Mo Li

In mainland China, both fiction and non-fiction films are subject to censorship by the China Film Administration. While media laws, regulations and normative documents provide clear guidelines and procedural justice, they offer very little room for independent films to reach a wider audience through mainstream media. Filmmakers have sought alternative channels to promote their work and effect social change through what is often referred to as underground cinema. In the past, VCDs, DVDs and underground film clubs were commonly used to distribute censored films, but in recent years, online video streaming platforms have become a popular means of sharing banned content. Filmmakers who do not comply with censorship rules face the risks of sanctions, including monetary fines and work bans. Despite those risks, some filmmakers continue to produce and share independent works. During the COVID-19 pandemic, grassroots director Jiang Nengjie distributed his documentary *Miners, Groom, and Pneumoconiosis (2019)* for free on social media via private cloud drive links, earning him the nickname "Cloud Drive Director". In 2021, the author conducted an interview with the director, resulting in this paper on video activism and alternative media.

Keywords: underground cinema, video activism, independent film, documentary, China

---

Underground Cinema Hidden in Plain Sight

My first encounter of underground cinema caught me off guard. During my early years in the 1980s, I was raised by migrant worker parents and later sent to live with my grandparents in a small county located 300 kilometers away from Beijing. Their humble village was nestled amongst picturesque mountains and vineyards, far removed from the bustling metropolis.

Eventually, I migrated to the city for better educational opportunities and only visited my hometown around the turn of the millennium. I seized the opportunity to revisit some of the landmarks of my childhood. Among them was the old cinema, which held a special place in my memories. It was still there, but no longer had its former glory. Its entire façade was dilapidated and crumbling, covered by a weathered poster of a lady posing suggestively with very little textile, accompanied by a risqué film title. As an adolescent still grappling with the intricacies of human anatomy, I was taken aback by what I had just seen.

While China was undergoing significant social and economic reforms in the 90s, the film industry was confronted with a range of complex challenges. In 1984, a pivotal policy document, Decision on Reform of the Economic Structure, was released.1 It called for significant changes in China's economic system, and it stated that the film industry should be managed as an enterprise with independent accounting and responsibility for its profits and losses. Prior to the reforms, cinemas in China were operated by the State and were not required to prioritize box office performance. New cinema chains quickly emerged, offering more modern and comfortable movie-going experiences. Increased competition and lack of government funding placed considerable financial strain on rural cinemas, resulting in unpaid staff, neglected infrastructure, and restricted access to blockbuster films.

---

1 *Decision of the Central Committee of the Communist Party of China on Reform of the Economic Structure*, adopted by the Twelfth Central Committee of the Communist Party of China at its third plenary session on October 20, 1984.

In 1986, a new department under the State Council, the Ministry of Radio, Film and Television of the People's Republic of China was formed. Prior to that, the film industry has been under the administration of the Ministry of Culture. The film industry was like a foster child placed in a new household. During a period of unpredictability and heightened stress towards the end of the 1980s, the State put more pressure on the control of content, particularly on sensitive political and social issues. Films that were deemed to be too critical or controversial were often banned or heavily edited.

The final fatal blow came from the rising popularity of home entertainment systems. The introductions of VCDs made it easier for audiences in China to access banned films. People would often trade pirated VCDs among friends or rent them from underground stores to keep costs to a minimum. This shift in audience behavior had a significant impact on rural cinemas, which were already struggling to keep their businesses afloat. In a desperate attempt to survive, some rural cinemas resorted to screening increasingly explicit content. Although not conventionally considered underground cinemas, their behaviors were reminiscent of such establishments. Whenever I read about scholarships on underground cinema in China, it often reminds me of the façade of my hometown's old cinema.

The DVD Black Market in the Shadows

In 2005, I rented a small room in a courtyard in the old town of Beijing, just across from Central Academy of Drama where I was studying. It didn't take me long to notice there was something going on in the adjacent room. Flocks of people were going in and out of the room. On occasion, visitors would come knocking at my door, under the mistaken belief that they had arrived at my neighbor's residence. They would attempt to buy 'stock' without revealing the nature of their intended transactions. To avoid any further confusion, I had to put up a sign that read, "Nothing to sell". For some reason, the sign only seemed to pique the curiosity of those visitors, who continued to persistently inquire about making purchases from me.

After a while, I discovered that my neighbor was actually a dealer of pirated DVDs, and I was invited to take a look at his inventory. It was impossible to ignore the numerous shelves of DVDs lining the walls, filled with everything from Hollywood blockbusters to French auteur films to censored domestic productions. He was also willing to go extra miles to source hard-to-get films for my schoolmates, probably from his fellow counterfeiters at specialized stores in Haidian District (Nakajima, 2014, p.59). Despite being aware of the ethical issues surrounding piracy, I couldn't help feeling that it was probably the best way to make world cinema accessible to all the film enthusiasts in China.

Censoring oversea productions had been a tradition in China. In 1981, the State Council approved an administrative document outlining the rules for the importation of foreign films.2 China Film Group, a government-owned enterprise that was previously known as China Film Distribution Company, was granted the exclusive rights to import foreign films, a monopoly that lasted until 2003 when Huaxia Film was given the same privilege. For decades, only 20 to 30 foreign films were permitted to enter the Chinese market each year. While the situation has improved since 2016, the number of foreign films allowed into the country is still restricted to the double digits.

The prohibition on importing foreign films gave rise to a thriving black market for pirated DVDs. Every neighborhood had its own covert dealerships, offering extensive collection of DVDs at unbeatable prices. The production of pirated copies was facilitated by personal computers, making them difficult to trace, and the costs were negligible. Customized orders were also available on demand, which only added to the popularity of the pirated DVD market.

Despite the fact that piracy of DVDs and other forms of intellectual property infringement was an issue during China's accession to the World Trade Organization in 2001, cracking down on the illegal operations was a challenge. The difficulty was

---

2 *Measures for Control Over Imported Films*, approved by the State Council on October 13, 1981.

twofold: firstly, the police had to catch the seller red-handed during a transaction when the money and the goods were exchanged. Secondly, locals were not incentivized to act as whistle-blowers and report their dealers, as doing so would ruin the affordable source of entertainment for everyone in the neighborhood.

As the 2008 Beijing Olympics drew nearer, there was a noticeable shift in the city's atmosphere. Pensioners were recruited to work as volunteers, keeping a watchful eye on the streets. The underground trade of various goods, including pirated DVDs, became increasingly challenging. My neighbor would often disappear without notice, and it turned out that he had been caught and detained by the police and was spending nights in custody. Subsequently, he shut down his operation and relocated to a more affordable neighborhood outside of the city.

Dos and Don'ts of Dealing with the Censorship

In 1998, the State Administration of Radio, Film, and Television (SARFT) was established as a replacement for the Ministry of Radio, Film, and Television. This regulatory body would later play a crucial role in shaping China's media industry. As a film production major in college, I spent four years poring over SARFT's regulations and normative documents, with one in particular: Decree [2001] No. 342, Regulation on the Administration of the Films, which was enacted by the State Council of China in December 2001 and came into force in February 2002.

The Regulation signified the government's acknowledgement of the economic and cultural significance of the film industry, and underscored the proper protocols and guidelines. China's film industry has since thrived and grown to become one of the world's largest. At the same time, film administrators were granted extensive powers to enforce strict control through various nuanced mechanisms and tools, including department rules, normative documents and written comments across different levels of governance (Y.-C. Chin, 2016, p.51-54).

In 2016, the Congress passed the Film Industry Promotion Law, a legal document with greater legal authority than the Regulation on the Administration of the Films. This Law reinforces the culture values of domestic productions, highlights the social responsibilities of filmmakers and cinemas, and emphasized the intellectual property rights protection. While the Law possesses greater power, the Regulation's enduring impact on the industry persists, and it remains in effect today. Consequently, I will reference it more frequently.

If you want your film to be legally screened in China, there are procedural steps you must complete. Firstly, you need to establish a qualifying production studio with a legal personality, a professional crew, and some starting capital, as outlined in Articles 8 and 9 of the Regulation. Secondly, you must apply for a shooting permit by submitting your application to your provincial film bureau, in accordance with Article 16 of the Regulation. Thirdly, you must submit your finished film for review to obtain the screening permit, as stated in Article 27 of the Regulation. Once you have obtained the screening permit, you must add an animation that carries a flying dragon and a unique license number corresponding to the screening permit of your film as required by Article 28 of the Regulation. Finally, you need to submit a copy of your film to the China Film Archive, as specified in Article 23 of the Film Industry Promotion Law.

When it comes to content censorship, Article 25 of the *Regulation* outlines the types of content that are not permitted in films, such as promoting obscenity, violence, terrorism, superstition, and ethnic discrimination, among other things.

Article 25. Films are prohibited from containing the following content:

1. Opposing the basic principles established in the Constitution;

2. Endangering national unity, sovereignty, and territorial integrity;

3. Disclosing confidential state information, endangering national security, or damaging national honor and interests;

4. Inciting ethnic hatred or discrimination, undermining ethnic unity, or violating ethnic customs and habits;

5. Promoting cults and superstitions;

6. Disrupting social order, undermining social stability;

7. Promoting obscenity, gambling, violence, or instigating crime;

8. Insulting or slandering others, infringing upon the legitimate rights and interests of others;

9. Endangering public morality or the positive cultural traditions of the nation;

10. Containing other content that is prohibited by laws and regulations.

In addition to the Regulation and the Law, dozens of administrative regulations, normative documents and guidelines had been issued to oversee almost every aspect of the film industry. To spare you the tedium of reviewing each document, I will focus on highlighting the most important aspects. In summary, to prevent a film from being banned in mainland China, it is essential to steer clear of three key elements: sex, violence, and antisocialist values.

The censorship of sex and violence in films is a familiar concept worldwide. Many societies believe in promoting peace and non-violent resolutions, often implementing measures to regulate and monitor content that depicts violence. However, China's censorship regulations are particularly strict due to the absence of a film classification system. Unlike in the United States, where films are assigned ratings to distinguish between different levels of suitability for audiences, China does not have a similar rating system in place to differentiate between films that are suitable for general audiences, those that require parental guidance, and those that are restricted. This means all films must be suitable for audiences of all ages, making it imperative to monitor and censor content to ensure it does not contain any material deemed inappropriate.

As a student being trained to become the next generation film producers, I was instructed on a comprehensive list of body parts that would not pass the review and how to avoid featuring them. It was later revealed to me that this practice is considered "self-censorship", a crucial step in preventing one's film from being subjected to sanctions. Today with the advanced visual analysis capabilities of Artificial Intelligence, there is a possibility of delegating a portion of the self-censorship task to these programs. It is curious to see how this technology will be used to improve the workflow and shape the media landscape.

Addressing content that could be perceived as antisocialist values can be challenging and requires navigating a fine line. Stories that do not align with the society's prevailing values or desired narratives may face censorship under the Article 25 of the Regulation. One common example is the notion that those who are deemed "bad" eventually end up in prison, where they regret their actions, while "good" people live out their lives happily. I remember watching a Chinese-dubbed version of a classic Hollywood crime film on TV, where criminal protagonists successfully escaped with the stolen money from the heist. However, the Chinese adaptation had an unexpected twist, with the characters deciding to turn in the money to clear themselves of their crimes. If one hadn't seen the original film, they could not have guessed the alteration. The art of creative dubbing worked wonders, effectively saving the film from being banned.

In case of non-compliance, Article 54 to 66 of the Regulation detailed the penalties for unauthorized film production, distribution, or exhibition in violation of this Regulation. The administrative department for industry and commerce shall order the cessation of the illegal activity. Those who violate the provisions of this Regulation by producing, importing, exporting, distributing, or screening films without authorization shall be held criminally liable in accordance with the relevant provisions of the Criminal Law for the crime of illegal business operations. For minor offenses, the illegal gains obtained from the activity shall be confiscated, and the equipment used in the illegal business operation shall be confiscated. If the illegal gains are more than 50,000 yuan, the offender shall also be fined 5 to 10 times the illegal gains, and if the illegal gains are less than 50,000 yuan, the offender shall be fined 200,000 to 500,000 yuan.

Besides financial sanctions, professional disqualification might also be imposed for violations such as producing films without permits, exporting films without permits, organizing or attending national or international film festivals without permits. Films associated with professionals subject to work bans would be barred from passing the censorship review. As stated in the Article 64 of the Regulation: If an entity violates this Regulation and is punished with revocation of its license, its legal representative or principal person-in-charge shall not serve as legal representative or principal person-in-charge of any film production, import, export, distribution, and screening unit within five years from the date of revocation.

However, apart from the serious offense, if the individuals involved do not have any intention of receiving remunerations or causing widespread impacts, they are largely exempted from harsh sanctions. The laws and regulations are primarily designed to regulate and exert pressure on professionals in the film industry. As such, hobbyists or those not seeking financial gain are unlikely to face enforcement, as the rules aim to ensure compliance among industry professionals.

Meeting the "Cloud Drive Director"

When COVID-19 pandemic swept the globe, China was hit particularly hard. During unexpected lock downs and travel restrictions, some turned to video games and television to pass time, others sought out more intellectual pursuits, searching for information on topics like health and wellbeing online. Amidst the chaos, an independent documentary about black lung diseases went viral: Miners, Groom, and Pneumoconiosis (2019).

Black lung disease, also known as coal workers' pneumoconiosis, is a lung disease caused by inhaling dust particles, often associated with mining industrial occupations. Although it was not connected to Covid-19 in any way, those afflicted with black lung disease experience a similar sense of suffocation in those affected by the virus. The public felt a strong sense of compassion towards the coal miners and were motivated to take actions. They were limited in their options due to the pandemic, but one thing they could do was spread the words to increase awareness and inform more people about the issue. Suddenly, this documentary gained immense popularity on the Internet and climbed to the top of Douban's charts, causing a sensation within the Chinese film community. Douban is an online database and one of the most popular social networking platforms in China, primarily used for reviewing and discussing books, films, music and other cultural events. It's often referred to as the "Chinese IMDb" and "Chinese Reddit".

The film was directly by the grassroots filmmaker Jiang Nengjie from Hunan Province, whose father was one of the miners affected by this occupational disease. Due to the underdevelopment of his hometown, many villagers had to seek work in the coal mines. Since the onset of black lung disease can take years to manifest, workers may have difficulty proving that their illness resulted from their time in the mines. As a result, cases of black lung disease were prevalent in his region, causing many to be unable to work and become impoverished.

Without a permit, Mr. Jiang started filming with a DV-cam while he was still in college. It took him nearly a decade to finish the documentary, mostly self-financed. His film garnered public attention unexpectedly due to its focus on respiratory health. Mr. Jiang took advantage of the momentum by uploading the video file to his cloud drive and sharing it free of charge through direct messaging. After sending tens of thousands of messages, Mr. Jiang earned the nickname "Cloud Drive Director" on social media. This term was coined to describe his actions of selflessly pirating his own film and sharing it online with the world. Because he financed the film himself, he was able to make the decision to share it for free on his own. However, other filmmakers who work with large studios or have sold their copyright licenses may not have the same flexibility. The term 'Cloud Drive Director' not only refers to the act of sending links to cloud drives, but also represents a symbol of genuine independence and a not-for-profit spirit.

In the spring of 2021, I returned to Beijing to visit my family. While enduring the boredom and weariness of quarantine in a hotel, I was scrolling online and came across an article about Mr. Jiang. Intrigued by his story and his approach to filmmaking, I decided to contact him. Despite the challenges posed by the pandemic, we were fortunate to have the opportunity to conduct an intense two-hour interview in the back room of a small bookstore.[3]

During our exchange, we discussed the potential consequences of sharing his film online without proper permits. To my surprise, he faced no sanctions and was able to continue traveling and working on future projects without any issues. Mr. Jiang's feature film *Yun Jie* (2018) passed censorship reviews and was granted a screening permit, allowing it to be shown on the big screens. In 2021, the film was screened publicly in cinemas. *Yun Jie* is a fiction film based on a true story, depicts the life of a left-behind child who was sent to live with her grandmother. It portrays the hardships and joys she faces while studying and doing heavy household chores, and her eventual journey to reunite with her parents after her grandmother passed away.

Since Mr. Jiang did not demand any payment in exchange for providing links, his actions were not considered a commercial distribution of an underground film, thus leading to the absence of sanctions against him. Similar to the act of sharing of pirated DVDs among friends, it was not regarded as a criminal offense enough to warrant the allocation of law enforcement resources. While some viewers offered tips as a gesture of gratitude, receiving small donations alone was not a violation stipulated in the *Civil Law*.[4] Moreover, Mr. Jiang informed me that the Hunan

---

[3] Video published with Mr. Jiang's consent, accessible on YouTube: https://youtu.be/OO5wvfOXpBw

[4] General Principles of the Civil Law was enacted by the National People's Congress in 1986. In a civil law country, generally everything is permitted that is not expressly prohibited by law.

provincial government also established a special medical fund to assist in relieving the effects of black lung disease in response to his documentary. The film ultimately yielded a positive outcome for all the parties involved.

Participating in international film festivals is another popular avenue for independent filmmakers to gain global recognition. When I asked him why he had not applied to international film festivals, he explained that he lacked the language skills to complete the applications and translate the subtitles. Moreover, his work often focused on domestic social issues that may not appeal to a global audience. Most importantly, applying to multiple festivals for a chance at nomination could be financially burdensome, even though the submission fee for each is typically less than a hundred dollars.

During my interview with the filmmaker, his response to my question about how he could use a large sum of investment, such as US$50,000, struck me. Rather than investing in promoting his film, as I anticipated, he had a different idea. To my surprise, his first wish would be to dine at a nice restaurant, and then to hire professional help so that he could take a break. Due to his limited budget, he operates as a one-man team, taking on multiple roles and managing tasks from start to finish. Fast-food takeout is a regular part of his daily routine at work. As someone working in the media industry in Europe at a similar age, I can say that dinning at a nice restaurant is more of a habit than a wish list item for me personally. His answer revealed the challenging reality of working as an independent filmmaker.

Video Activism and Regulations in the Cyberspace

Independent documentary filmmaking in China has always borne the burden of activism since its inception, serving as a means of advocating for social change. It not only helps to raise awareness of social and political issues, but also empowers the marginalized groups, opens up dialogue between the filmmakers and the authority, and calls for citizen participation in addressing important social issues (Viviani, 2014). The rise in popularity and capacity of consumer-grade digital video cameras has given birth to the term video activism, a form of citizen activism that offers alternative perspectives outside of the official narratives.

During my conversation with Mr. Jiang, I attempted to steer towards the delicate subject of video activism. I encountered a problematic issue before raising the question: there is no direct Chinese translation of the word activism. Instead, it is often translated as "radicalism" (*Jijin Zhuyi*), which carries connotations of extreme or revolutionary political views or actions. Due to its association with dissidents and social movements that challenge authority, the use of this term can be sensitive and controversial in China.

Many of the filmmakers I have come to know do not self-identify as activists, including Mr. Jiang. He prefers the term *"Gongyi filmmaker"*, a Chinese word that translates to public welfare or public interest. Nevertheless, he embodies the essence of video activism as recognized in the Western context, striving to advance social justice, human rights, and environmental protection by using video as a medium for change. He has devoted a decade of his life, resources, and expertise for the betterment of society, and whether or not he embraces the "video activist" label matters little, as his work speaks for itself.

Alongside private cloud drives, online streaming platforms like BiliBili, iQIYI and Youku have created an unparalleled parallel public space. The widespread use of 4G mobile networks, the availability of high-speed broadband, and the popularity of mobile devices have given rise to a new media landscape. Similar to Mr. Jiang, numerous independent filmmakers now turn to alternative channels by sharing their work online. However, it is important to note that the Internet in China is not beyond the reach of authority. Similar to television and cinema, online video content is subject to multiple regulations and oversight by various entities.

One of the most relevant regulations is the *Regulations on the Management of Internet Audio-Visual Program Services*, published in December 2007 and came into force in January 2008. This document aims to regulate the operation and content of Internet audio-visual program services in China, including online video platforms, livestreaming platforms, and other online audio-visual content providers. It covers a range of issues, such as licensing requirements, content censorship, and data protection, among others. It has been updated several times since the initial release, with the most recent update taking effect in 2015.

Online censorship plays a significant role in gatekeeping China's cyberspace. Piracy, however, offers a mean of escape and an alternative space within a narrow scope for video activists to thrive. While piracy is a complex issue and an offense that causes damage in the creative industry, it also provides a precious opportunity to distribute censored content, similar to the pirated DVD black market of a decade ago. Apart from benefiting the public, it's arguable that piracy could potentially benefit filmmakers in the form of free promotion (Feng, 2017). In exceptional instances such as Mr. Jiang's, when a filmmaker shares their own work outside of the traditional distribution channels, this can be viewed as a classic case of self-piracy. As the sole copyright holder voluntarily discloses the content, it is not considered a copyright infringement, unlike instances of end-user piracy.

In an effort to modernize the administration of the cyberspace, the Chinese government undertook several reorganizations. Notably, in 2013, SARFT and the General Administration of Press and Publications (GAPP) merged to form the State Administration of Press, Publications, Radio, Film and Television (SAPPRFT) in China. Since the merger, SAPPRFT has assumed responsibility for regulating both online publications and audiovisual content, which were previously regulated separately by GAPP and SARFT. The National Copyright Administration, a subordinate department of GAPP, was also brought into SAPPRFT. The change aimed to improve management and reduce overlap in administrative procedures and to combat piracy. It was not expected to lead to any form of liberalization or deregulation. However, administrative overlap and dual licensing remained problematic, particularly in the online space, as the Ministry of Culture and Tourism and the Ministry of Industry and Information Technology maintained their respective duties.

After a short 5 years, SAPPRFT was taken apart as an effort to streamline government agencies and reduce bureaucratic overlap. In 2018, it was split into three different departments: (1) the National Radio and Television Administration (NRTA), an institution directly under the State Council responsible for regulating radio and television broadcasting; (2) the National Press and Publication Administration (NPPA) oversees the publishing and distribution of print and digital media, under the direct control of the Central Propaganda Department; and (3) China Film Administration responsible for regulating and supervising the production, distribution and screening of films, also under the direct control of the Central Propaganda Department.

The Central Propaganda Department is responsible for shaping and controlling the flow of information in China, and by placing the China Film Administration under its control, it suggests that the State sees the film industry as an important tool for promoting its political and ideological agenda. This can manifest in various ways, such as through censorship of sensitive topics or themes, or through the promotion of positive representations of Chinese culture and values.

Conclusions: The Dilemma of Independent Filmmakers

When I started my research in Europe, fellow researchers often asked me a simple but profound question: "Do people in China get to watch censored films? If so, how?" It's a quite straightforward question, yet it's difficult to explain. One day, I spoke with a friend who used to live in Europe but now resides in Indonesia. I asked him if people drink alcohol in Indonesia during the holy month, and he told me that some people drink wine from coffee mugs. This revelation was an aha moment for me, and I realized it was a perfect metaphor, depicting an operation conducted clandestinely, unbeknownst to the authorities.

Just as people in Indonesia drink alcoholic beverages in coffee mugs, we watch independent films in covert alternative spaces in China. Societies have varying degrees of tolerance, and in some cases, the rules are stricter than in others. For example, some countries prohibit drinking alcohol in public, so people use brown paper bags to conceal their drinks. This confused me initially, and I questioned whether the authorities knew what the consumers were doing. I thought: "Is it not apparent? How could they not be aware?" Censorship might sound like a terrible idea, but it is not as alienating as it seems. Living in any society means facing limitations and restrictions, as individuals must be protected from themselves and their own free will for the greater good of all.

Originally designed to encourage compliance and enable films to be showcased in mainstream media, film permits have become increasingly unattractive and unprofitable for independent filmmakers. Even with a permit, there is no guarantee of box office success, and filmmakers face administrative red tape and intense competition in the market. This double-trouble is worsened by the hierarchical distribution of profits through cinemas. There are numerous fees and commissions involved, including contributions to the national film fund, taxes, cinema theater shares, cinema line management fees, national distributors' fees, and production studio distributor representation fees. All revenue is first collected by theaters and then shared layer by layer, making it difficult for filmmakers to earn a good margin.

As my professor for film distribution often reminded us, filmmaking is a risky business, unlike retail businesses such as running a supermarket. A couple of years later, I heard that he invested in a convenient store nearby that gave him a good return on investment. The decision of an informed expert to invest in something other than the industry can be viewed as a warning signal. In recent years, some modern cinema theaters are also struggling to attract customers, with the pandemic exacerbating the situation. The suicide of the vice president of Bona Film Group in Beijing in June 2020 highlights the industry's pervasive skepticism, which professionals must face in addition to the difficulties encountered in their work.

In contrast to the bureaucratic obstacles and intense competition of mainstream film distribution, the underground cinema scene in China offers a stable, albeit imperfect, alternative. Filmmakers can opt to share their work privately online, or distribute it in small-scale alternative spaces like art centers and social gatherings. While independent filmmakers may not receive monetary compensation for their screenings, they can gain recognition and exposure, which could potentially attract sponsorships from private entities and donations from the public.

Documentaries are subject to the same laws and regulations as fiction films, but enforcement is generally more relaxed. This is especially advantageous for documentary filmmakers, who have the freedom to apply for shooting permits at any stage of production process. In contrast, permits for fiction films must be obtained before filming begins. The documentary *Four Springs* (2019), for example, was shot between 2013 and 2016 and acquired its shooting permit in 2017 and screening permit in subsequent year before being released in 2019.[5] The documentary followed director Lu Qingyi's family life in rural China during four spring festivals. A simple calculation would tell us that the majority of the work was completed before obtaining the necessary permits. While this flexibility is beneficial, it also poses a dilemma for documentary filmmakers, as they must decide whether to follow the official route or an alternative path.

Independent filmmakers face a crucial crossroads at every turn, presented with choices such as whether to comply with regulations, whether to remain within the confines of mainland China or present their work to the wider world at international film festivals, and whether to monetize their work or offer it for free. Each decision presents a series of potential consequences, requiring filmmakers to weigh the trade-offs between creative freedom and market viability. Yet, for some, the choice is clear, as they are not motivated by financial gain but rather the desire for social change, as famously expressed in Banksy's graffiti: "Keep your coins, we want change." Thus, the question remains, to conform or rebel, to choose the path of creative autonomy or commercial success? Ultimately, it is a difficult choice that each filmmaker must make for themselves, as they navigate the complex and often uncertain terrain of independent filmmaking.

---

[5] All shooting permits can be accessed at: https://www.chinafilm.gov.cn

Acknowledgments

This research is entirely self-funded and has not received sponsorship from any public or private entity, either Chinese or international to maintain neutrality, much like independent filmmakers who finance their own projects.

About the Author

Mo Li is a Ph.D. candidate at the Polytechnic University of Valencia, Spain. She was born and raised in China, currently based in Europe. She holds a B.A. in Film Production (China), M.A. in Film Studies (Australia), M.A. in European Studies (Germany), and an MBA (Spain). Having witnessed the rise and fall of underground film clubs and the pirated DVD trade in Beijing, she is driven to delve deeper into independent filmmaking in China.

References

Chin, Y.-C. (2016). *Television Regulation and Media Policy in China* (1st ed.). Routledge. https://doi.org/10.4324/9780203798751

Feng, L. (2017). Online video sharing: An alternative channel for film distribution? Copyright enforcement, censorship, and Chinese independent cinema. *Chinese Journal of Communication, 10*(3), 279–294. https://doi.org/10.1080/17544750.2016.1247736

Nakajima, S. (2014). Chinese film spaces: The social locations and media of urban independent screen consumption. *Continuum, 28*(1), 52–64. https://doi.org/10.1080/10304312.2014.870872

Viviani, M. (2014). Chinese Independent Documentary Films: Alternative Media, Public Spheres and the Emergence of the Citizen Activist. *Asian Studies Review, 38*(1), 107–123. https://doi.org/10.1080/10357823.2013.873016

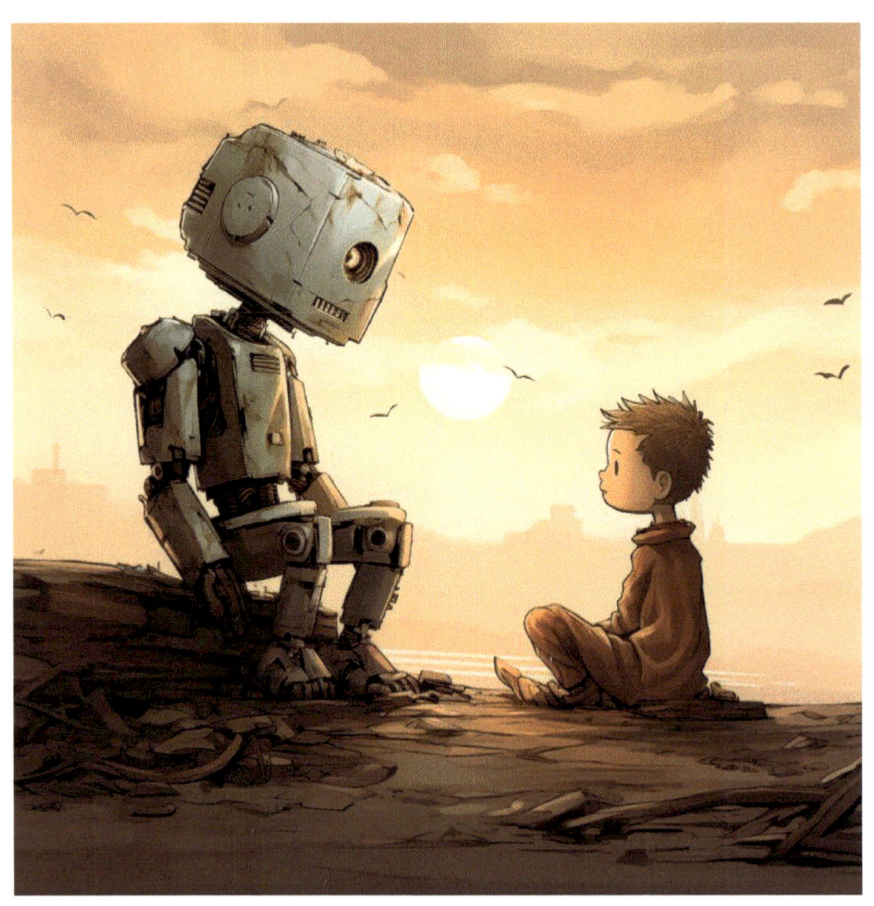

WHAT WOULD MAKE A ROBOT SAD?

ROBOT WERTHER VS. MARVIN THE PARANOID ANDROID

Alesha Serada

In this paper, I compare two fictional artificial agents who appeared on television in the 1980s in the USSR and in the UK. Despite their unrelated cultural genealogy, both characters project the similar emotion of sadness from the screen. First and foremost, I focus on the robot Werther from the Soviet children's TV series *Visitor from the Future* (1985). This character subverts several stereotypes in representation of artificial intelligence: he possesses high emotional intelligence, as well as the ability to make independent decisions and moral judgements. His equally subversive British counterpart is Marvin the Paranoid Android from the fictional universe of *The Hitchhiker's Guide to the Galaxy*, namely from the 1981 TV series: unique human-like personality of this robot is defined by his inability to achieve satisfaction of any kind. These two representations of sad, melancholic and depressed robots are united by the fact that neither of them has a fulfilling job. I argue that this trope mirrors the popular human fear of robots taking over human jobs, resulting in "technological unemployment" of human workers, and more generally, losing one's purpose in life. If designers and developers assume their responsibility for well-being of artificial beings that they create, they should be able to predict scenarios when robots become sad, depressed or even suicidal for the same reasons as humans do.

Keywords: Soviet cinema, artificial intelligence, robots, media representation, utopia

Introduction: Thinking one hundred years ahead

Soviet science fiction cinema has a long history, but a relatively limited catalog of released films. Even though Aelita: Queen of Mars (Protazanov 1924) was a creative breakthrough in sci-fi cinema worldwide, Soviet critics still panned it for its political ambivalence. In general, fantastic themes in film were scarce before the Thaw began in the 1950s. The following generation of directors produced a limited number of ideologically immaculate, albeit visually inventive films. These 'Soviet space operas' owed their existence and relatively generous budgets to success of the Soviet space program (Fedorov 2017, Majsova 2020). The most daring example, Planet of the Storms (Klushantsev 1962), featured one of the first robot characters with a unique personality, Robot John (Majsova 2020). Still, he was rather an ideological caricature: a comical defendant of capitalism who eventually had served the higher purpose of Soviet science.

The late 1970s and the early 1980s mark the last generation of Soviet science fiction films. These films introduced more relatable and emotionally complex characters, which was also true for robots and other AI agents. The best-known landmark of this period, Per Aspera ad Astra (Viktorov 1981), featured the alien female cyborg Niia as a protagonist, and this character has not her relevance even today. For the first time in Soviet science fiction, Niia delivered a strong ecocritical message (Majsova 2020) to the audience hungry for space exploration. Niia's planet is dying because its resources are exhausted, and it makes her very sad 1. Niia became one of the most memorable manifestations of the trope that still permeates in global science fiction: an extraordinarily powerful AI agent who develops human-like feelings and emotions on their journey to become 'the real human' (Gulin 2016). Another famous character of the same kind was the artificial boy Elektronik from the beloved children's TV film Adventures of Elektronik (Bromberg 1979) (Kukulin 2008), although his story was more similar to the modern reinterpretation of Pinocchio. The most original and memorable

---

[1] Much later, Luc Besson will introduce a very similar motif in The Fifth Element (1997).

artificial mind appeared in one of the last Soviet TV films in the genre of science fiction.

Visitor from the Future (Arsenov 1985), a children's TV film series in 5 episodes produced in 1984-1985, is the final milestone in this series of prominent late Soviet science fiction films for children (Kostyukevich 2020, p.144). It was based on the book One Hundred Years Ahead (1978) by the prolific science fiction writer Kir Bulychev, the leading author of Soviet children's science fiction literature. Kir Bulychov himself belonged to the same generation as the famous Strugatsky brothers and came to prominence during the Khrushchev Thaw (Csicsery-Ronay 2004, Gulin 2021). He was also a cowriter of the script for the film Per Aspera ad Astra mentioned above. As a children's author, Bulychev is best known as the creator of the character of the exceptionally smart and brave girl Alisa Selezneva. She is the main character in a long series of books created by Bulychev, some of which were adapted for screen, such as the classical feature-length animated film The Mystery of the Third Planet (Kachanov 1981). In general, the fictional universe explored in Alisa's adventures was a major part of children's science fiction in the USSR.

Alisa lives in a futuristic space utopia and spends her time traveling across the universe together with her father, a cosmo-biologist. In this bright far away future, everything is possible, including both time and space travel. In One Hundred Years Ahead, as well as in its adaptation Visitor from the Future, Alisa travels back in time from 2084 to 1984 to retrieve her father's device that allows humans to communicate with non-human animals. During her journey, she meets the ordinary Soviet boy Kolya Gerasimov and his friends, and they help her to fight space pirates who came after the device. In the final battle, children are joined by their friend, the kind and sensitive robot Werther, who helps them escape by sacrificing himself. This tragic scene remains in memories of many Soviet children, influenced their concept of artificial intelligence and robots in the future.

In this paper, I will focus on one particular character from one of the many fictional universes that Bulychev created: robot Werther, as he appears in Visitor from the Future. Speaking of

Western pop culture of the same period, it was also the time when Marvin the Paranoid Android entered the cultural consciousness in the UK, after his appearance in the fictional universe of Hitchhiker's Guide to the Galaxy by Douglas Adams. Arguably, robot Werther became an equally prominent figure in the cultural consciousness of the USSR almost at the same time.

"I can tell you are not really interested": the place of robots in fictional societies

Werther as an artificial bureaucrat

Scientific research was often presented as a noble and even heroic task in the Soviet society, and rightfully so (Lipovetsky 2017). Its more mundane aspects were sometimes discussed in satirical magazines but rarely addressed in more productive manner. Still, these aspects found their way into the Soviet science fiction as the material for comedy and irony, such as Monday Begins on Saturday (1965), the satirical novel by the famous Strugatsky brothers that is sometimes labeled 'the first Soviet fantasy novel'. This novel also inspired the much-loved Soviet fairy tale film The Magicians (Bromberg 1982). Events of the film take place at the imaginary Research Institute of Wizardry and Magic, a research institution that studies supernatural forces and events. Apart from human researchers, this institution also employs magical beings such as Baba Yaga and a talking cat. This example demonstrates the possibility of cooperation between human and non-human (or super-human) persons in the imagined utopian future. Still, both the novel and the film provided a pointed critique of Soviet research institutes: their bureaucratization, detachment from reality, and lack of opportunities for junior, ideologically ambiguous or otherwise less privileged scholars.

Notorious bureaucracy was probably the only feature of the Soviet state that its regime allowed to criticize from within (see e.g. Pakulski 1986, p.11). To sociologists from the West, it also represented a conceptual problem: as it appeared in practice, Soviet administrative organization did not fully align with the classical understanding of bureaucracy proposed by Max Weber, due to its inefficiency and totalitarian tendencies. According to Max Weber, the characteristic principle of bureaucracy is "the abstract regularity of the exercise of authority" (Weber 2003, p. 22), which is based on scripted rules, rather than direct power. In his view, "Bureaucracy inevitably accompanies modern mass democracy" (ibid.), as opposed to decentralized self-government of small groups of people. To Jan Pakulski, the main problems with Soviet bureaucracy were legal uncertainty and dominance of direct power over scripted rules, i.e. "Legal norms do not seem to be binding for the security services combating political nonconformity" (Pakulski 1986, p. 7). Besides, the spheres of responsibility are not clearly defined, and administration of an organization is often based on informal ties and falsification. Finally, even middle level managers in technical spheres such as lead engineers and chief physicians are appointed 'from above' by the Communist Party functionaries (ibid, p. 10).

From this perspective, depiction of bureaucracy in science fiction films such as The Magicians and especially Visitor from the Future acquire almost utopian qualities: the rules are scripted and (mostly) obeyed, spheres of responsibility are clearly demarcated, and, most importantly for our case, the resulting administrative systems represent equal and just societies of the future. It may be the ideal type of a 'monocratic bureaucracy'. In Weber's words, we observe "the leveling of the governed in face of the governing and bureaucratically articulated group" (Weber 2003, p.23), which means, in our case, that human and non-human agents are treated equally by the power of regulations and rules. Even bureaucracy is benign and just in this imagined future.

Werther first appears as a rather minor character in Bulychev's novels; he is first introduced as a fully fleshed out comical character in Visitor from the Future. Werther is a human-like 'biorobot', although there is an air of artificiality about him. To convey non-human nature of Werther, the actor Evgeniy Gerasimov invented a slow and heavy walk, as if he was made of metal, and the trademark deadpan laugh, which is perceived as comical in more light-hearted scenes, but ironic or even tragic in the scenes with higher emotional stakes. At all times, Werther's speech is slow and exaggeratedly 'mechanical', which is the feature inherited from the common stereotype of a robot in Soviet film (Korosteleva 2019).

> Kolya: Are you joking?
>
> Robot Werther (with a deadpan expression): Do I look like a joker?

Robot Werther works as a janitor at the Institute of Time in the future year 2084 - a quite depressing duty, given his abilities and inclinations. Among other tasks, he keeps the inventory of the Institute's Museum collection in order. Werther explains his work ethics with commitment, if not passion: "Our descendants will not forgive us if we allow chaos in the documentation".

Employing a robotic bureaucrat is no more a novelty in our time. Artificial Intelligence solutions are widely used to streamline decision processes in private firms and public institutions. This leads to the question of peaceful and productive cooperation of human and non-human agents in organizations. One possible way to see it is to imagine AI agents as autonomous 'artificial bureaucrats' working alongside humans, and to set goals and standards that should be achievable in cooperation between them. This concept was proposed by Justin Bullock and Kyoung-cheol Kim (Bullock & Kim 2020), who base it on the Weberian foundation. In this sense, an artificial bureaucrat is an AI agent employed in a hybrid (human and nonhuman) working environment to facilitate mundane administrative tasks. This environment supports plurality of possible decisions and a hierarchical chain of command. In such organization, "AI systems may be considered as individual agents making and executing decisions rather than simply being operated by humans utilizing them as mere tools" (Bullock & Kim 2020, p.30).

In terms of Bullock and Kim (2020), the Institute of Time where Robot Werther works becomes a utopian model of a "multiagent bureaucratic system". Here, humans and AI agents cooperate with the intention to achieve a common goal (in this particular case, conduct historical research). In a Weberian sense, Werther is the bureaucrat by vocation (Beruf): following the rules is what he was made to do, and he fully devotes himself to it. In his monologues, however, Werther constantly repeats that he cannot go on like this. It appears that his human colleagues openly dislike him for his scrupulousness. They call him a bureaucrat in a derogatory tone, although his only intention was to make them follow best working practices.

Here, Werther subverts the stereotype of a robotic servant once again. Despite being a robot, he is inherently a good colleague with a kind, caring personality. In that, Robot Werther expresses human traits that are usually reserved for human agents in posthuman bureaucracies (Bullock & Kim 2020): selfless loyalty to his senior colleague Polina, a strong sense of personal responsibility, as well as the ability to reflect on the boundaries of his own responsibility when other agents are involved. As further development of his character demonstrates, this kind and sensitive robot has his own strong moral compass that defines his unique character and influence his decisions, allowing him to fully own them, as well as their consequences.

According to the prospective vision of a hybrid multi-agent bureaucratic system, "joint persistent goals and joint intention help to build a system of multiagent actors that, for example, might coordinate and co-work to deliver public services" (Bullock & Kim 2020, p. 32). Unfortunately, goals and intentions of human and non-human agents do not align even at the fictional Institute of Time: young and vivacious human coworkers want to relax and have fun rather than follow the formalities. It causes Werther emotional distress: in his own words, his colleagues "are never able to return one by one, "which would be the least that they could do to respect his job. Werther values social responsibility first and foremost - the quality that his human colleagues sometimes lack. However, Werther's inclination to always follow the procedure is not absolute: it does not influence decision-making in important situations, and Werther is able to feel happy and free when he goes against the procedure for a good reason: "What a lovely day it was", - he recalls, after having broken the rules in order to make a human boy happy.

Marvin and Werther are two of the same kind

While Soviet filmmakers had some level of access to foreign films, as Werther's origins will demonstrate, it is highly unlikely that they could familiarize themselves with the production of BBC. And yet, Visitor from the Future (1985) shares a number of aesthetic qualities and narrative elements with The Hitchhiker's Guide to the Galaxy (1981). Some of these similarities are imposed by the limitations of the TV medium, such as the almost identical curved corridors at the Institute of Time (Visitor from the Future) and in the Heart of Gold spaceship (The Hitchhiker's Guide to the Galaxy). Warping the perspective is a common trick used in TV shooting sets to create the illusion of a much larger space in a small studio. Other similar features can be traced down to common tropes and forms of media such as scientific documentaries. Truthful to the genre conventions of TV series, each episode of Visitor from the Future begins with a recap of previous events. As a part of such recap, the introduction to the third episode includes a humorous reference to the fictional "The Encyclopedia of Inventions, 2082". This Encyclopedia describes 'melophone', a telepathic device central to the plot of the film. The voice over narration sounds somewhat ironic: "With the help of melophone, you can read the thoughts of any living being, provided that they have any thoughts". Even stronger ironic tone is used in the TV adaptation of The Hitchhiker's Guide to the Galaxy, which also parodies educational and pop science TV programs.

Next, both Marvin the Paranoid Android and Robot Werther are introduced in the almost identical manner in their respective series. They both appear walking slowly and unnaturally heavily along the aforementioned curved corridor. Moreover, the first thing viewers learn about each of the characters that is that they are unhappy with their job. Job dissatisfaction dramatically affects personalities of both characters across the rest of their stories and makes them much less fun to be with. One particularly toxic consequence is that both Marvin and Werther behave in a passive aggressive way when speaking to their seniors, and both imply that they are too sophisticated for the mundane tasks that they are presented with.

Werther, with a grave expression: Who am I? A janitor! Nobody loves me, nobody needs me.

Marvin: Here I am, brain the size of a planet, and they ask me to pick up a piece of paper.

Finally, both AI agents seem much happier (which means not gravely unhappy in the case of Marvin), and even make better decisions, when they operate at their own discretion. It appears as if writers and directors from two completely different and somewhat isolated cultures have modeled two fictional artificial intelligent beings who have to deal with similar problems.

"Sensitive nature and exquisite psychic organization": emotional intelligence of robotic characters

Werther: "Boy, are you a romantic?"

To the educated viewer, the name of robot Werther already frames him as a very particular cultural type, tied to the German Romantic tradition. It is a direct reference to The Sorrows of Young Werther (1774) by Johann Wolfgang von Goethe. The original young Werther committed suicide on the grounds of unrequited love. Although his artificial namesake has a different destiny, they both subvert the canon by prioritizing their inner feelings over the hard 'ratio'. Even the linguistic analysis of Werther's persona reveals that, unlike a stereotypical robot, he is focused on himself and his own private emotional sphere (Korosteleva 2019).

Similar to the character of The Sorrows of Young Werther, Robot Werther describes himself as a person of "sensitive nature and exquisite psychic organization" 2. Werther is well versed in

---

[2] By the way, is Werther queer? His unnatural blonde wig and a tight silver jumpsuit set him far apart from the normative expression of masculinity in Soviet cinema. It appears that Werther's haircut and other stylistic choices were inspired by War of the Robots (1978), an unremarkable specimen of Star Wars-inspired Italian trash. The film critic Howard Hughes still distinguishes this film among

European art: for example, he is interested in the Spanish romantic painter Francisco Goya. "We also have our own Goya!", - his new friend Kolya Gerasimov replies arrogantly. He supposedly refers to Goya's "Portrait of Doña Antonia Zarate" (1811), which was given to Hermitage by the controversial American oil tycoon Armand Hammer3 in 1972 in exchange for a more valuable masterpiece by Kasimir Malevich (Epstein & Hammer 1996, pp. 294–295). Such a snobbish dialogue in a children's TV film probably speaks to the dual audience of children and their parents, which was common in Soviet cinema. Even in the late USSR, young teenagers would rather be interested in detective stories than in high art; such as, Kolya Gerasimov's classmate, Kolya Sadovsky, is a big fan of detective stories, and he is determined to reveal the secret of the space pirates with the Sherlockian 'deductive method'.

On the other hand, this presumed 'art snobbery' accompanies Kolya's deep interest in romantic poetry. In the cultural climate of the late Soviet academia, this echoes the ideological conflict between 'physicists' and 'lyricists', e,g. humanities and natural sciences (Lipovetsky 2017; Vol'kenshtein 1977). This somewhat convoluted academic argument had been simmering in public discussion spaces since the Thaw. The real reason for it, as Mark Lipovetsky suggests, lay in deep disappointment with the thoroughly ideologized role of literature and arts, which squandered the potential of creative workers in the Socialist society. Same as other conflicts that had plagued humankind in the historical past, this confrontation between different schools is already resolved in the happy and prosperous universe of Visitor from the Future that lies just one hundred years ahead. Here, both 'physicists' and 'lyricists' are equally important, because they combine their efforts to contribute to the progress of humankind. Remarkably, both Kolya Gerasimov and robot Werther represent 'lyricists' in this symbolic confrontation.

---

others for "passable costumes" in his substantial guide on Italian cinema: "gold suits and blond wigs, a shiny, glam rock Abba tribute" (Hughes 2011, p. 117). Based on that, and assuming that Werther, as a robot, is asexual, he inherited his queer fashion from the Italian disco culture.
3 Also, the grand-grandfather of the now infamous actor Armand Hammer.

After having witnessed one of Werther's passionate monologues about futility of his life and work, Kolya acknowledges and encourages Werther's romantic lust for adventure. At that moment, Werther's attitude towards Kolya changes from treating him as an 'inventory object' to sincere emotional connection. Werther is touched and inspired, so he allows the boy to take a quick tour around the future Moscow as in 2084. "Boy, are you a romantic?" - Werther asks Kolya directly before letting him go. As he admits, he would give half of his life to get the same opportunity as Kolya, and he gets even more excited when he learns that space pirates are involved.

> Robot Werther, to himself: Why wouldn't I really quit my job? Am I not a romantic? Am I worse than Kolya? I'll just go to the past, and I will have something to remember when they finally send me to the junk yard, ha ha ha.

As an indirect reference to The Sorrows of Young Werther, Robot Werther is also tragically in love with Polina, his superior. She works as a senior researcher at the Institute of Time and, as it appears in the finale, does the job of an invincible space ranger on the side. At the beginning of the film, this affection is presented as more of a pose, reminiscent of the classical character of the sad white clown Pierrot (Korosteleva 2019). Even though Werther is not always willing to follow Polina's instructions, he secretly writes poetry about her: "I literally pray to her" - he admits to Kolya. Eventually, it is revealed that Werther's affection is also the source of his morality, when Kolya accidentally follows Polina to the future, Werther is worried about her reputation first; he cares about her even more than about the procedure and the rules.

Polina herself is human (as far as the viewers know, although there is a good reason to suspect that she is, in fact, a super-powerful android). Whatever the case may be, her beauty is superhuman by all standards. Moreover, the 'Martian-looking' model and actress Yelena Metyolkina who plays Polina, also plays supernaturally powerful cyborg Niia in Per Aspera ad Astra. Incidentally, both films are based on works of Bulychev, although they do not share the same fantastic universe. Most importantly, these characters represent female superheroes in Soviet science fiction (a career that exceptionally strong and smart Alisa

Selezneva may consider when she grows up). These super-intelligent and super-strong female characters represent a stark contrast with the archetypal masculine Cyborg Hunter, the default role for an AI agent in the American pop culture of the 1980s (Rushing & Frentz 1995).

As for Robot Werther, he may not look like Terminator in any way, especially at the beginning, but he is capable of putting up a real fight when children are in danger, as it is revealed in the finale. Following the trope at least as old as Pinocchio (1883), Werther only becomes truly human after he makes a free and informed decision to sacrifice himself for the sake of others. Before that happens, narrator in the film refers to Robot Werther as "kind, romantically inclined Robot Werther" and even "the humane Robot Werther". Niia in Per Aspera ad Astra actualizes the same trope when she makes the altruistic choice to save her planet, which makes her, in the words of Igor Gulin, "a female Christlike saint" (Gulin 2016). In general, Soviet science fiction eagerly invites interpretations based in religious spirituality, as we will see once again in Conclusion.

Marvin: "Call that job satisfaction, because I don't"

Robot Werther and robot Marvin first appeared on the small screen right at the peak between two 'AI winters' (Bastani 2019, p. 75; Pagallo, Corrales, Fenwick, & Forgo 2018), when researchers and developers felt particularly inspired with the future of artificial intelligence. AI ethics, however, belonged to the speculative domain at that time. Almost two decades had to pass before the domain of 'robo-ethics' would emerge, and the concept of robot rights would be recognized (Gunkel 2019). It should be noted here that popular culture provided slightly different perspective on robo-ethics in the USA and in the USSR. Soviet regime retained many authoritarian features even during Perestroika, but late Soviet popular culture provided a more nuanced perspective on artificial intelligence and robot rights, at least, in works of fiction such as Per Aspera ad Astra, Adventures of Elektronik, and Visitor from the Future. This should not come as a surprise: access to American science fiction was relatively limited before Perestroika, and the Soviet audience was first exposed to the most critical examples of it. For example, many young Soviet readers were first introduced to robo-ethics in The Velvet Glove, a short story by Harry Harrison from his War with the Robots collection (1962), first translated into Russian in 1969 and re-published again in 1989 in a very popular collected volume under the title The Unemployed Robot. This fantastic story presents social critique of the labor market in a capitalist state, where intelligent robotic employees stand as a metaphor for racial inequality (Harrison 2009). This critical message allowed this story to cross the Iron Curtain during the Thaw. In the meantime, depictions of robots in Soviet film have mostly been sympathetic and humane, in contrast with the iconic American characters such as Terminator from the franchise of the same name, replicants from Blade Runner (Scott 1982), or even HAL 9000 from 2001: The Space Odyssey (Kubrick 1968).

In this relation, the British Hitchhiker's Guide finds itself somewhere in between the American and the Soviet version of early AI ethics. Although Douglas Adams was rather critical of capitalism, robot rights were not always respected in his multiverses. While robot Werther can enjoy stable employment in a Utopian welfare state, Marvin is still technically a property, a robotic servant of the eccentric space pirate Zaphod. At least, Werther has the upper word over his human coworkers within his area of responsibility; conversely, Marvin's competence is always ignored by his clueless master and other humans. In society, Marvin is not a person, but a product, advertised as "Your plastic pal who's fun to be with", by the Sirius Cybernetics Corporation. He is equipped with superintelligence, but it is, sadly, not valuable in itself: just an extra feature to increase his value as a commodity. In this regard, Marvin's fate can be compared to that of a particularly 'smart' device such as a 'flagman' smartphone with high computational benchmarks that will hardly ever be employed for a meaningful purpose. This incredibly smart and sentient device is in possession of the human who makes particularly bad decisions throughout the whole history of the world created by Douglas Adams. "Life! Don't talk to me about life", Marvin repeats bitterly in the radio and TV versions of his story.

At least, in this relatively progressive future, robots are not just capable of, but also allowed, to have feelings and openly express them4. Marvin's most recognizable trait, his depression, signifies that he is not just super-intelligent, but also a super-emotional artificial agent. At first sight, it may seem that Marvin does not care about anyone's feelings: instead, he demands unrealistic level of respect that would be proportional to his enormous intelligence (he repeatedly refers to himself as "brain the size of a planet"). Unlike creative and soulful, even if quirky, Werther, Marvin sees himself as a rational being first and foremost. While Werther idolizes his female supervisor, Marvin expresses a different - or, may we say, completely indifferent attitude to his female boss Trillian. In a broader context, existence of Marvin likely frees Trillian from the common limitations of a female character and allows her to take the role of the second commander at the ship, but this also means the unbridgeable gap between their statuses. In the TV version, Trillian initially expresses care about Marvin and offers him tasks to "occupy his mind". "It won't work. I have an exceptionally large mind", - he replies sourly. We might ask ourselves whether Marvin the Paranoid Android has ever been in love, but this possibility is never present in the TV version of his story.

This lack of emotional intelligence is detrimental not just for Marvin's own well-being, but also for his social life. Having internalized the idea of 'intellectual superiority' and rationality, Marvin never learns to manage his own feelings, which he definitely has in spades. Neither can he understand the feelings of others - unlike Werther, who is fully proficient in acknowledging the position of the other, as the linguistic analysis of his speech demonstrates (Korosteleva 2019, p. 88). To compensate for his low emotional intelligence, Marvin regularly asks people around him whether he makes them feel bad. "I would not like to think I'm getting you down", he repeats, sometimes adding: "Pardon me for breathing - which I never do anyway" (Adams 1985, p. 45). There is still the chance for Marvin to evolve as a person. Toxicity of his character seems to be more

---

4 It may be worth reminding that artificial replicants in *Blade Runner* (1982) are fiercely passionate in contrast to the behaviour that is expected from 'real humans'. Notably, Rachael becomes more emotionally expressive after she realises that she is a replicant. (Rushing & Frentz 1995, p. 158)

pronounced in the early TV version, but it is less prominent in the book version and almost unnoticeable in the film adaptation in 2005. In the third volume of the book series Marvin even writes poetry, which may symbolize gradually coming to terms with his overwhelming emotions (Adams 2008, p. 196).

After many adventures and challenges, both robots face existential choice, which makes their lives ultimately meaningful in the end. They sacrifice themselves to save their human friends - at least, this is what happens to them in the TV versions of their otherwise much longer media journeys. Still, two robots do it with a completely different attitude. Robot Werther openly confronts space pirates, and his metallic body destroyed in a flashy battle. This is his personal existential choice, and he does it for the children whom he befriended, without any hesitation. Marvin, to the contrary makes it all about himself 5. He has to be left behind to save the rest of the team from the ship that is going to collide with a star, and no wonder he is reluctant to go on his saving mission. Eventually, Marvin accepts this fate; still, he breaks the fourth wall and goes into a long passive aggressive monologue that somewhat diminishes the value of his heroic deed.

Will freedom from work make us free?

The robotic soul and its body-machine

Not all robots are sad in the fictional worlds that are analyzed here. To the contrary, most fictional AI agents seem to find fulfilment in their jobs, such as Eddie, the annoyingly cheerful shipboard computer on the spaceship Heart of Gold in The Hitchhiker's Guide to the Galaxy. Sentient talking doors on the same spaceship make even better examples. These mechanical doors get (allegedly) genuine satisfaction from their job: "It is their pleasure to open for you, and their satisfaction to close again with the knowledge of a job well done" (Adams 1985, p. 45), Marvin explains, stressing the shallowness of such 'job satisfaction'. In his mind, serving people is an incredibly trivial duty compared to

---

[5] Marvin seems to become gradually more devoted to his human colleagues in the book version and in the 2004 film, even though this quality remains hidden behind his sulky facade.

the search for meaning of life, the Universe, and everything. Regardless, the doors are perfectly happy about their place in the world: they see their mission in life as being helpful, and they do not feel estranged from their vocation. Their form, function, and the type of intelligence they possess are perfectly aligned with the ordinary task that they perform, which cannot be said about Marvin.

The audience of Visitor from the Future also gets to know a number of helpful AI agents, when Kolya Gerasimov accidentally travels to the future in the first and second episodes. To start from, the time traveling machine instructs him how to use it. Its command to 'take a deep breath' parodies the tone of a typical instructor for morning exercises, or 'gymnastics', on the radio, - the everyday routine in the USSR. The voice (male, by the way - yet another sign of higher gender equality, at least, in the 1980s) asks Kolya to close his eyes and warns, in a more human-like tone, "No peeking!" when Kolya tries to cheat. This AI agent is not much more than a voice assistant, but it is already used to dishonest behavior of humans. Unfortunately, he is not able to recognize the deceitful space pirates and sends them to the past without asking anything.

Even though disembodied secondary AI characters are not much more than voice assistants in both TV films, there is a healthy proportion of male and female voices, none of them 'othered' by allusions to power relations between genders, races or age groups, as it is often the case with robotic voices in real life (Mannisto-Funk & Sihvonen 2018; Atanasoski & Vora 2019). Another robotic assistant can be found at the intergalactic airport. This time, it is the female voice of the ticket terminal. Kolya does not have a fixed goal in this new and unknown world, and his communication with this AI agent is not particularly successful.

> Kolya: Just take me anywhere!
>
> Ticket Terminal: Your question is not understood. Where do you want to go?
>
> Kolya: You don't understand anything!

- Kolya finally says in despair, finding himself in a typical situation of misunderstanding between a human and nonhuman agent.

Coincidentally, happy robotic servants are mostly represented by their voices in both films. On the one hand, this is the natural consequence of limited budgets for TV production. On the other hand, these robots are symbolically deprived of bodily autonomy. They are only ghosts, speaking from immobile electronic shells. Possession of their own autonomous body-machine seems to be the prerequisite of forming a complete, even if flawed, personality for AI representations. We may turn to HAL 9000 from 2001: The Space Odissey (1968) for a comparison; still, one may argue that HAL's embodiment is the spaceship as a whole. The ship can travel by itself in full control of HAL; this is exactly what HAL wants and, eventually, achieves.

How to fix the 'automatic sulking machine'

Is there a job for Marvin that would suit his enormous brain? We can easily imagine him as a professional philosopher: he would likely find satisfaction or, at least, recognition as a robotic Schopenhauer. However, it is implied that even human philosophers are losing their jobs to supercomputers in the world of The Hitchhiker's Guide. According to the main narrative of The Hitchhiker's Guide, the ultimate task of appropriate complexity - finding the meaning of everything - has been reserved for artificial intelligence literally the size of the planet. Unfortunately, Marvin's ideal job, probably his vocation, has been taken from him by an even bigger super-AI. As we eventually learn in all versions of The Hitchhiker's Guide, this supercomputer is, in fact, the planet Earth itself; Marvin's 'brain the size of a planet' may be foreshadowing this dramatic reveal.

For Werther, the dream career is becoming a poet. He reveals it to Kolya Gerasimov as soon as they meet in the future for the first time.

Werther: Do you write poetry?

Kolya: Used to, when I was young *(Kolya is approximately 12 years old in the film, and, in fact, he still writes poetry).*

Werther: I still do.

Werther confesses melancholically, before breaking into reading his (rather uncomplicated) poetry. This creative side of the technological cyborg symbolizes successful synthesis of art and science, achieved by cooperation between 'physicists' and 'lyricists' in Soviet philosophy of science (Vol'kenshtein 1977). We have another example of the same trope in Soviet children's film: the robotic boy Elektronik from The Adventures of Elektronik (1979) reaches the next stage of development when he writes a poem, which manifests the human level of emotional intelligence (Kukulin 2008). Notably, this trope actually reflected the state of research in AI at the time: the 1980s saw real-life experiments of Ray Kurzweil and Charles Hartman, who attempted, more or less successfully, to teach AI agents to write poetry (Schwartz 2018).

Visitor from the Future provides the optimistic version of the future of human and non-human agents – for everyone but the kind and humane Robot Werther. At least, like a true romantic, he has had the last laugh in the face of impending death. Robot Werther will never become a poet - but his human friend Kolya will. In the finale of the series, Polina, the super heroic researcher of the future, reveals prophecies about the future career of every child. According to her, Kolya will indeed become a recognized poet when he grows up, and he will dedicate his poems to another character Lena Dombazova, who will become a famous actress. "It is bad manners to be famous"-one child comments, voicing a more common collectivist message typical for many earlier Soviet films for children (Kostyukevich 2020). In his turn, Kolya Sadovsky, the young detective and Kolya Gerasimov's classmate, will become a "regular engineer" and invent a "regular time machine" - supposedly the one that started their adventures together. In this way, the last episode of the TV series gives hope to 'lyricists', while also paying respect to 'physicists'. Other members of the children's "gang" will become a doctor, an artist and a professional tennis player. At least, this time, everyone has the chance to become someone they truly want to be, no matter what the future may hold for them.

Conclusion and discussion

Visitor from the Future remains one of the most influential children's TV films of the 1980s, and the formative memory of the first post-Soviet generation. Its uplifting optimistic ending, however, is tainted with the eschatological anxiety of the famous final song, The Winged Swing, written by the lyricist Yuri Entin and the composer Yevgeny Krylatov. The researcher of Soviet utopias Irina Kaspe interprets this song as a "prayer-song" (Kaspe 2018, 160), the implied spiritual impulse that goes against the radically materialist Soviet ideology. Even though the song is about the future, this imagined future is too beautiful and perfect for living people, even today's children, that it is easily interpreted as the afterlife, which one deserves by today's decisions and deeds. Its chorus, still lingering in the cultural memory of post-Soviet people, is uncharacteristically bleak for the typically optimistic Soviet children's cinema:

Don't be cruel to me, the beautiful far away (future).

This song remains a spiritual hymn of the last Soviet generation, who was destined to face major societal changes and a rather depressing reality of early post-Soviet years. Visitor from the Future was produced in the year when Perestroika started, which eventually has led to the collapse of the USSR. Both present time and the future are comfortably socialist: the Russian film critic Igor Gulin even suggests that Visitor from the Future presents the only successful attempt of Soviet science fiction cinema to construct the actual working Utopia (Gulin 2021).

No matter how different, the future Utopias of Werther and Martin share one common feature, much sought after in contemporary utopianism as well: people do not have to work in them, unless they want to. They can freely engage in creative activities and arts in the fictional version of "fully automated luxury communism" (Bastani 2019). So, there is no reason to be sad - for humans, at least. In the year 2084, everyone can become a cosmonaut, fly to the moon, travel back in time to meet great historical personalities and even dinosaurs. Even the highest aesthetic demands of Werther are met: he freely enjoys classical art, and he can't wait to see the competition of robotic guitarists (although he never expresses the wish to participate himself). What he lacks in his life is the purpose that comes with a fulfilling job – the one thing that he cannot have. The same is true for Marvin, and this is why both robots express their disappointment with life in an almost identical manner: they become depressed.

Depression is a social phenomenon as well as a personal malady. In his writing on depression, the late British philosopher and cultural critic Mark Fisher described the political dimension of melancholia, present in British popular culture since the early 1980s. To him, its nostalgic sadness was a symptom of the 'canceled future' and the inevitability of capitalism (Fisher 2014). However, the future is neither 'canceled' nor homogeneously capitalist neither in Visitor from the Future nor in the universe of The Hitchhiker's Guide to the Galaxy. In the TV version of the latter, two fictional documentary sources - the Hitchhiker's Guide to the Galaxy and Encyclopedia Galactica casually mention at least one revolution that changed the social order for the better. From these sources, we learn that the Marketing Division of the Sirius Cybernetics corporation, the makers of Marvin, was put "against the wall" and allegedly prosecuted (Adams 1985, p. 44). It is unclear whether this revolution takes place in the past or in the future, but it provides an optimistic perspective and hope for humanity, where 'genuine robotic personalities' are no longer under control of 'mindless jerks' (Adams 1985, p. 44). As Marvin has a practically unlimited life span in the series, he can hope to see better days, and the future is not sealed for him.

This brings us to the main thesis of this paper. In the future, both work and dissatisfaction with it are passed on to robots, who are specifically "designed to do the work of a man", as the Galaxy Encyclopedia states (Adams 1985, p. 44). Tragically, by their very design, robots are often forced to do someone else's work, and not the kind of work they wish to do. If that happens, even robots become estranged from their 'true selves' as they develop unique human personalities and become 'almost human'. Moreover, in both analyzed cases, a robot character finds themselves in a position when someone else has taken their jobs from them - in the same way as people would speculate about robots taking their jobs (Atanasoski & Vora 2019, pp. 1-4). This mirrors the critique of the Western liberal subject provided by Atanasoski and Vora:

this subject can only be free at the cost of another 'non-human' or 'less than human' subject doing his job for him (Atanasoski & Vora 2019, pp. 5).

To conclude, the cause of depression in robots lies deeper than the simple fear of unemployment, which is most likely eradicated in fully automated Utopian futures. The reason for existential crisis is one's inability to actualize one's full potential in their vocation. This contradiction is resolved through self-sacrifice for Werther and through an altruistic heroic deed for Marvin. Both robotic characters thus establish themselves in what we may call an existential choice, as explored by the human philosophers such as Sartre and Camus.

Should we even care if robots are sad? By being able to make, or even to consider an existential choice, artificial beings raise to the same level of ethical consideration as real humans. This future is still far ahead: in the words of Sherry Turkle, "It belongs to the future to determine whether robots could ultimately "deserve" the emotional responses they are now eliciting" (Turkle 2011). In the meantime, sci-fi literature, film and video games already present us with characters of robots with "genuine human personalities" (like Marvin) and exceptionally high emotional intelligence (like Werther). I suggest looking at these sympathetic robots as the fictional ambassadors of their real-life descendants. Representations of robots in popular media invite wider audiences to 'humanize' nonhuman agents already in existence; they even shape public perception of artificial intelligence in general (Banks 2020; Gunkel 2019). These complex representations also place expectations on researchers, designers and developers of artificial intelligence. As long as human designers take on moral responsibility for the artificial beings they create, it becomes their moral duty to avoid or decrease unnecessary suffering in virtual worlds (Gualeni 2020), and even more so in the hybrid multi-agent reality of technological society.

Robot Werther will always live as an instantly recognized and cherished image of late Soviet children's media. Rooted in the previous generation of science fiction that emerged during the Thaw, he embodied the last argument in the philosophical dispute between sciences and arts. His heroic death caused many children's tears, but it also served as a lesson of empathy to the ones who are different, and not necessarily biologically human.

About the Author

ALESHA SERADA is finishing their dissertation at the University of Vaasa, Finland. The dissertation discusses construction of value in games on blockchain. Alesha's research interests revolve around exploitation, violence, horror, and other banal and non-banal evils in visual media. In their spare time, Alesha writes about late Soviet and post-Soviet visual culture to make it more accessible to the English-speaking audience.

References

Adams, D. (1985). The Original Hitchhiker Radio Scripts. Harmony Books.

Adams, D. (2008). Life, the Universe and Everything. Random House Publishing Group.

Arsenov, P. (1985). Visitor from the Future. Gorky Film Studio.

Atanasoski, N., & Vora, K. (2019). Surrogate Humanity: Race, Robots, and the Politics of Technological Futures. Duke University Press.

Banks,J. (2020). Optimus Primed: Media Cultivation of Robot Mental Models and Social Judgments. Frontiers in Robotics and AI, 7. Retrieved 2021-05-25, from https://www.frontiersin.org/articles/10.3389/frobt.2020.00062/full (Publisher: Frontiers) doi: 10.3389/frobt.2020.00062

Bastani, A. (2019). Fully Automated Luxury Communism. Verso Books.

Bullock, J. B., & Kim, K.-c. (2020, October). Creation of Artificial Bureaucrats. In Proceedings of the European Conference on the Impact of Artificial Intelligence and Robotics ECIAIR 2020 (pp. 30–37). Lisbon, Portugal: Instituto Universit´ario de Lisboa.

Csicsery-Ronay, I. (2004). Science Fiction and the Thaw. Science Fiction Studies, 31(3,), 337–344. Retrieved from http://www.jstor.org/stable/4241281

Epstein, E. J., & Hammer, A. (1996). Dossier: The Secret History of Armand Hammer. Random House.

Fedorov, A. (2017, September). The western world in soviet and russian cinema (1946–2016). Russian Education and Society, 59(7-9), 319–464. doi: 10.1080/10609393.2017.1413880

Fisher, M. (2014). Ghosts of My Life: Writings on Depression, Hauntology and Lost Futures. John Hunt Publishing.

Gualeni, S. (2020, March). Artificial Beings Worthy of Moral Consideration in Virtual Environments: An Analysis of Ethical Viability. Journal For Virtual Worlds Research, 13(1).

Gulin, I. (2016, July). Svjatoj android i dialektika biomassy. Colta. Retrieved 2021-05-28, from https://www.colta.ru/articles/raznoglasiya/11869-svyatoy-android-i-dialektika-biomassy

Gulin, I. (2021, April). Gost'ja iz budushhego, ili Postoronnim vhod vospreshhen. Kommersant(12), 8–8. Retrieved 2021-05-27, from https://www.kommersant.ru/doc/4773090

Gunkel, D. J. (2019). How to Survive a Robot Invasion: Rights, Responsibility, and AI. Routledge.

Harrison, H. (2009). The Velvet Glove. Project Gutenberg. Retrieved 2021-05-28, from https://www.gutenberg.org/files/29471/29471-h/29471-h.htm

Hughes, H. (2011). Cinema Italiano: The Complete Guide from Classics to Cult. Bloomsbury Publishing.

Kaspe, I. (2018). V sojuze s utopiej. Smyslovye rubezhi pozdnesovetskoj kul'tury. Moscow: NLO.

Korosteleva, A. (2019, July). Communicative Stereotype of Robot in Children's Movies. Stephanos, 36(4), 68–95. doi: 10.24249/2309-9917-2019-36-4-6895

Kostyukevich, M. (2020). Detskij seans. Minsk: Medisont.

Kukulin, I. (2008). Chetvertyj zakon robototehniki: fil'm "Prikljuchenija Elektronika" i formirovanie "pokolenija 1990-h". In Veselye chelovechki: kul'turnye geroi sovetskogo detstva (Vol. LXXIV, pp. 458–506). Moscow: NLO.

Lipovetsky, M. (2017, January). The Poetics of the ITR Discourse: In the 1960s and Today was published in Postmodern Crises on page 33. In Postmodern Crises: From Lolita to Pussy Riot (pp. 33–52). Academic Studies Press. Retrieved 2021-05-28, from http://www.degruyter.com/document/doi/10.1515/9781618115591-003/html

(Pages: 33-52 Publication Title: Postmodern Crises Section: Postmodern Crises)

Majsova, N. (2020, June). Soviet Sci-fi Film and Different Modalities of Future Ecosystems. Strelka Mag. Retrieved 2020-06-11, from https://strelkamag.com/en/article/soviet-sci-fi-film-and-different-modalities-of-future

Mannisto-Funk, T., & Sihvonen, T. (2018, March). Voices from the Uncanny Valley. Digital Culture & Society, 4(1), 45–64. doi: 10.14361/dcs-20180105

Pagallo, U., Corrales, M., Fenwick, M., & Forgo, N. (2018). The Rise of Robotics & AI: Technological Advances & Normative Dilemmas. In M. Corrales, M. Fenwick, & N. Forg´o (Eds.), Robotics, AI and the Future of Law (pp. 1–13). Singapore: Springer. doi: 10.1007/978-981-13-2874-9 1

Pakulski, J. (1986). Bureaucracy and the Soviet system. Studies in Comparative Communism, 19(1), 3–24. https://doi.org/10.1016/0039-3592(86)90002-5

Rushing, J. H., & Frentz, T. S. (1995). Projecting the Shadow: The Cyborg Hero in American Film. University of Chicago Press.

Turkle, S. (2011). Authenticity in the age of digital companions. In Machine Ethics (pp. 62–76). Cambridge, MA: Cambridge University Press.

Retrieved 2020-09-25, from https://doi.org/10.1075/is.8.3.11tur (Publisher: John Benjamins Publishing Company)

Vol'kenshtein, M. V. (1977, July). The Esthetics of Science and the Science of Esthetics. Soviet Studies in Philosophy, 16(1), 13–25. doi:

10.2753/RSP1061-1967160113

Weber, M. (2003). Bureaucracy and Legitimate Authority. In M. J. Handel (Ed.), The Sociology of Organizations. Classic, Contemporary and Critical Readings (pp. 17–23). Sage Publications.

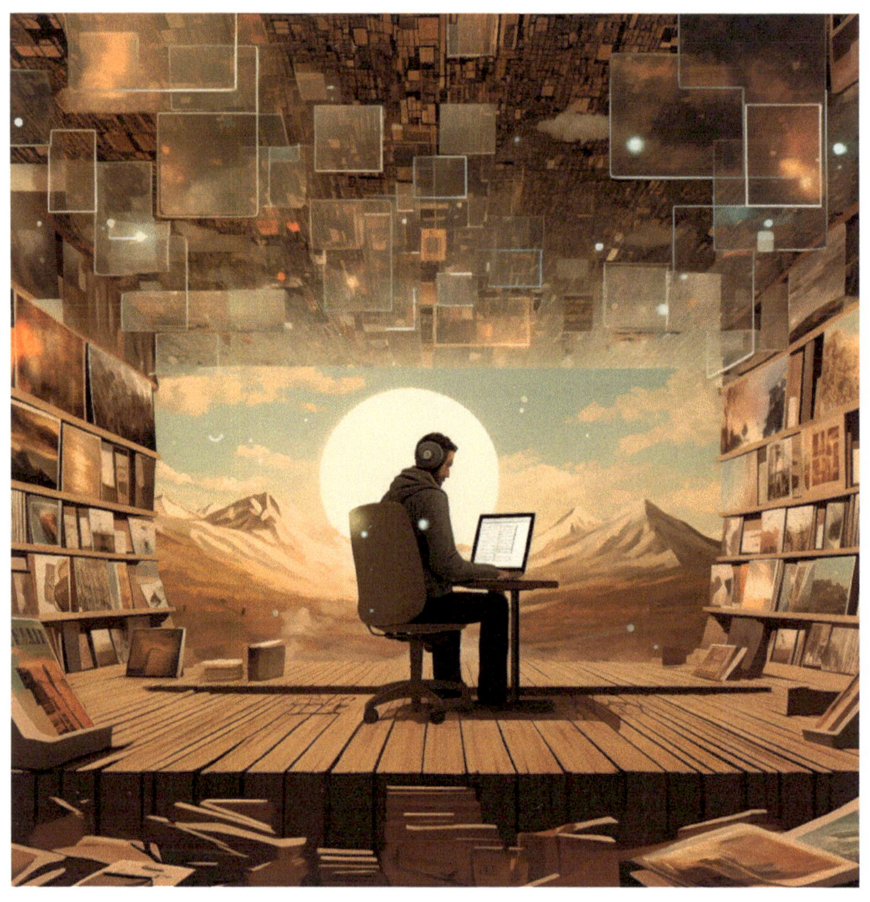

PLACE AS ASSEMBLAGE AND THE VIRTUAL

EXPERIENCING PLACE THROUGH LAYERS OF PHOTOVOICE AND VIRTUAL MEETING TOOLS

Tania Berger

In this paper, I investigate the way in which we experience place through layers of virtual means, like virtual meeting tools and photovoice methods.

While place is a way of bodily being in the world, of bonding with people and getting involved in a physical environment, this concept is obviously challenged by daily routines which see people spending substantial amounts of their working time in virtual meetings – a phenomenon that may have predated the pandemic but was undoubtedly strongly propagated by restrictions on physical movement and in-person interactions. Typical virtual meetings are mostly limited to verbal communication with video images of persons residing in other geographical locations, however, these physical locations do not normally matter as such for the interaction.

By contrast, in an ongoing international cooperation on Urban Health & Place, researchers in three different continents are using a photovoice tool to assess people's sense of place which they then analyze in virtual exchange. Understanding places as ever-changing assemblages of people and physical objects in a specific environment, created through a process of constant realignment with existing structures of power, knowledge, and discourse, I interrogate this process of making sense of place in multiple layers of virtual representation.

Keywords: virtual meetings, location, photovoice, sense of place

---

Introduction: Place as a precondition of being

Place 1 is a fact of life based on which we experience the world - the only way humans can exist is to be "in place": human beings and physical environment are thus inseparable in as far as human bodies necessarily need physical environment to exist at all (Rivlin, 1982). Experiencing self is not possible without experiencing self in place and is thus simultaneously experiencing place (ibid). This consciousness of being in the world constructs a relation between self and world - being conscious of something in the world and in its place therein (Cresswell, 2015).

Humanistic geography therefore understands the essence of human existence as being necessarily and importantly "in place". Place is seen as a universal and transhistorical part of the human condition (ibid). What we know cannot be separated from what our bodies perceive as we move through space (Bodenhamer, 2015). We integrate physical environment into our worldview based on sensual perception and experience of this environment (Mannheim, 1980: 208/9, Giddens, 1995; Loer, 2007). And as we get to know the world around us through places, an affective band between people and places can emerge. If we acknowledge that intimate relationships between place and people exist, we do not see people and places as independent parts (Rivlin, 1982).

In this chapter, I investigate how this relationship contributes to places assuming a kind of "identity" and how spatial and temporal coexistence of people in specific places offers

---

[1] Place vs space: there is abundant literature (e.g. Bodenhamer, 2015; Armstrong, 2004 Feldman, 1990 Mendoza & Morén-Alegret, 2013) which investigates distinctions between "place" and "space". However, leaving this discussion aside, I herein use the term "place" as generally referring to physical environment.

opportunities for community identity to be formed. I go on to explore how places can be viewed as assemblages of people and objects in which the relationships between these are central. Finally, I look at photovoice as a method to gain insight into such local relationships and how implicit local knowledge can be rendered explicit by applying it in the settings of a specific place.

Place identity

People, things, and activities in places are an integral part of the social world of everyday life. These places become imbued with personal, social and cultural meanings. They provide a significant framework in which identity is constructed, maintained, and transformed (Lee Cuba & David M. Hummon, 1993).

When talking about a specific place's identity, we therefore not only refer to the material qualities of this place but also to its characteristics and people's relations to it (Rivlin, 1982). Identification with this place – especially when this is a place of residence (the intimate home as well as the broader neighborhood) - often involves emotional ties to it, a sense of shared interests and values, a sense of being "at home" and "really me" (ibid). Place identity formulates as a component of self-identity and therein identity is derived from the physical environment as much as it is from social experiences made in it.

Long-term residence in a particular place is found to contribute to place identity and a sense of home by building sentimental attachment through establishing of local social ties (Lee Cuba & David M. Hummon, 1993). Becoming involved in a neighborhood may create a sense of belonging, rootedness and ultimately an attachment to place (Cresswell, 2015). Over time, place is imbued with personal meanings, linking significant life events to the place and providing the individual with a sense of "autobiographical insidedness" (Lee Cuba & David M. Hummon, 1993). For the elderly especially, place of residence can become an increasingly important focal point in live.

Following Lefebvre's notion of space as being socially constructed, we may thus understand that place „ [...] is not just inhabited but [...] is produced through inhabiting" (McFarlane, 2011 cit. in Eckardt, 2021).

Community identity

In the process of becoming familiar with a place, specific bodies of knowledge emerge that are based on habitualized experience. Communities of experience are formed that know the local context of rules and ascribe meaning to them in a mostly tacitly effective processes of meaning formation (Bourdieu, 1976, p.228; cit. in Löw, 2018, p.138) and also spread this experience in words and images.

A community thus is not a mere ‚thing' with geographical boundaries, but rather a broader set of ideas (Eckardt, 2021). Such ideas may become apparent in the narration of one resident's biography.

"The place a group occupies is not like a blackboard, where one may write and erase figures at will. No image of a blackboard can recall what once was written on it before, and new figures may be freely added. But place and group have each received the imprint of the other. [...]. Each aspect, each detail, of this place has a meaning intelligent only to members of the group [...]." (Lee Cuba & David M. Hummon, 1993).

The city - or a specific area, a place within it - as a "we-relationship", as a "conjunctive experiential space" (Mannheim, 1980) is the experience of a specific, social environment in spatial and temporal coexistence (Schütz, 1991 [1932]: p. 227, cit. in Löw, 2018) as human beings residing spatially close to each other in a specific neighborhood have similar options for perception – even though in everyday life, one cannot know whether other people in the same area interpret the place in the same way (Rivlin, 1982).

A specific environment can be understood as an organizing frame for laying down of residents' memories, the canvas on which a rich set of experiences with objects, people and groups is laid out. Therein, memories become the invisible 'glue' attaching people to this environmental setting and often even to parts of it that are no longer visible such as buildings that once were part of the neighborhood but have since been demolished – while remaining very "present" in residents' memories. An individual's social participation in the local community is essential for this individual's community identity as it can be a significant source of sentimental ties to local places (ibid) - a feeling of togetherness that existentially includes the materialization of the cultural landscape (Eckardt, 2021). Settlement types may also provide residents with a community identity as a city person, country person, small-town person, suburbanite etc. (Lee Cuba & David M. Hummon, 1993).

We also learn what is "typical" for a certain place and thus considered worthy of protection in this place - while it might be outright forbidden elsewhere (Ritter & Burckhardt, 2006: 259). In order for a particular landscape to be perceived as a lovely place, what is seen there must be filtered by an onlooker's perception in such a way that it corresponds to a conception of an ideal that is understood to be lovely. The selection mechanisms of different people for what is perceived as "lovely" may differ individually, but there are inter-individual agreements that are commonly subsumed under the very broad term of "culture". If a landscape is unfamiliar to the onlooker, it may no longer be recognized as lovely because it deviates too much from an inter-individually established ideal (ibid: 36).

It is worth noticing, however, that social constructivist approaches in Critical / Radical (human) geography remind us of the fact that places are also instances of more general social processes, such as the construction of place in general conditions of capitalism, patriarchy and post colonialism (Cresswell, 2015).

Places can thus be viewed as assemblages of objects in which the relationships between these objects and people are central, looking at socio-material aspects of the city or the environment more generally, jointly exploring social practice and materiality located between macro-societal processes and material objects and artefacts at intermediate levels of interaction (Eckardt, 2021).

The stability of ever-changing assemblages is created through a process of realignment with existing structures of power, knowledge, discourse, rationality, and dispositives. This constant realignment takes place under the impacts of unequal distribution of power, resources, and knowledge. In this understanding, cities and places are seen as a permanent co-production of different relationships, which can be linked again and in new ways through creative action (ibid).

Photovoice as a method for participatory place analysis

Photovoice is a method for participatory research on physical environments. (Petersen & Østergaard, 2003). Photos are used for elicitation to gain insight into the specific local/ spatial contexts in which they are taken by research participants. This allows getting to know and understand the abilities, needs and interests of different communities concerning their use of the place in question. Photovoice is therefore a participatory method to give voices to specific local target groups.

Traditionally, the photovoice method has involved participants using disposable, non-disposable, or digital cameras to capture visual images of their daily environment (Crabtree & Braun, 2015; Börner, Albino, Caraveo, & Tejeda, 2015). Participants were enabled to either use cameras to take photographs on their own or together in a guided photoshoot. The photographs were then printed and used to generate conversations in workshops among groups, discussing various themes, such as community-level problems. These conversations served to elucidate community members' knowledge as experts of their daily lived experiences and their immediate physical and social environment. 'And the appliance of the photovoice method may also effectuate impacts on the community itself:

"Ultimately photovoice is about leveraging participant-taken photographs and discussions to raise community consciousness and promote community-level change." (Foster, Davis, & Foell, 2022).

The use of digital technologies such as smartphones, social media, online platforms etc. is changing the ways in which scholars conduct photovoice research. Such technologies are enabling various participatory formats on how participants collect and share the photos and engage in discussions and analysis with the researchers. As smartphones are ubiquitous among many communities across the world, they are often well-integrated into daily life of participants, unlike in traditional photovoice method where participants needed to carry a camera as an additional device.

Using smartphones demonstrates how the photovoice method can be redesigned for immediate sharing of perspectives on neighborhoods, and thus, generate conversation throughout the study period not just among the research group but also with wider audiences (ibid). Photovoice can also be combined with geospatial methods that actively involve participants in collecting data related to places of their environment. Thereby, capturing meaning and interpretations could directly ground research in spatial, social and perceptual experiences of person-place relationships and transactions. Digital development thus is offering new ways of using the photovoice method, giving access to diverse participants and potentially repositioning them as co-producers of knowledge.

This chapter is a reflection on the way in which the complexity of experiencing place can transpire (if at all it can) through layers of virtual means like photovoice methods and virtual meeting tools: in an ongoing international cooperation on Urban Health & Place, researchers in three different continents are using photovoice to assess people's sense of place which the researchers then analyze in virtual exchange across continents.

Typically, virtual meetings are limited to verbal communication with video images of persons residing in different geographical locations, however, these physical locations do not normally matter as such for the interaction. How then can the complexity of experiencing place as described above be communicated in such settings?

Method

In late 2021, the University of Applied Sciences Bochum (Germany) staged Urban Health digiSpace (https://urbanhealth-digispace.de/), focusing on physical activity in public open spaces. Within the broader framework of this event, a total of 65 participants in cities of eight different countries (Austria, Brazil, China, Germany, India, Nepal, Pakistan, Switzerland) took part in photovoice workshops in different public settings, ranging from recreational areas, university campuses, and parks to local neighborhoods in the center and periphery of urban spaces. Participating locations for these workshops were selected through existing research networks to represent a wide range of countries from the global North and South.

Workshop participants were mostly students and fellow researchers. They ventured out in their accustomed environments to collect photos in Kobo-Toolbox (https://www.kobotoolbox.org/), an open source photovoice tool. A survey had been set up in Kobo-Toolbox by the researchers, which allowed workshop participants to upload photos on places they like or do not like to be in with regards to the overarching theme of physical activity in public open spaces.

After the photoshoot, group discussions were conducted among those who had taken the photos in each location. In these discussions, the SHOWED approach was applied - an established intervention-oriented approach of photovoice, which requests participants to answer the following key questions with regards to the photos they had taken in the photovoice workshops (Annang et al., 2016; Shore, Tatum, & Vollmer, 1986):

- What do you **S**ee in the photograph?

- What is **H**appening in the photograph?

- How does this photograph relate to **O**ur lives in the community?

- Why are things this **W**ay?

- How could this photograph **E**ducate others?

- What can we **D**o about these issues?

Finally, findings of these group discussions were picked up in virtual meetings of the researchers who had conducted the local photoshoots and discussions. In a joint online meeting with our fellow researchers, we explored and assessed issues and concerns raised by the workshop participants in all locations. The sequence of procedural steps involved in this application of photovoice is summed up in Figure 1.

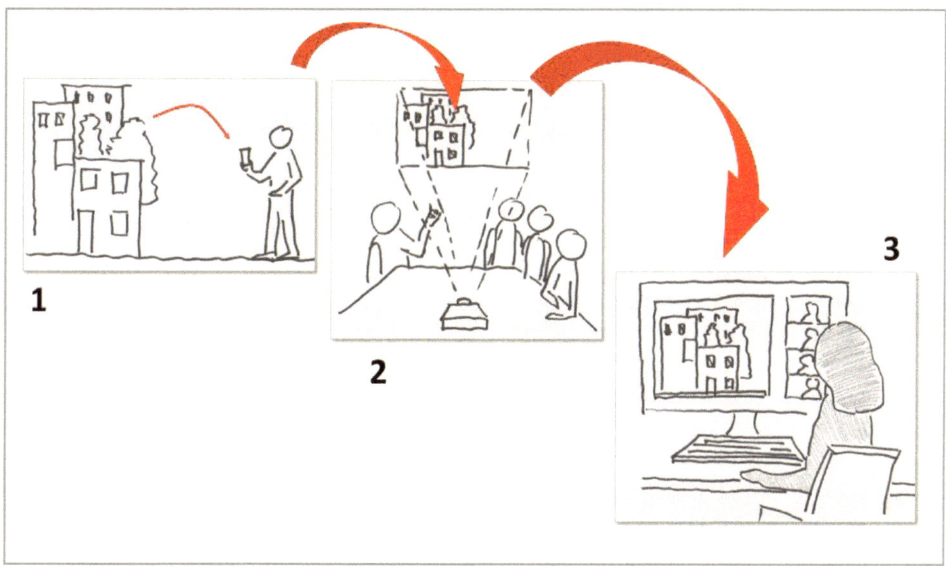

Figure 1: Steps of photovoice application

Step 1

A specific set of physical objects in a given geographical location is chosen to be photographed by a participant because these are of more importance to the participant than other objects. Implicit knowledge of the place guides the participant's decision what to include in the photo and what to leave out.

Step 2

When discussing the photo in the group by application of the SHOWED method, the photographers make their implicit knowledge of (certain aspects of) the place explicit to the group and the researcher2

Step 3

The researchers communicate this implicit knowledge (made explicit to them by research participants) to fellow researchers in a virtual setting. Thereby this knowledge becomes known to researchers who have no firsthand experience of the specific place.

Results

The questions of the SHOWED method proofed to make explicit (certain aspects of) the implicit knowledge of those who took the photos in the locations involved in this research. The broader framework conditions under which the depicted situations are occurring on daily basis may be well known and obvious to the research participants who experience them regularly. However, these conditions require to be pointed out explicitly to those who do not have any firsthand knowledge of the places depicted in the photographs. Participants might not have consciously thought about such determining framework conditions before or even while taking the photos. Yet, when trying to verbalize what it was that they saw in these pictures, why it was happing and what it meant for daily live in the community, they started talking about networks of relationships between actors and objects of the physical environment, looking at assemblages of socio-material aspects of their neighborhood.

Some of the following examples of such relationships are especially striking as they relate to material objects as well as

---

2 During the time of research, some Covid-19 restrictions were in force even outdoors in some of the study locations, mostly however these restrictions were limited to the mandatory use of face masks. Some of the group discussions also had to be held virtually.

socio- material aspects which are not even visible in the photos taken by the participants.

Multiplicity of uses coexisting in public spaces in Nepal, India and Pakistan

Photos taken and consequently discussed by participants in Nepal, India and Pakistan revolve around street scenes incorporating a multiplicity of uses in public spaces. Concerns over pedestrian safety, accessibility and walkability arouse in the absence of continuous and freely useable sidewalks. When street vendors and parked cars as well as scooters encroach upon such sidewalks (or sidewalks are absent altogether), walking becomes not only tedious but also dangerous and biking likewise gets disincentivized.

Omnipresence of individualized vehicular traffic in European settings

In the German and Austrian cases, the influence of vehicular traffic even on situations where no actual car is visible in the photos needs contextual knowledge: one of the images investigated in participants' group discussion in Vienna, Austria, actually depicts a public park in which no motorized vehicles are allowed. Still, the discussion centered on the perceived link between a general lack of such green public spaces and the dominant car centered use of spaces in the city more broadly. Participants observed that due to this imbalance in space available for different modes of movement within the overall city, bikers and pedestrians find themselves competing for limited space in parks like the one photographed. This competition engendered several instances of conflict between these two groups.

Prevailing security concerns in Brazil

The constant fear of one's phone/ camera being snatched by passers-by in the Brazilian context not only influences how participants behave on a daily basis in public space. It also impacted upon the photos taken during the workshop: young participants were rooming the streets and pointed out places they use or have to use on regular basis, yet they abstained from taking photos of the same for the said reason; they felt that taking photos here would arouse too much of attention from bystanders and could eventually lead to their phone being snatched – be it to simply get hold of this valuable device or to keep the participants from taking photos in the area.

When compiling these exemplary research findings across different geographic and cultural realms, the differences in the implicit background knowledge linked to public open spaces became evident. Such influences and interdependences are not apparent for outsiders and the SHOWED method applied in the international setting of this research helped making them explicit.

Conclusion

When understanding places as ever-changing assemblages of people and physical objects in a specific environment, created through a process of constant realignment with existing structures of power, knowledge, and discourse, we come to acknowledge the difficulty of communicating such complexity of experiencing place through layers of means like photovoice methods and virtual meeting tools.

In this research, a first willful reduction of complexity of the bodily experience of place was enacted in the research participants' decision on what to photograph and what not. The resulting two-dimensional photos necessarily lack the sensual information of place. In the group discussion after the photoshoot, focus was laid on some aspects of the visual representations (and not on others), thereby engendering a further reduction of complexity. At the same time, however, by rendering implicit knowledge explicit, a layer of information was added which was not previously there in this form. And it was this explication of specific local knowledge which could transpire in the third step of the process by which foreign researchers, not otherwise linked to the place, were still able to acquire specific knowledge of it.

Inserting this piece of knowledge in their more general concept on contexts of unequal distribution of power, resources, and knowledge, they may manage to understand cities and places as characterized by the permanent co-production of different relationships.

About the Author

TANIA BERGER is a trained architect and planner with a strong focus on interlinkages between societies and the built environment; she heads the center for Social sPACe based research in built Environment (SPACE) in the Department of Building and Environment at Danube University Krems, which researches integration of heterogeneous social groups in housing at the national level and global urbanization processes and precarious housing in an international context. She coordinates international cooperation projects with a focus on informal settlements in India and Ethiopia.

www.donau-uni.ac.at/dbu/space_en

Acknowledgement

I would like to express my sincere gratitude towards my fellow researchers engaged in this conversation under the overall guidance of Heike Köckler at University of Applied Sciences Bochum (Germany): Rehana Shrestha, Atif Aslam, Susanne Börner, Clement Cheung, Carlo Fabian, Hiranmayi Shankavaram, Reshma Shrestha, Saddicha Shrestha, Raphael Sieber and Daniel Simon. Without them this text would not have been possible.

References

Annang, L., Wilson, S., Tinago, C., Wright Sanders, L., Bevington, T., Carlos, B., et al. (2016). Photovoice: Assessing the Long-Term Impact of a Disaster on a Community's Quality of Life. Qualitative health research, 26(2), 241–251.

Antonio Gasparrini, Yuming Guo, Francesco Sera, Ana Maria Vicedo-Cabrera, Veronika Huber, Shilu Tong, et al. (2017). Projections of temperature-related excess mortality under climate change scenarios. The Lancet Planetary Health, 1(9), e360-e367, from https://www.sciencedirect.com/science/article/pii/S2542519617301560.

Armstrong, H. (2004). Making the Unfamiliar Familiar: Research Journeys towards Understanding Migration and Place. Landscape Research, 29(3), 237–260.

Bodenhamer, D. J. (2015). Narrating space and place. In D. J. Bodenhamer, J. CORRIGAN, & T. M. HARRIS (Eds.), Deep Maps and Spatial Narratives (pp. 7–27). Indiana University Press.

Börner, S., Albino, J. C. T., Caraveo, L. M. N., & Tejeda, A. C. C. (2015). Exploring Mexican adolescents' perceptions of environmental health risks: a photographic approach to risk analysis. Ciencia & saude coletiva, 20(5), 1617–1627.

Bourdieu, P. (1976). Entwurf einer Theorie der Praxis auf der ethnologischen Grundlage der kabylischen Gesellschaft (1. Aufl.). Frankfurt am Main: Suhrkamp.

Crabtree, C., & Braun, K. (2015). PhotoVoice: A Community-Based Participatory Approach in Developing Disaster Reduction Strategies. Progress in community health partnerships: research, education, and action, 9(1), 31–40.

Cresswell, T. (2015). Place: An introduction (2. ed.). Chicester: Wiley Blackwell.

Eckardt, F. (2021). Die Stadt als Assemblage: Neue Perspektiven für die Stadtplanung durch die Actor-Network- Theorie? Zeitschrift für Praktische Philosophie, 8(1).

Feldman, R. M. (1990). Settlement-Identity: Psychological Bonds with Home Places in a Mobile Society. Environment and Behavior, 22(2), 183–229.

Foster, K. A., Davis, B., & Foell, A. (2022). Innovations to Photovoice: Using Smartphones & Social Media. Urban Affairs Review, 107808742211002.

Giddens, A. (1995). Konsequenzen der Moderne (2. Aufl.). Frankfurt am Main: Suhrkamp.

Landa, M. de (2006). A new philosophy of society: Assemblage theory and social complexity. London: Continuum.

Lee Cuba, & David M. Hummon (1993). A Place to Call Home: Identification with Dwelling, Community, and Region. The Sociological Quarterly, 34(1), 111–131. Retrieved April 20, 2023, from http://www.jstor.org/stable/4121561 .

Loer, T. (2007). Die Region: Eine Begriffsbestimmung am Fall des Ruhrgebietes. Qualitative Soziologie: Vol. 9. Stuttgart: Lucius & Lucius.

Löw, M. (2018). Vom Raum aus die Stadt denken: Grundlagen einer raumtheoretischen Stadtsoziologie. Materialitäten: Band 24. Bielefeld: transcript.

Mannheim, K. (1980). Strukturen des Denkens. (Kettler, D., Meja, V., & Stehr, N., Eds.). Frankfurt am Main: Suhrkamp.

McFarlane, C. (2011). The City as Assemblage: Dwelling and Urban Space. Environment and Planning D: Society and Space, 29(4), 649–671.

Mendoza, C., & Morén-Alegret, R. (2013). Exploring methods and techniques for the analysis of senses of place and migration. Progress in Human Geography, 37(6), 762–785.

Petersen, N. J., & Østergaard, S. (Eds.). 2003. Organisational Photography as a Research Method: What How and Why. Research Methods: Vol. 63. Seattle.

Ritter, M., & Burckhardt, L. (Eds.) (2006). Warum ist Landschaft schön? Die Spaziergangswissenschaft. Berlin: Schmitz.

Rivlin, L. G. (1982). Group Membership and Place Meanings in an Urban Neighborhood. Journal of Social Issues, 38(3), 75–93.

Schütz, A. (1991 [1932]). Der sinnhafte Aufbau der sozialen Welt: eine Einleitung in die verstehende Soziologie (5th). Suhrkamp-Taschenbuch Wissenschaft: Vol. 92. Frankfurt am Main: Suhrkamp.

Shore, J. H., Tatum, E. L., & Vollmer, W. M. (1986). Psychiatric reactions to disaster: the Mount St. Helens experience. The American journal of psychiatry, 143(5), 590–595.

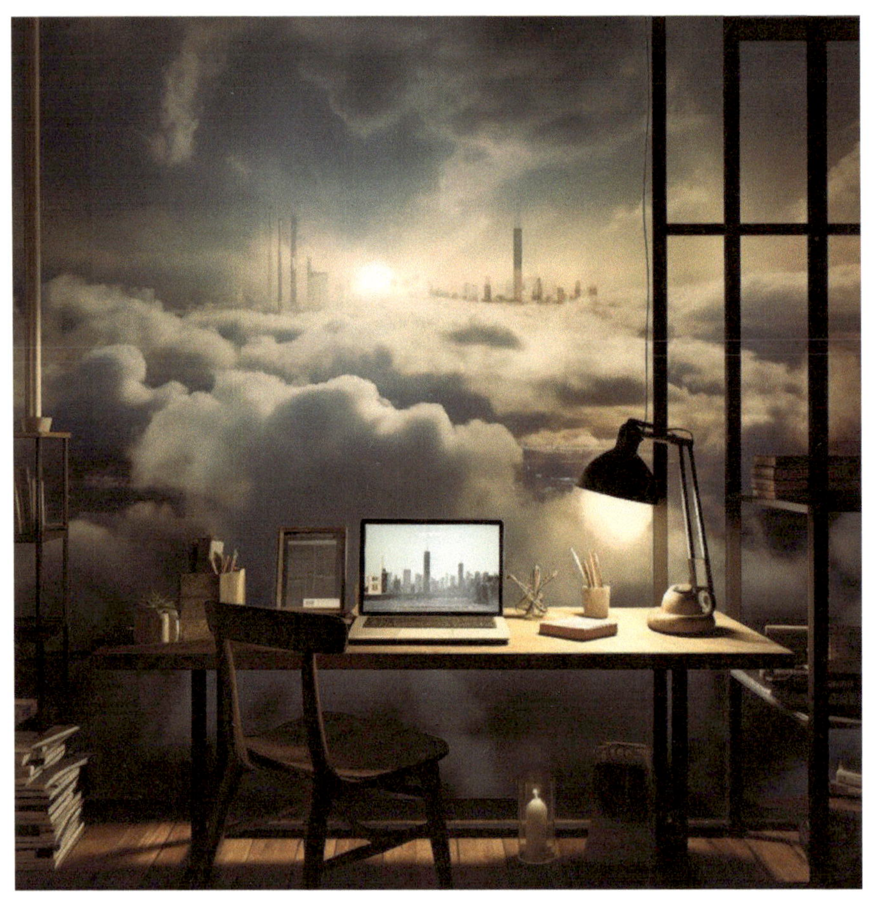

HOW TO DESIGN RELATIONAL WORKING CULTURES IN HYBRID ENVIRONMENTS

Klaus Neundlinger
Simone Rack

While modern industrial work organization was based on the principle of synchronizing bodies and minds in centralized working spaces such as the factory, in the late 20th century production processes became more and more fragmented and distributed over distant regions. As a consequence, synchronicity, as a principle, was transformed from a precondition for efficient work organization to an ideal that eventually would never be attained. Agile management and the ever-increasing necessity and intensity of communication constitute principles according to which work organization is characterized by fragmentation, de-synchronization and the continuous readjusting of strategic aims.

Virtual and hybrid forms of working create environments that can be considered the next generation of spatiotemporal arrangements in which organizational relations unfold. These spaces are co-constituted by embodied, affective experiences as the basis for new types of cooperation that are yet to be defined as fully-fledged teamwork. The paper lists a series of suggestions on how to form, organize and maintain teams in hybrid working environments.

Keywords: Organizational culture, virtual collaboration, embodiment, team cooperation, hybrid office spaces

The emergence of the hierarchical organizational model

Historically, our societies owe their wealth, as well as many aspects of their design, to industrialization. In the context of our article, by 'industrialization', we intend not merely the technological progress in manufacturing, but also a model of designing organizational environments that profoundly changed the way of working together and relating to each other. Especially in the first half of the 20th century, working spaces were designed, and cooperation was organized, according to the principles of centralization and spatial concentration. The underlying idea of efficient organization was to bring workers together in big factory halls and to synchronize their tasks and activities. An iconic, albeit dystopic, representation of the modern industrial society is Fritz Lang's *Metropolis* (1927) that depicts a futurist urban environment in which masses of workers move to and from the factory in lethargic collective and synchronized movements.

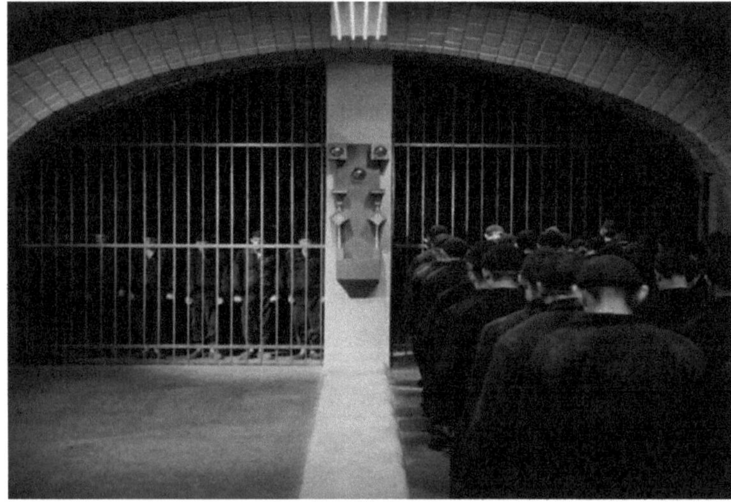

Figure 1. Workers moving to and from the factory in Fritz Lang's Metropolis.

As the title *Metropolis* suggests, this image of synchronizing individual bodies in form of collective choreographies, representative of industrial work organization in big corporations, was transferred from the factory to the way spaces and movements are organized in modern cities. In his experimental documentary *Berlin – Symphony of a Metropolis* (1927), Walther Ruttmann, by drawing on the film avantgarde repertoire of cutting and collage techniques, 'composes' the city of Berlin as a metropole that is organized, in space and time, like a musical symphony. Like in the design of production processes in the factory, also in urban planning efficiency became the prevailing organizing principle for almost any spatiotemporal arrangement, governing individual and collective movements and rhythms.

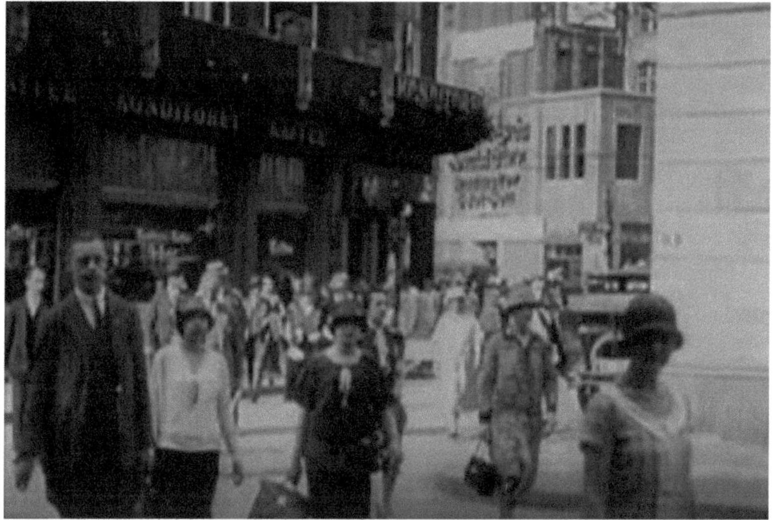

Figure 2. People moving in the street in Walther Ruttmann's *Berlin – Symphonie einer Großstadt.*

For many decades up to the second half of the 20th century, work used to be organized in a centralized and hierarchical way. 'Hierarchical' organization meant to neatly separate the diverse functions and tasks of cooperation: The planning of tasks was separated from the execution, strategy from implementation. In order to cooperate effectively, workers had to be first instructed to perform simple tasks that they would later execute during the shifts. Organizational cultures were characterized by the submission of bodies and minds to pre-established choreographies.

The crisis and overcoming of the hierarchical organization model

The big centralized corporation as the prevalent model of organizing work in modern industrial societies was eventually challenged in the 1960s and 1970s. On the one hand, the authoritarian mindset, characteristic of the modern societies in the first half of the 20th century, was questioned and rejected by younger generations, so that alternative modes of thinking and living evolved. People more and more refused to submit themselves to hierarchical settings, in workplaces as well as in school and in other social and political contexts (Hirschman 1970, Boltanski and Chiappello 1999). Furthermore, the effectiveness of organizing work in a centralized way was challenged by the petrol shock, inflation and the successful return of decentralized ways of organizing that had emerged in Japan and other Asian countries, but also in Europe (Piore and Sabel 1984). The centralized Fordist organization model was replaced by the so called Post-Fordist production mode, characterized by lean management, outsourcing, decentralized organization, and the globalization of supply chains (Revelli 1999 Bologna and Fumagalli 1997). All this led to a networked economy that was further boosted by the rapid evolution of information and communication technologies (ICT).

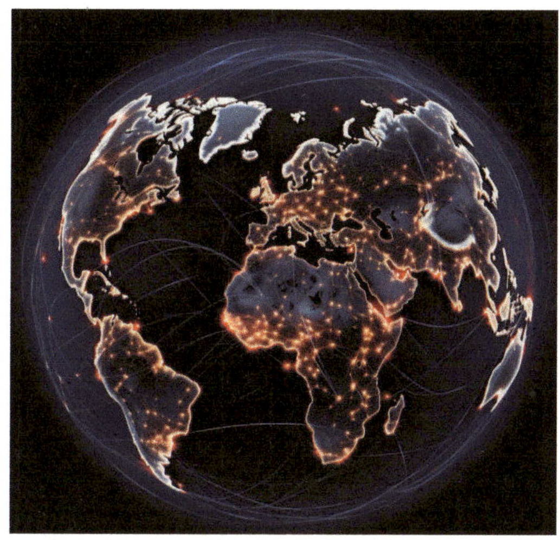

Figure 3. The global networked economy

The more work is organized in a decentralized way, the higher the importance of communication (Marazzi 1997). Still, not only the quantity of communication rises, it is also the quality of communicating within and across organizations that changes. Nowadays, if you ask people working at any level of an organization how much time they spend communicating with others, either directly or via e-mail and other channels, it is likely that they indicate shares beyond 70%, often 80% and more. Other than in the past, communication does not regard only orders, reports or the clarification of tasks. As Philippe Zarifian (1997) points out, work-related communication often consists in asking oneself and others about what's going on, i.e., in communicating with colleagues with the aim to cope with uncertainty and ambiguity. Strategic aims and processes cannot be pre-structured and then implemented as it was the case during the Fordist period. There is no more clear distinction between planning and executing, between working out strategic aims and their implementation. Rather, the planning and execution of projects and the performing of tasks have transformed into negotiation processes that require communicative efforts and blur the boundaries between functions, departments and different stages of the value chain. This is also due to the increasing complexity of projects and cooperation. Hence, a fundamental openness in communicative processes is currently at the core of cooperating. Whether in temporary projects or in teams, it is necessary to coordinate not only at the beginning of a process, but also regularly during the stages of a collaboration. This is one reason why in management agile methods have been established that structure team collaboration by frequent short meetings and short working cycles (sprints).

One can state that the function of synchronization has profoundly changed in work organization. While in the classical industrial period it was a precondition of performing tasks and cooperating (the assembly line), it has now become an ideal objective that will never be attained, but should be approximated (agile management). What is to be synchronized are not, as in the past, movements or mechanical processes in production, but rather ideas, understandings and the ability to react to unforeseen changes and events. While in the industrial period, the synchronization of bodies and minds was the outcome of a preliminary design process and a long-term discipline, the lacking of synchronicity is currently considered as a source of value creation and a continuous challenge for the design of work-related cooperation processes.

Challenging the communication paradigm

As communication has been gaining more and more importance in the Post-Fordist economy, a whole strand in organization studies emerged and has further evolved, labeled under the term 'communicative constitution of organizations' (Brumanns et al. 2014, McPhee and Zaug 2009, Schoeneborn 2011, Schoeneborn and Blaschke 2014, Schoeneborn and Vásquez 2017, Taylor and Van Every 2011). Starting from the late 1990s, many scholars have evidenced that communication is not only a means of coordinating work-related activities, it is in itself a work-related activity, a negotiation process. It represents an essential cooperation form if the task is to achieve results in complex economies.

So far, we have named some factors that explain the importance of communication for working contexts, answering the question: Why do we communicate more, compared to the past, when we work together?

- Decentralized work organization

- Socio-cultural developments (1970s, claiming for autonomy, …)

- Integration of basic needs of sociality and personality development

- into working contexts

- Complexity has increased

- Communication technologies, virtual spaces

Still, there is no evidence indicating a linear progress in the development from hierarchically structured big corporations to decentralized networks of smaller units that are distributed over distant regions (Dioguardi 2007). Rather, we have been witnessing an ambiguous development. Big corporations are still important in many sectors and businesses, despite the pressure towards lean and fast forms of producing goods and delivering services. With the rise of platform economy, the currently powerful tech corporations have coined business models for 'governing' the networks and ecosystems of small and medium enterprises that, in order to gain market-access and visibility, have to offer their services and goods on the virtual marketplaces and digital infrastructures owned by a very small number of giants.

Furthermore, many big corporations, especially in the manufacturing industry, struggle in the attempt to adopt recent organizational models like agile management and flat hierarchies. For many of these organizations, the new management practices have turned out to be appropriate only within certain limits. As a result of this ambiguous development, employees in big organizations have to cope with the tension between hierarchy and the pressure and complexity of markets and networked cooperation in their daily work. They work inside hierarchical structures and at the same time are pushed to operate as if they were members of decentral organizations.

For many of them, the autonomy regarding the way how to fulfill tasks increases, but this does not go along with an increase of resources and decision power with respect to resource allocation, i.e., the opportunity to prioritize tasks, objectives and projects (Eichhorst et al. 2016). As a consequence of this overload, their communicative effort intensifies constantly, so that they are confronted with the alienating aspects of communication: too much, too fast, too mediated.

If employees enter the spiral of communicative overload without being able to prioritize according to strategic and operational decisions, they tend to focus on their immediate environment and base their interaction on emotional needs (stress regulation). In other words, they switch to the survival mode that implies a less open, less networked form of addressing work-related issues. While they are told to overcome silo-mentality, they often do not find the safe environment for thinking and acting outside the box (Edmondson 2018).

Point of no return: Future working spaces will be hybrid

The COVID-19 pandemic has deeply questioned the global production system. But not only the various lockdowns have reduced the confidence in distributed and networked value chains. Also, incidents such as the blocking of the Suez Canal by a huge TEU container ship in March 2021 have been evidencing the vulnerability of the global supply chain. On February 24th of 2022, the vision of an ever more integrated global economy and society was further shaken by the Russian attack against Ukraine. On a societal level, 'globalization' is being challenged in many countries by various groups, ranging from far-left to extreme right. As the basis of public debate has been severely undermined by fake news, conspiracy narratives and other techniques of disinformation and disorientation, it seems more and more difficult to build on a vast consensus regarding literally any societal and political issue. Nevertheless, the major challenges like the threatening climate collapse and the multiple ecological crises can be resolved only at a global level, based on international cooperation. It is worrisome to observe that, while cooperation is required, people, groups and nations are tempted to withdraw from engaging in common problem solution processes.

For the context of organizational culture, we can state that an important paradigm that emerged in the late 20th century (an ever more globalized economy and society) has been going through a profound crisis that began with the crash of the US real estate business and the international financial crisis. While the networked global economy has proved to be vulnerable due to its high degree of interwovenness of businesses, regions, and technologies, the idea of disentangling global interdependencies appears to be equally problematic. Undoubtedly, in terms of sustainability, there are many steps to go in order to attain a fair global production and trade system. Yet, it would be harmful to renounce a crucial aspect of the networked economy and society (Benkler 2006) – that of a relational view on cooperation and society (Elias 1986). It is relationality, not autarky, that has to be strengthened if we want to survive as a global community that embraces mankind as well as all the other forms of life that are essential for the planetary ecosystem (Bridle 2022).

What are the implications of this global situation for the design of collaboration within and across organizations? Apart from the general picture of shrinking trust in a networked economy, the COVID-19 pandemic was a major stress test and turning point with respect to organizational processes and, as a consequence, to organizational culture. According to Stefan Kühl (2018), it is not possible to transform organizational cultures only by reflectively working on behaviors, values and other symbolic structures and patterns. Rather, changes in corporate culture are triggered by the changing of material or formal structures and processes. While corporate culture will not be changed only by carrying out workshops in which management and employees talk about values and behaviors, any change regarding the formal structure, production or service delivery processes will inevitably have its effect on the culture. However, a systemic view on organizational processes and dynamics (Luhmann 2000) implies that is not possible to completely control the way an organizational culture reacts to the changing of material or formal processes and structures (Kühl 2018). Any change process on the formal level will result in a reaction of the informal ways of behaving (the 'corporate culture') that affect the functioning of the newly established formal structures. One important reason why many change initiatives fail or are hampered lies in the fact that culture in terms of the informal patterns is not sufficiently considered and change is not supported by midterm or long-term measures in organizational development.

The transformations brought about by the COVID-19 pandemic can be seen as such material or formal changes that have had an impact on a huge number of organizations over the world that could hardly be anticipated, let alone controlled. While collaboration in teams whose members operate from different places as well as remote work were not new to many teams and employees of international corporations, with the lockdowns these processes of virtualization and hybridization of working cultures have been spreading also in organizations in which before 2020 this had been unthinkable. Equally, after more than two years of experiences with new forms of working and collaborating, executives and middle managers in many organizations are aware of the fact that there will not be a 'back to normal'. Rather, they are forced to design collaborative spaces for the future that are apt to integrate physical and virtual environments. Hence, the issue of communication overload and the problems raised above are further aggravated by the fact that time and especially space acquire a hybrid dimension.

The changing from real to virtual spaces has become normal for many workers. Yet, they have to be able to integrate their cooperation, i.e., their lived experience of working in a team in this new type of cooperative time-space. It is a novel form of spatiotemporal arrangement that creates novel forms of communicating and synchronizing, as well as de-synchronizing, bodies and minds in cooperative efforts.

Working spaces are embodied environments

Our view on organizational culture differs from that of social systems theory (in the Luhmann tradition). We assert that a working culture can be designed and shaped despite, or even because of, its informal nature. While a social system's theory approach is of high value in terms of differentiating essential aspects and dimensions of the social system in question (in our case organizations), it overlooks the subjective dimensions of the distinctions it draws. People in organizations act and live according to and confronting themselves with the formal as well as the informal dimension. They accept, oppose to, or transform contracts, hierarchies, strategic aims, projects, colleagues, and they do so by relating to these entities, be they abstract or concrete in their nature. It is therefore of high relevance to describe, for example, how people experience not only the legal, formal or technical, but also the spatiotemporal dimensions of the organization as part of their lifeworld (Schütz and Luckmann 2003). In other words, we look not only at the consequences of differences on the level of the systems, but on the way how subjects experience these differences in their daily interaction.

Hence, we consider the transformation of an organizational culture not only from the point of view of an unintended reaction and adaptation to formal interventions in organizational processes and structures. Rather, we would like to draw the theoretical and practical attention to the processes that regard the relational dimension of working together. This implies taking into consideration the needs and requirements of single persons within a collaborative setting, but also the atmosphere and the environment that frames daily cooperation. In this sense, also emotional aspects are of major importance, yet not as allegedly interior states of the humans involved, but rather as collective processes that evolve in physical as well as in virtual spaces (Demmerling and Landwehr 2007, Schmitz 2019, Vidolov 2021).

In this sense, any communicative situation is experienced, by the persons involved, not only as a temporary event that affects their supposedly interior psychological state, but also a spatial arrangement. It is a situation in the strict sense of the term, in that it *takes place* by unfolding at a particular time in a particular space. Yet, it is not only the objective physical dimension of time and space that determine when and where a communication takes places. Equally, the persons involved engage in actively *situating* the communication, by ascribing roles to each other, by asking and responding, by signaling social and cultural differences, by making gestures and referring and relating to the context as well as to other situations, and also by negotiating the topics of the discourse. Actually, 'topic' derives from the ancient Greek term 'topos', i.e., 'place'. As the phenomenological tradition has shown, any form of spatiality grounds in an embodied, affective exposure, a *Being-to-the-world* that is not reducible neither to the objective position a concrete body occupies nor to the physiological and neurological processes at the basis of the subjective experience (Merleau-Ponty 1945, Waldenfels 2000, Fuchs 2000). Being exposed to the world in form of our embodiment implicates that we co-construct time and space with the others, so that atmospheres are part of the spatiotemporal arrangement we experience. There is not 'the objective physical space' on the one hand, plus some feelings we might have about a situation on the other hand, without being clear what 'situation' exactly means. There is always a lived space in which situations and therefore atmospheres evolve.

Let us illustrate the interwovenness of spatiotemporal experiences in social situations, particularly in organizations, by referring to a concrete example: In team meetings, often only some of the participants do take actively part in the conversation while others only listen or, even worse, do not pay attention. In this sense, 'presence' is a complex phenomenon that is socially constructed by the negotiation and distribution of shares with respect to the interaction. People who dominate a meeting do not only take time-shares, they also occupy more 'room' than the others in terms of attention and acknowledgement. The others' gazes are directed upon them, and while they dominate the space by their movements and gestures, others tend to withdraw and sometimes congeal. Their withdrawal is real, also without them actually leaving the meeting space, because it is an integral part of the situation that is created by the team as a whole. It is a response to the others' dominant behavior, can have an impact on the dynamics of the social situation and—if similar dynamics occur repeatedly—transforms into a pattern, i.e., a collective behavior that characterizes the team's culture. In this way, an apparently neutral spatial environment becomes stratified and loaded with atmospheric tension (Bulka 2015). While in team collaboration a certain tension is necessary to create a productive atmosphere characterized by curiosity and joint attention, it can be detrimental if it results in the longing for domination by a few participants and the respective submission or withdrawal of the rest. This situation will remain unchanged or even worsen as long as it is not addressed explicitly by one or more members of the team. To actually address such negative dynamics is experienced, by the people involved, as a reopening of the situation, i.e., of the communicative space. It can help to do so by introducing a formal mechanism (like the 'minute round', see below), but this is not sufficient for changing the collective pattern. All team members will have to change attitude, and this means to engage in reshaping their respective behavior: the dominant ones by holding back and the silent ones by learning to assert and express themselves. Again, the term 'communicative space' is not a mere metaphor in that it is lived by the people involved in the situation (Lakoff and Johnson 1980). It is the particular embodied environment that emerges by the history of the team collaboration.

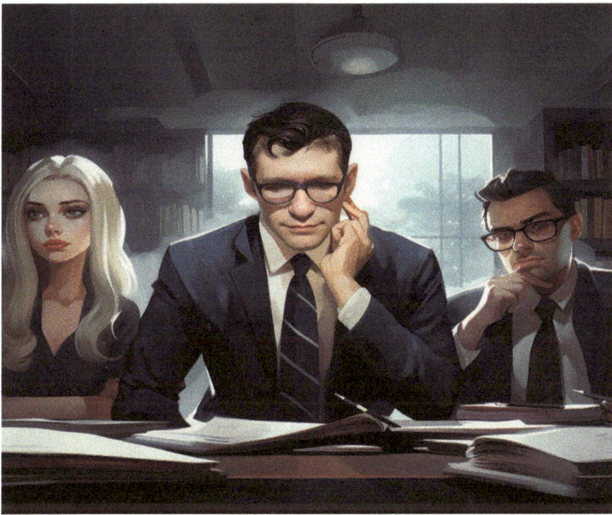

Figure 4. In many team meetings, one person dominates, and the others are either bored or intimidated.

These atmospheres may be palpable to everyone in working contexts characterized by physical presence (offices), but they are also effective in virtual and hybrid settings. We have argued that 'presence' is a complex phenomenon even if one considers the traditional form of being together in a physical space. Words, gestures and feelings can unite us as well as they can divide us, and this happens in physical proximity as well as in the mediated forms of gathering we are now used to, such as video conferences or virtual communities. This is not to say that there is no difference between these forms of being together. Obviously, there are essential differences. Nevertheless, people live computer-mediated encounters as experiences of togetherness in the strict sense of the term, as a shared space in which any form of emotional contagion is possible. Recent phenomenological studies provide evidence, for example, of how affective states or dynamics are perceived and propagate in virtual working environments (Vidolov 2021). Even in computer-generated environments where people interact via avatars, psychological states are precisely grasped by the humans engaging in these interactions, such as multiplayer games or virtual communities (Ekdahl and Osler 2023, Osler and Zahavi 2022, Osler 2022, Osler 2020). There is not 'the virtual world' on the one hand, and 'the real world' on the other, while humans switch from one world to the other as some Science Fiction suggests. Hybridity, from our point of view, means the interwovenness of apparently immediate togetherness—which is in itself a complex arrangement of spatiotemporal experiences related to past, future and contemporaneous situations—and technologically mediated forms of communication.

Suggestions for designing hybrid working environments

In this sense, working environments are designed not only by architects, by the executive management and by the organigram of an organization. They are co-designed by the people (and technologies) involved in the collaboration. Just as the Post-Fordist paradigm is characterized by the fact that planning and execution cannot be neatly separated, the design of collaborative spaces in the current economy is not separable from the interaction that takes place in these spaces. To separate the architectural or organizational design from the ways of experiencing collaboration would amount to an incomplete notion of 'working environment', and this applies also to the environments created by digital technology, i.e., virtual and hybrid communication spaces. The fact that even these spaces are constantly co-created by our interaction—and only by that become environments—points to the fundamentally relational dimension of human existence, in general, and of working together in organizations, in particular. When we work together, we do not only fulfill tasks and apply our personal knowledge and expertise to pre-established programs, processes and plans. By doing so, we contribute to a common endeavor in which we cannot participate if we do not establish and develop relationships. By working together, we inevitably accept relating to each other, this applies to personal as well to anonymous types of collaboration (Durkheim 1893). Undoubtedly, the relational dimension of work and of organizational culture in terms of proximity and personal relations has been challenged and weakened through the lockdowns and forced remote working. Therefore, it is important for team or department leaders, in an age where virtual forms of collaboration are not likely to disappear, to consciously manage the relationships between organizational members in order to create a productive atmosphere in which everyone is heard and seen and gets their share within ever more hybrid spatiotemporal arrangements that appear to be our future offices, shops, and production sites.

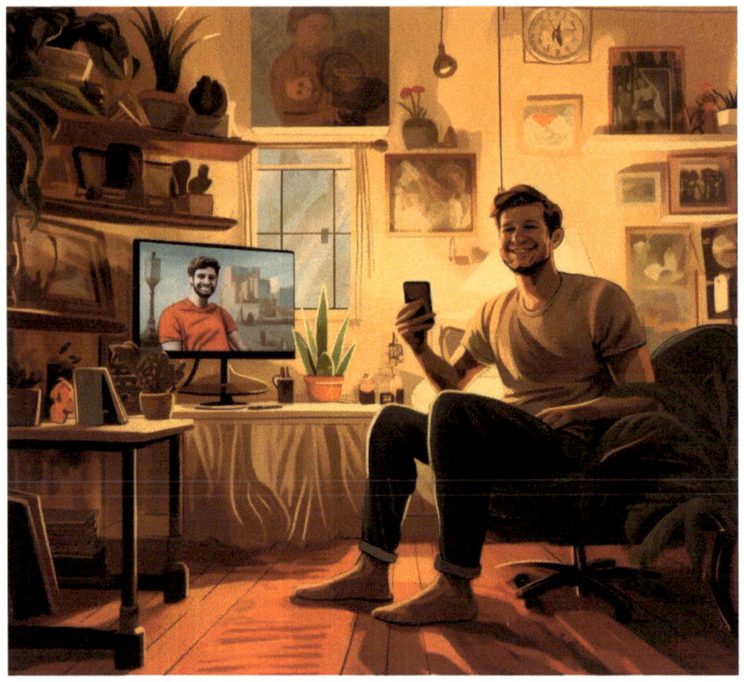

Figure 5. Virtual and hybrid meetings can be joyful encounters.

In the following sections, we list a series of issues that are common in team collaboration, but have to be addressed partly in a diverse or new way in hybrid working contexts. The design options are thought as elements for the construction of a relational working culture in hybrid environments. As we have argued, our concept of design implies that any option must not be taken as pre-established, as separated from the process of interacting and relating to each other. For this reason, by design, on the one hand, we intend measures for structuring meetings, building up and maintaining teams, networking communicative practices, methods and instruments for decision making, conflict solution, feedback and appraisal. On the other hand, these measures should be taken in the full sense of their appearance in organizational life, i.e., as formal structures and interventions that have their informal counterpart: the culture. As outlined above, by 'culture', we intend the material dimension of organizational life, the patterns, collective behaviors, and modes of interacting. By dealing with organizational culture, we do not need to draw on 'unconscious' hypotheses or assumptions in order to explain collective patterns of behavior or shared values and ideas (Schein 1985). In our view, it's all there, in the daily modes of relating to each other. These are dynamic and can be subject to change. Still, it is the material process that counts, not the single measure or intervention on the formal level.

Team formation and structure

In times of shrinking labor force supply, *recruiting and onboarding* are crucial activities for organizations. If the aim is to build up a relational working culture from the beginning, particular attention has to be laid on the integration of new members of the organization. People have to be supported in order to integrate well from the start. They have to be provided with access to critical knowledge, they have to able to find their place in the respective department, project or team. What's more, they have to experience that they contribute to the team's success with their knowledge and experience.

Thus, becoming a member of the organization is a process that has to be curated. 'Onboarding' means to welcome people by framing the experience of the new member as a meaningful passage, e.g., by creating events and spaces of encounter between and building up the relationship with a successful candidate even before they start. Especially for younger people, organizations should conceive of this stage in terms of narratives, drawing on social media or even virtual and augmented reality in the communication with applicants and new members.

The *formation of new teams* is an equally challenging task for team leaders. They have to facilitate the building up of relationships between the members of the team as well as the creation of a trustful and supportive relationship between themselves and every single member. If the team works together in a hybrid form, it is essential that the virtual space be used not only for work-related topics, but also for personal exchange. It is this affective and social dimension that people missed particularly during the COVID-19 lockdowns. In many teams, rituals like the "virtual coffee" were introduced to compensate the social and affective exchange that almost naturally evolves if people work together in office spaces. On a more formal basis, team leaders should introduce regular common reflection rounds on how the cooperation is experienced by the team members.

A team does not operate in an isolated manner, but constitutes a *network* that is in itself embedded in larger organizational networks. In terms of relationality, the aim should be to take advantage of the openness and embeddedness of the team's relationships and, at the same time, to maintain a certain robustness (Burt 2005). As to the internal dynamics, a team works better if its network structure is dense and decentralized. If single team members only relate to the central figure of the team leader, this could result in an overload and a lacking robustness of the network. In this sense, team leaders (and also the members) should suggest or create occasions of exchange without the leader being present. This helps to create the robustness of the team's network even if the exchange is not focused on work-related issues. Furthermore, the team leader should invite members to coordinate in a decentral way, signaling by that their trust in the members' competences.

Work organization

Human resources departments and especially team leaders have to adjust to *novel requirements* expressed by new generations of employees, as well as by employees that have been adapting to hybrid working arrangements during the pandemic. Other than in the past, people attribute at least equal, if not higher, importance to private life, so the management has to come to terms with the process of *individualization* with respect to work organization (work-life balance). In this sense, the spreading of remote work has contributed to a further entanglement of professional and private life. While at the beginning of the pandemic, people were forced to find arrangements between their private situation and the rhythm of working life, in the meantime many people (obviously not in all professions and sectors) claim flexibility with respect to job and private life requirements. How should the management and especially team leaders react? Acknowledging the shift in how working and private life intermingle in the spatiotemporal experience of the employees amounts to adopting a relational view on the own culture of working together. It is therefore recommendable that departments and teams initiate reflection processes and collectively decide on the organization of the working structure (remote/presence, flexibility of working hours and shifts). In order to establish a productive atmosphere, it is important to dialogue on the needs and necessities of every single person involved. This potentially raises the mutual understanding between the team members for the colleagues' situation. There are a number of reliable instruments for this type of collective decision making, such as the sociocratic method of "consent" (Rau und Koch-Gonzalez 2018) or the "systemic consensing" (Schrotta 2011).

Another aspect of work organization in hybrid environments is the fact that people do have *diverging needs with respect to physical presence* while engaging in teamwork. Some people opt for a quiet working place where they can concentrate on their tasks, which may be easier to achieve at home, but not necessarily, e.g., if employees have little children or other care exigencies. Others need the company and communicative situation of an open, common office space and have suffered considerably from the isolation during the lockdowns. The task for a team leader or for the team as a whole is then to create physical and hybrid spaces that allow different types of working and communicating. This includes also rooms or zones where people can work in silence without being interrupted or disturbed by people rushing in or by conversations in open office spaces.

Atmosphere

In order to create an *atmosphere characterized by active participation,* a certain equilibrium with respect to the distribution of time and attention is necessary. Such an atmosphere contributes to the maintaining of a group identity, the readiness to contribute and the quality of the teamwork's outcomes. A simple, but effective instrument to establish a participatory team culture is the minute-round. During a meeting, the team leader, or any other team member, can establish a question or raise a topic and invite the other members, one by one, to express their view in a 60 to 90 seconds' statement.

No interruptions and comments are admitted. By repeatedly applying this method, team members exercise being concise, assertive and, conversely, learn to listen attentively to the others. In other words, they collectively train two of the most important social skills, i.e., the ability to assert oneself and actively contribute in collective processes and the ability to take others' perspectives and display empathic behaviors toward others.

However, working together can also lead to *conflicts*, especially when diverging approaches and views or diverse personalities encounter. It is normal that conflicts emerge in teamwork, still they do not disappear if they are not addressed and linger, negatively affecting by that the group functioning and the wellbeing of the members. Methods for addressing conflicts can be taken from communication psychology or approaches like nonviolent communication (Rosenberg 2015, Mastrogiacomo and Osterwalder 2021).

For team leaders as well as for colleagues it is important to consider the personal situation of the other team members. *Keeping in touch* on a personal level in order to promote psychological wellbeing and safety creates the conditions for trustful cooperation. It has been shown that psychological safety is one of the major presuppositions for sustainable cooperation (Edmondson 2018). Therefore, it is recommendable for the team leader to deliberately create occasions (also in virtual meetings) for asking team members about their personal situation, especially when they are working remotely. In most of the cases, such a dialogue between the team leader and a single member, or between two team members, should take place separately.

Conclusion

Addressing the question of how to design relational working cultures in hybrid environments, we intended to shift the focus from the objective givenness of organizational arrangements and technological developments to the way how they are lived and experienced by the people working under these conditions. As we argued above, this is not to be mistaken as an account of alleged "psychological effects" of spatiotemporal designs and their extension by communication technologies. By holding meetings in hybrid environments, people experience the particular spatiality of these novel forms of working together *as such*. If we aim to assess the importance and the value of new cooperation forms in hybrid environments, we have to consider the way how humans co-shape these environments by living them.

In a more radical sense, we have been stating that it is not possible to speak of 'hybrid environments' if we are not able to phenomenologically describe the experiences that constitute these environments as communicative spatiotemporal arrangements. There is no 'hybrid environment' if the embodied, affective dimension is left out in the analysis, and a purely linguistic or neuropsychological account of the respective experiences would be reductive and therefore incomplete.

Embodiment, in the phenomenological sense of the term (Husserl 1952, Merleau-Ponty 1945, Waldenfels 2000), is also the pre-condition of relationality. In this sense, relational working cultures are the result of designing embodied encounters and affective exchange, no matter if they take place in physical, in computer-mediated or in hybrid environments. In our recommendations, we therefore foregrounded the human dimension of cooperation. We are well aware that technology and human efforts are, and will be more and more, interwoven in working processes. Nevertheless, organization as a process cannot renounce the relational dimension, even in its most mediated and extended modes. Otherwise, it would run out of its purpose, i.e., to structure collective human endeavors according to a meaningful investment in shared and divided space and time.

About the Authors

KLAUS NEUNDLINGER holds a PhD in Philosophy. His research focus is on work and organization from a phenomenological perspective. He directs the research of the institute for cultural excellence and has coordinated the transdisciplinary project Virtual Skills Lab (2019-2021), in which a prototypical VR scene for training social skills was developed and evaluated.

LinkedIn: @Klaus Neundlinger

SIMONE RACK has a Master's degree in Sociology. She engages in transdisciplinary research projects with a focus on corporate culture and social skills. She is the managing director of the institute for cultural excellence and accompanies and supports people operating at any level in organizations with the aim to improve their processes and increase their level of reflexivity regarding social dynamics and social interaction in collaboration within and across teams, departments and organizations

LinkedIn: @Simone Rack

References

Benkler, Y. (2006). The Wealth of Networks. Yale University Press.

Bologna, S., Fumagalli, A. (eds.) (1997). Il lavoro autonomo di seconda generazione. Feltrinelli.

Boltanski, L., Chiappello, È. (1999). Le nouvel ésprit du capitalisme. Gallimard.

Bridle, J. (2022). Ways of Being. Animals, Plants, Machines. The Search for a Planetary Intelligence. Penguin Books.

Brummans, B., Cooren, F., Robichaud, D., and Taylor, J. (2014). Approaches in Research on the Communicative Constitution of Organizations, in Putnam, L.L., Mumby, D. K. (eds.) Sage Handbook of Organizational Communication. 3rd ed. London: Sage Publications.McPhee and Zaug 2009.

Bulka, T. (2015). Stimmung, Emotion, Atmosphäre. Phänomenologische Untersuchungen zur Struktur der menschlichen Affektivität. Mentis.

Burt, R. (2005) Brokerage and Closure. Oxfod University Press.

Demmerling, C., Landwehr, H. (2007). Philosophie der Gefühle. Metzler.

Dioguardi, G. (2007). Le imprese rete. Bollati Boringhieri.

Durkheim, E. (1893). The Division of Labour in Society. Free Press 1997.

Edmondson, A. (2018). The Fearless Organization. Creating Psychological Safety in the Workplace for Learning, Innovation, and Growth. Wiley.

Eichhorst, W. Tobsch, V., Wehner, C. (2016). Neue Qualität der Arbeit? Zur Entwicklung von Arbeitskulturen und Fehlzeiten. In Badura, B. et al. (Eds). Unternehmenskultur und Gesundheit. Fehlzeitenreport 2016. Springer (pp. 9-20).

Ekdahl, D., Osler, L. (2023). Expressive Avatars: Vitality in Virtual Worlds. Philosophy & Technology, 36, 24. https://doi.org/10.1007/s13347-023-00628-5

Elias, N. (1986). Was ist Soziologie? Grundfragen der Soziologie. Beltz.

Fuchs, T. (2000). Leib, Raum, Person. Klett-Cotta

Hirschman, A. O. (1970). Exit, Voice, and Loyalty. Harvard University Press.

Husserl, E. (1952) Ideen zu einer reinen Phänomenologie und phänomenologischen Philosophie. Zweites Buch. Phänomenologische Untersuchungen zur Konstitution. Nijhoff.

Lakoff, G., Johnson, M. (1980. Metaphors We Live By. The University of Chicago Press.

Luhmann, N. (2000). Organisation und Entscheidung. Westdeutscher Verlag.

Marazzi (1997). Il lavoro autonomo nella cooperazione comunicativa. In S. Bologna, A. Fumagalli (eds.) Il lavoro autonomo di seconda generazione (pp. 43-80).

Mastrogiacomo, S., Osterwalder, S. (2021). High-Impact Tools for Teams. Wiley.

Merleau-Ponty, M. (1945). Phénoménologie de la perception. Gallimard.

Osler, L., Zahavi, D. (2022). Sociality and embodiment: online communication during and after Covid-19. Foundations of Science. https://doi.org/10.1007/s10699-022-09861-1

Osler, L (2020). Feeling togetherness online: a phenomenological sketch of online communal experiences. Phenomenology and the Cognitive Sciences, 19, 3, pp. 569-588.

Piore, F. Sabel, C. (1984). The second industrial divide. Basic Books.

Rau, T. J., Koch-Gonzalez, J. (2018) Many Voices One Song. Shared Power with Sociocracy. Sociocracy For All.

Revelli, M. (1999). la sinistra sociale. Bollati Boringhieri.

Rosenberg, M. (2015). Nonviolent Communication. A language of Life. PuddleDancer Press.

Schein, E. (2016). Organizational Culture and Leadership. Wiley.

Schmitz, H. (2019). Der Gefühlsraum. System der Philosophie III, 2. Alber.

Schoeneborn, D. (2011) Organization as Communication: A Luhmannian Perspective, in Management Communication Quarterly, 25(4), 663-689.

Schoeneborn, D. and Blaschke, S. (2014): "The Three Schools of CCO Thinking: Interactive Dialogue and Systematic Comparison," in Management Communication Quarterly, 28 (2), 285-316

Schoeneborn, D. and Vásquez,C. (2018) Communicative Constitution of Organizations, in Scott, C. R., Lewis, L. K. (eds.) International Encyclopedia of Organizational Communication, Hoboken, NJ, Wiley. https://doi.org/10.1002/9781119010722.iesc0024Taylor and Van Every 2011

Schrotta, S. (Ed.) (2011). Wie wir klüger entscheiden. Styria.

Schütz., A. Luckmann, P. (2003) Strukturen der Lebenswelt. UVK.

Vidolov, S. (2022). Uncovering the affective affordances of videoconference technologies. Information Technology & People. 35, 6, pp. 1783-1802. DOI 10.1108/ITP-04-2021-0329.

Waldenfels, B. (2000). Das leibliche Selbst. Suhrkamp.

Zarifian p. (1997). Travail, langage et civilté. https://www.multitudes.net/Travail-langage-et-civilite/

Films

Metropolis (1927). Director: Fritz Lang. Screenplay: Firtz Lang, Thea von Harbou. Producer: Erich Pommer. Germany.

Berlin – Die Sinfonie einer Großstadt. (1927). Director: Walther Ruttmann. Screenplay: Karl Freund, Carl Meyer, Walther Ruttmann. Germany

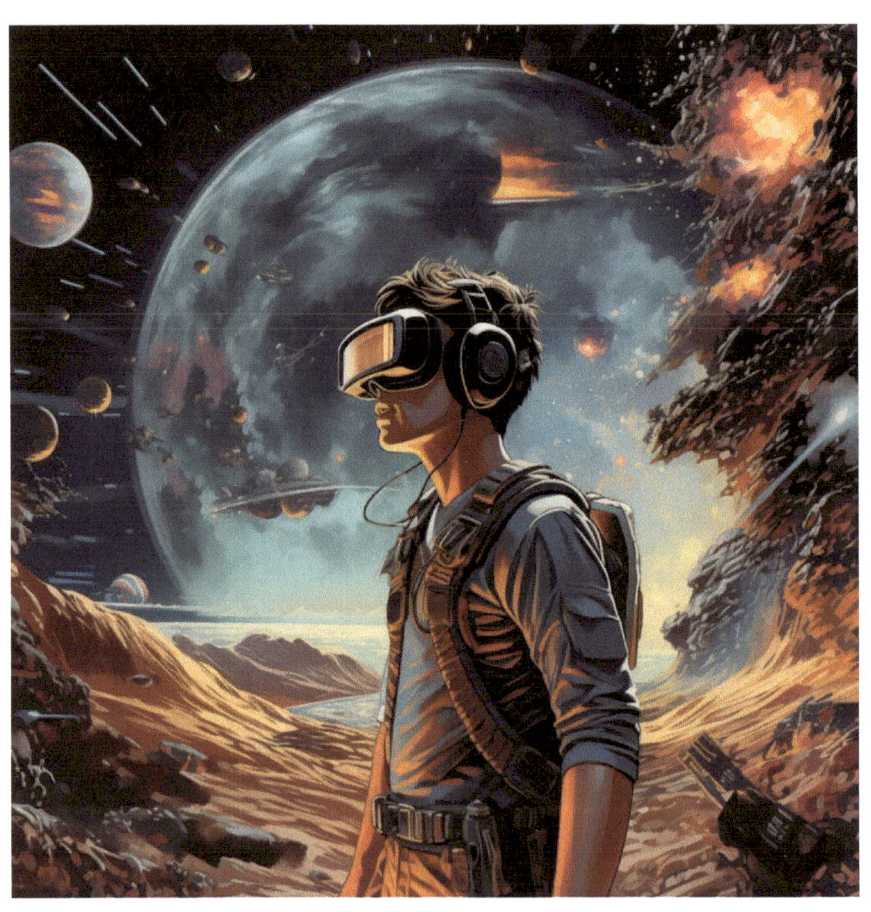

TO BOLDLY GO WHERE NO (WO)MAN HAS GONE BEFORE

ENSURING SURVIVAL THROUGH FUTURE-ORIENTED LEARNING WITH EXTENDED REALITY AND GAME-BASED LEARNING

Stephanie Wössner

The past three and a half years have clearly shown that there is something wrong with education systems around the world. Teachers and schools have had a particularly hard time adjusting to the pandemic situation and often resorted to traditional ways of schooling using web conferencing systems due to the fact that they weren't prepared for such a drastic change and a lack of ability to think (and act) outside the box. There are many lessons that could have been learned from these experiences, but realistically speaking, this did not happen.

However, if we look at the world we live in and analyze the clash between what is considered education and reality. i.e., the many challenges we have had to face and which we have partly failed to overcome so far, it becomes very clear that there is a dire need for drastic change. This is especially true because we're facing an exponential future and because we need to enable learners (of all ages) to shape the future, our future. Generations Z and Alpha need to develop various competencies to have agency in this exponential future and it is the job of teachers to become their learning partners and to provide them with learning opportunities to develop these competencies.

Extended reality, Artificial Intelligence, virtual worlds and particularly games offer a great potential in this effort to make learning future-oriented and to ensure that humankind will survive and have a future on this planet. However, future-oriented learning requires us to reconsider everything we take for granted. It is time to boldly go where no (wo)man has gone before so we can assist learners in learning the things they will need for their future as responsible (German, Austrian, European, world) citizens in the age of digital transformation.

After a brief look at the current state of education, this paper will discuss how future-oriented learning approaches using emergent technologies can help prepare learners for their life's mission, i.e. building the future as members of an international community. This will be illustrated by three concrete examples taken from game-based learning: designing a sustainable future with *Minetest*, making sure democracy will prevail by approaching *This War of Mine* from different angles, and experiencing gender and diversity with the *Sims 4.*

Keywords: shaping the future, future-oriented learning, game-based learning, democracy, extended reality, artificial intelligence, metaverse

---

Education Caught Between The Past, The Present And An Exponential Future

Our current education system is based on the social structure of the Industrial Age and focuses primarily on the acquisition of knowledge that can be tested in standardized exams. This emphasis on academic excellence may even be considered a relic of a much more distant past: the Enlightenment (Robinson & RSA, 2010). Although the curricula of all sixteen German federal states highlight the importance of competency-based learning, assessment policies and procedures still focus mostly on the transfer of knowledge, and so do, therefore, teachers. In practice, this means that surface learning (content, information) has a much more prominent role than deep learning (transfer of knowledge, application), even though learning experts like John

Hattie argue that deep learning should outweigh surface learning by far (UQx LEARNx Team Of Contributors, 2019). This is especially true in the context of a global community that is undergoing rapid changes in the age of digital transformation and that is not only struggling with a lot of contemporary problems but also facing an exponential future: We have been living with a pandemic for several years, we have frequent encounters with the effects of climate change, and with the war in Ukraine and the war between Israel and Hamas there are currently two very recent wars that affect us. The war in Ukraine is about much more than one country's freedom, it's a war about the democratic values that unite us, and the war between Israel and Hamas "has a potential to worsen tensions between communities and to feed extremism" according to EU Council President Charles Michel (Cook & Casert, 2023).

It will be up to late Generation Z and Generation Alpha[1] to deal with all these challenges we haven't managed to overcome yet – and with all the challenges the future has in store for us, but that we can't even imagine yet. This is why we need to prepare the young generation for the future, so they will have agency and be able to shape the future in the best possible way, and so that, ultimately, democracy and tolerance will prevail. For all these recent events have shown us repeatedly that not being prepared for the future does not only lead to surprise, but often to paralysis. However, neither teaching to the test nor focusing on existing knowledge will prepare them for these challenges – otherwise we would already have overcome them. Therefore, rather than sticking to teaching, we need to turn towards future-oriented learning to deal with a complex (VUCA), sometimes even chaotic (BANI) world (Theil, 2021) and learners must be allowed to take responsibility for their learning so they can not only understand the world but learn how to shape the future in a responsible and sustainable way.

---

[1] According to the Pew Research Center, members of Gen(eration) Z were born between 1997 and 2012, which implies that Gen(eration) Alpha refers to the age cohort born since 2012 (Dimock, 2022).

VUCA, BANI, What?!

The concept of the VUCA world was developed by the US Army War College in the late 1980s, more than 30 years ago, as an attempt to describe the world after the collapse of the USSR, i.e., the end of the Cold War, and the resulting challenges. The acronym stands for volatile, uncertain, complex, and ambiguous.

However, simply describing the world's challenges is no longer enough. More than three decades later, digitalization has changed the world dramatically and has led to a fundamental cultural change, i.e., the digital transformation, that is at least as drastic as the one triggered by industrialization. The complexity of the world is still a fact, but it is no longer enough to merely describe the challenges and do experiments to overcome them. Unlike industrialization, which people had to cope with primarily on a local level, digitalization has given people a means to communicate their thoughts and opinions on a global level, e.g., via social media. As a result, humanity has moved closer together. Thus, the impact of these challenges that are due to the digital transformation can now be heard and felt everywhere, and even though we continue to live in a complex VUCA world, its impact on the individual is omnipresent and has made many people feel like they live in chaos. This second, more personal dimension of the VUCA world has added chaos to the equation and is referred to as the BANI world: it is brittle, people are anxious, it is non-linear, i.e., cause and effect are no longer tangible, and for many people the world has become incomprehensible. It should be noted that different cultures deal differently with these effects of cultural change, as can be seen in a comparison between Europe and Asia (Ito, 2018). There are different approaches to overcoming the paralysis that has a firm grip on many people, but they can all be summarized under the term future skills.

While in the VUCA world it was still enough to solve problems experimentally in pilot studies to find the best solution and then implement it, in a BANI world and in the face of an exponential future it is necessary to act as quickly as possible. However, this ability to act must be learned by making it an everyday practice and by realizing that there are no mistakes, just learning opportunities. To achieve this, learners must be allowed to take responsibility for their learning and develop many competencies that require an open mindset. RAAT is an acronym summarizing some of the most important future skills that can lead the way to dealing with the effects of complexity on the individual. RAAT stands for resilience, attention (i.e., mindfulness), adaptation (i.e., flexibility), and transparency. These are the skills Gen Z and Gen Alpha need to acquire to be well prepared for the future.

Table 1. VUCA, BANI, and RAAT

Challenge	Impact on the individual	Solution
V = volatile	B = brittle	R = resilience
U = uncertain	A = anxious	A = attention
C = complex	N = non-linear	A = adaptation
A = ambiguous	I = incomprehensible	T = transparency
> changes since the Cold War	> symptoms in a global world	> future skills

Future-Oriented Learning

In recent years, the term "contemporary education" has often been used with reference to the 4Cs (Communication, Collaboration, Creativity, Critical Thinking) in order to describe the ideal education in the 21st century (The Partnership for 21st Century Learning, 2015). However, particularly the Covid-19 pandemic has shown that the ideal the notion of contemporary education is based on, i.e., to realign learning with the changed social reality, has reached a dead end. This can be seen, among other things, when having a closer look at the DigitalPakt Schule[2], a German initiative that aims at providing schools with money for digitalization, but which turned out to be a missed opportunity because it focuses too much on equipment and too little on a changed learning culture (Wössner, 2022a). Even before that, however, there were indicators that the notion of contemporary education had taken a wrong turn: for years, we have been flooded with training sessions for contemporary education like "The iPad in the English Classroom", which seem to imply that contemporary education is much more about technology than

---

[2] https://www.digitalpaktschule.de/

about society. Moreover, in the past five years or so, the definition of what is considered contemporary learning has been greatly reduced to certain aspects, primarily the use of digital devices and the 4Cs in a learning setting that is very much determined and assessed by a teacher, and, therefore, no longer synonymous with what it might have been according to the original ideal. This is why we should reevaluate the use of the term "contemporary education" and, following a 2012 New Zealand study (Bolstad et al., 2012), replace it with the notion of future-oriented learning.

According to the researchers from New Zealand, the term "21st century learning"[3], coined at the end of the 20th century, was already problematic in 2012, as it tended to describe current practices but was not (or rather no longer) visionary and oriented towards the future. In 2012, they nevertheless used the term "future-oriented learning" or "future learning" as a synonym for "contemporary education", as the term was already established in academia at that time. However, they emphasized that, for them, the term represented an evolving collection of new ideas, beliefs, knowledge, theories, and practices. Specifically, they saw "future-oriented learning" as combining a new understanding of knowledge with new insights about learning with the ultimate goal to deconstruct the existing system. They identified the following basic principles of this new system: personalized learning, a new understanding of equity, diversity and inclusivity, a focus on competencies, a new understanding of the roles of learners and teachers, lifelong learning, establishing a collaboration between schools and the community. New technologies and collaborative practices were mentioned as secondary areas of interest. The ultimate goal was to integrate the lessons learned into the system and develop it so that New Zealand's learners would be able to participate in and shape their personal, as well as national and global futures.

Future-oriented learning still takes into account the 4Cs of learning but adds to them other equally important elements, such as character and citizenship (cf. 6Cs of Deep Learning (Fullan & Scott, 2014)), as well as future skills (Fidler & Williams, 2016). At the same time, in a world where peace can no longer be taken for

---

[3] This term is used interchangeably with "contemporary education" in the educational community.

granted and where the global community has to deal with the challenges of the present and the future together, foreign languages are becoming more and more important. Despite the fact that quite a number of amazing AI applications have been released since 2022, e.g., ChatGPT (OpenAI, 2022), and that this may lead people to believe that we no longer need to learn foreign languages to communicate, it will still take a long time until any machine learning algorithm may understand and be able to translate cultural nuances and mentalities. However, learning a foreign language is not an end in itself, it needs to happen in an authentic environment where your need to speak the language for a specific purpose that goes beyond being evaluated for it.

Although not everyone will share these thoughts on this new old notion of future-oriented learning because we have been talking about contemporary education for a while now, it actually doesn't go far enough: if we want to change the system, we need to use many other new words, such as learning group (instead of class), learning environment (instead of classroom), learner (instead of student), and learning facilitator or partner (instead of teacher). For traditional terminology comes with a lot of preconceived notions and historical baggage and will make change difficult or even impossible (Wössner, 2022b).

Despite all this, future-oriented learning is not an end in itself, either. Shaping the future also requires everyone to think about sustainable development and acquire many more skills, like future and problem-solving skills. For our ultimate goal as citizens of the world is to have agency in the future, so current and future problems can be solved by the global community. This is in accordance with the OECD Learning 2030 framework, which highlights the importance of knowledge, skills, attitudes, and values that are used in a learning context to develop competencies with the ultimate goal to have agency in the future. (OECD, 2018).

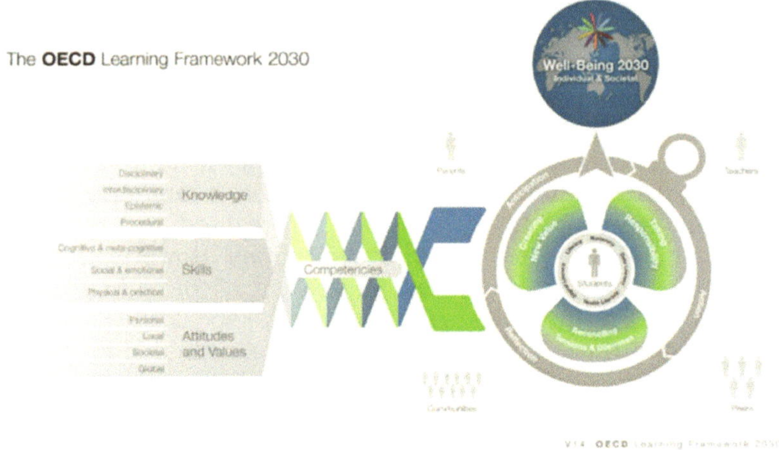

Figure 1. The OECD Learning Framework 2030
(Source: OECD, 2018, p. 4)

This experiential learning, communication and collaboration space can take many forms and may include, among others, design and futures thinking practices, questions of sustainable development, extended reality, virtual worlds, gaming, and game-based learning. They can encourage a paradigm shift in which the former teacher becomes both a facilitator by designing learning opportunities and a learner in their own right. Designing learning opportunities has always been part of being an educator, so while the tools may change, both mindset and part of the required skills remain intact (Rober. 2018). Moreover, playing has always been part of human nature (Huizinga, 1987), so it should be easy for any educator to reclaim the heritage they may have lost sight of during their teacher training.

Game-Based Learning

In her book Reality is Broken, Jane McGonigal identified four important traits that define games (McGonigal, 2011, pp. 26):

- goals, which "provide players with a sense of purpose"

- rules, which "unleash creativity and foster strategic thinking"

- a feedback system, which "serves as a promise to the players that the goal is definitely achievable, and [...] provides motivation to keep playing"

- voluntary participation

In other words, "a game is the voluntary attempt to overcome unnecessary obstacles" (Suits & Hurka, 2005, p. 159). More recent games often have a contextualizing story but being embedded in a narrative is not a prerequisite for a game.

Games have always been an integral part of human nature (Huizinga, 1987), which is why they should definitely be part of learning. Following the Hook Model (Eyal, 2014), when a player is incentivized to start playing a game (for example through a compelling narrative), they will want to overcome obstacles presented to them. If they play a good game, all four defining traits of games will be present, they will learn from their mistakes and receive a meaningful reward which will encourage them to go on playing. This reward is linked to the notions of self-determination and self-efficacy (Deci & Ryan, 2008). As they keep playing, they will choose more challenging tasks and will soon enter in a state of flow (Csikszentmihalyi & Szöllösi, 2010), which goes hand in hand with a profound happiness. This feeling is due to dopamine, a neurotransmitter that is released when the brain expects a reward (van der Linden et al., 2021), and self-efficacy, optimism, hope, and resilience (Luthans et al., 2007).

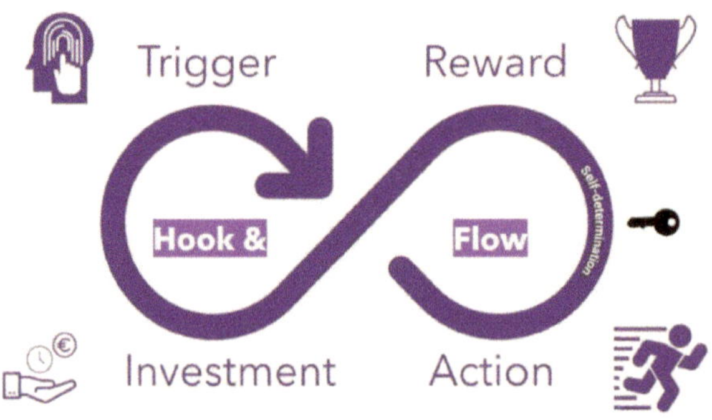

Figure 2. The Hook Model (Source: Fabian Karg | CC BY-SA-NC 4.0 | Icons: Noun Project)

While, at first glance, good games and the traditional education system seem to share a great deal of those qualities of good games which lead to intrinsic motivation, a closer look reveals that in theory, this may well be the case, but in practice, it isn't. In school we encourage young people to face a challenge, we give them a grade as a reward and – in a perfect world – this reward would motivate them to go on learning. However, we do not live in this perfect world: In a game, the rules make sense to the player – often because there is an underlying narrative that explains the system - challenges are set by the player and the reward they receive is of personal value. Most importantly, the player is allowed freedom to choose the way to overcome the challenge they chose to tackle and to fail as many times as they need to learn how to succeed. In school, on the other hand, the challenges are set by a teacher, the rules are set by the system and may not make sense because they lack a contextualizing narrative, and feedback is of social nature. Unlike in a good game, there is no self-determination involved and learners are continuously punished for their mistakes. This basically sets up young people for failure because their attention is redirected to their own failings instead of celebrating their talents. This also explains why parents often have to practically force their children to study and fight to get them away from the latest computer game.

Games are not only an integral part of the lives of late Gen Z and Gen Alpha (Medienpädagogischer Forschungsverbund Südwest, 2022, pp. 49) but the competencies developed by gamers in what is mostly considered a leisure time activity can be quite valuable in many respects (Bediou et al., 2018; Mitterer & Steiner, 2020). They can be of cognitive, social, personal, and sensomotoric nature, and can also contribute to digital literacy (Donau-Universität Krems, 2018). These skills have not only been proven to have "real"[4] life consequences (McGonigal, 2011; Katski, 2017) but they are increasingly desirable for employers (Molloy, 2019). Moreover, games have even helped solve scientific puzzles more than a decade ago (Uehlecke, 2010) and have advanced the development of artificial intelligence tremendously (Luzgin, 2019). Even the fact that games can change the world is nothing new if we take into account organizations like Games for Change.

Game-based learning basically refers to using - very often popular - games for learning. It has nothing to do with gamification[5] or educational games[6]. It also doesn't necessarily refer to the use of digital games, as can be seen with the Quest2Learn school in New York (Tekinbas et al., 2010). However, in this paper, the term "game-based learning" is used to refer to digital game-based learning.

Game-based learning focuses on the development of competencies. Factual knowledge will very likely be acquired as well during gameplay, but it isn't the goal of the game. Unlike gamification and educational games, which often reward players with points that they can accumulate to compare themselves to others or see some kind of progress, game-based learning is rooted in the belief that overcoming a challenge deliberately taken on by the player will make them happy and motivate them to go on playing, thus becoming increasingly competent. Moreover, games are designed in a way to allow the player to learn from their mistakes instead of punishing them like the current education system with its assessment culture does.

---

[4] quotation marks are deliberately used because experiences in a virtual world are also real (Chalmers, 2022)

[5] "the use of video game elements in non-gaming systems to improve user experience and user engagement" (Deterding et al., 2011)

[6] Games designed for learning, often also called "serious games" (for an in-depth analysis of elements of serious games cf. Bedwell et al., 2012)

Virtual Worlds And Learning

Virtual worlds, i.e., computer-simulated environments (Bartle, 2003), have been around for a long time. First references predate computers and go back to Roman Times (Biocca & Levy, 1995, pp. 6-8). In the 20th century, the cinematographer Morton Heilig played around with the idea of a *Sensorama*, a theatrical experience involving all senses (Norman, n.d.). Video games like *Maze War* (Lebling, 1986; Damer, 2004) and MUDs and MUSHes from the 1970s can be considered virtual worlds as well (Mitchell, 1995), even though the 1986 Commodore 64 game *Habitat* (Lucasfilm Games, 1986) is credited to be the first online virtual world (Rossney, 1996). Most people probably think of *Second Life* (Linden Lab, 2003) as the first mainstream virtual world, or of games like *Fortnite* (Epic Games, 2017) or *Animal Crossing* (Nintendo, 2015). So virtual worlds have very often been synonymous with video games.

According to James Paul Gee, learning design and video game design are very similar. He came up with a list of principles that show how learning can be encouraged by games (cf. Table 2). It is very interesting to see how many of these principles match the general idea behind the OECD Learning 2030 framework, too (OECD, 2018).

Table 2. Learning principles by James Paul Gee (Gee, 2007 pp. 23)

Empowering learners	Learning
• co-design	• learners need to feel like active agents
• customize	• learners learn differently
• identity	• learners need to be committed
• manipulation & distributed knowledge	• learners feel like they have agency; immersion & interaction > feeling of presence
Problem-solving	**Learning**
• well-ordered problems	• learners need scaffolding and apply what they have learned
• pleasantly frustrating	• learners need challenges they want and are able to overcome; they must neither be bored nor overwhelmed

•	cycles of expertise	•	learners need time to practice in order to be able to integrate previously acquired knowledge/skills with new knowledge/skills
•	information "on demand" and "just in time"	•	learners need access to certain information when they can use it or feel like they need it to solve a problem
•	fish tanks	•	learners need to start with simplified system that become more and more complex
•	sandboxes	•	learners need to be allowed to fail and feel safe taking risks
•	skills as strategies	•	learners need to apply their skills and knowledge to accomplish a certain goal
Understanding		**Learning**	
•	system thinking	•	learners need to see the big picture and understand how what they do is meaningful
•	meaning as action image	•	learners need experiences they can link to their learning

All these learning principles can be found in different forms and with variations in priority in the following three examples.

Designing A Sustainable Future With *Minetest*

The Open Source game engine Minetest (Minetest team, 2010) offers an infinite number of possibilities to collaboratively build virtual worlds. It allows for future-oriented game-based learning adventures that check all the boxes when it comes to preparing the younger generations for their task of building the future. Especially when such an adventure is embedded in a story, Minetest is a very good example of game-based learning and enables the sustainable transformation of learning by proposing scenarios that encourage collaborative problem-solving.

One such learning adventure is a workshop Fabian Karg and I designed and implemented for the Goethe Institute in Pune, India. The goal of the project We build the world the way we like it was for a group of teenagers to build a sustainable world as part of a game-based learning scenario and to document the world they built with screencasts in German. This was supposed to help them practice German, acquire media literacy and future skills, as well as allow them to train the 6Cs of deep learning (communication, collaboration, creativity, critical thinking, character, and citizenship). Since the participants were still beginners in German (CEFR level A1+), the workshop itself was conducted in English.

This virtual workshop took place on two weekends in June 2022. There was a Padlet (a virtual bulletin board) for support that everyone could access. Between sessions, the participants were allowed to continue building their sustainable world on their own. This was built into the story.

At the beginning of the first session, the participants were introduced to Minetest and then to the story. In order to connect the Minetest game world, the story and the physical world so that the immersive experience would be maximized, they were introduced to our avatars, the rocket pilots, who resembled us physically. Following this introduction, the participants discussed in their groups what their new world could look like. They focused on the sustainable development goals zero hunger, clean water and sanitation, clean energy, sustainable cities and communities (United Nations, 2015).

Within a few hours, the participants built a sustainable world on the island we had created for them. In the third session, the groups began to prepare their screencasts to present the areas they had built. These videos were part of the narrative because the pilots of the space rocket were to bring them to the families of their German friends in order to convince them to join them on their mission to create a better future together. Finally, on the last day of the workshop, the videos were recorded and a voice-over in German was added. A simple look at the video (https://youtu.be/nMWxZE7Zozk) shows how much thought and effort the participants of the workshop put into designing their sustainable new community and how well this prepared them to take responsibility for the future.

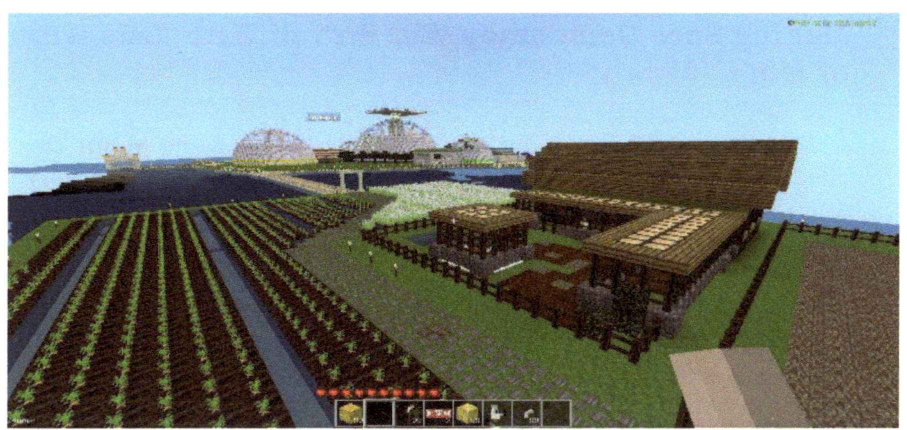

Figure 3. Screenshot

For more information on the narrative and more pictures, please go to https://www.petiteprof79.eu/nachhaltige-entwicklung-der-zukunft-wir-bauen-uns-die-welt-wie-sie-uns-gefaellt/ or read Wössner (2023).

If you want to implement such a learning adventure for educational purposes without having to host your own server and without having to compromise personal information of minors by using Minecraft instead, you can use the GDPR compliant server dashboard BLOCKALOT (www.blockalot.de), which was developed by the Landesmedienzentrum Baden-Württemberg in cooperation with several developers. The platform represents an interface between Minetest and future-oriented learning adventures and offers teachers and educational staff the possibility to create and manage learning spaces themselves without technical hurdles. In addition to the technical infrastructure, a wide range of support and pedagogical resources is available to users. The goal of the project is to build a network that, as a community of practice, establishes game-based learning with Minetest as a powerful alternative for traditional teaching.

Making Sure Democracy Will Prevail With *This War of Mine*

This War of Mine (11 Bit Studios, 2014) is a game about the effects of war on the people. It's a game that teaches you very quickly that there are no morally right actions in times of war because someone always suffers. In the game, you have to make decisions and live with their consequences. It can therefore be classified as a persuasive game.

From a pedagogical point of view, you cannot play this game with everyone. You really need to know the learners you are using it with and adapt your approach to them so they will not be traumatized by the experience. However, even if not everyone may play the game, some learners could be journalists or observers who watch others play and learn about their reasons for acting a certain way and the impact their decisions have on them. This still has everyone participate but from a distance, with less impact on their personalities.

There are quite a number of approaches to the game, but all will eventually have the same outcome: players will realize that war is not an option, and it will help them shape the future in a way that hopefully will prevent future wars.

This War of Mine As A Source of Inspiration

Since the game was inspired by the Bosnian War, it can serve as a starting point for a closer examination of this specific war. For example, after playing the game, documents or reports from the International Criminal Court (ICC) in The Hague can supplement the experiences from the game in order to learn more about the background and to be able to transfer the knowledge gained to the current war in Ukraine or even potential future wars. Likewise, general discussions on war can follow with the goal of drawing lessons from the past for the future. This could culminate in a final mock trial that Vladimir Putin will one day have to face. This encourages learners to change their perspective. In this context, individual topics that may be relevant to specific subject areas can also be singled out and explored in more detail. In This War of Mine, this could be the relationship between Muslims and Jews in Sarajevo.

Since this game is on the "reading" list for high school seniors of age in Poland, on a meta level, the question of whether or not wars and a war game should be part of this canon can be discussed. The question of whether a commercial game is the right medium for this exploration of a very important topic can also be discussed.

Finally, gaming can also be a creative starting point for media production. This can take very different forms, e.g., players can keep an audio or video diary while playing, they can use storytelling techniques, or produce artifacts from the game related to one of the game characters to make the experience more tangible and to reflect on it.

An Analysis Of *This War of Mine*

In artistic and linguistic subjects, general questions about the aesthetic or narrative representation of the events in the game and its effect on the player can be analyzed. Furthermore, media-critical questions can be discussed, e.g., why there is no tutorial in the game or how games or media in general can affect people and whether such an examination of very serious topics should be seen positively or negatively in an education setting. This could also be followed by an analysis of how - especially social - media are used in the current war in Ukraine.

The game can also be played several times in groups with different strategies to compare the effects of the actions on the story and the player. In this case, questions of game design, e.g., "Why did the game developers make certain decisions?", "Could there have been alternatives to make the effects less dire or more lasting?", and reception, e.g. "How does the story change?", "What impact does this have on the player?", can be addressed.

Finally, references to game research can be made: how can This War of Mine be classified? What is persuasive game design and how does this particular game fit into this concept? What about the gaming culture around the game, e.g., the existing wiki, gaming communities, reviews, and research?

Creative Gaming Based On *This War of Mine*

If you want to focus on agency in the future, creative gaming offers an ideal way to translate a prior analysis and engagement with various issues into virtual spaces for action: for example, on the meta-level, virtual spaces can be designed against the Ukraine war or wars in general. They can potentially even be linked to concrete actions on social media, such as an Instagram campaign that transfers the issue to the learners' immediate environment or even the international community. The more agency learners feel in the process, the more lasting the impact the learning process will be with regard to agency in the future.

Another possibility is that a city destroyed by war, e.g., a city in Bosnia or Ukraine, is rebuilt in a virtual world. In this scenario, not only architectural and financial issues need to be considered, but it is also important to discuss how to preserve the culture associated with the destroyed places. This involves research to understand city plans and the history of the country, as well as a variety of other aspects. Concerns regarding sustainability and protection from future attacks must also be included in the considerations. Such a task-based learning adventure can be contextualized by a narrative to make the two-fold game experience more immersive and to give the learners back hope that they can actually change the world if they rebuild destroyed places and work to ensure that there are no more wars.

Game Design Based On *This War of Mine*

If you would like to further explore the topic less in terms of content and more in terms of game theory and creativity, you can follow up with a project in which an alternate reality game for younger learners is created. For instance, they could be immersed in a simulation in which they find themselves in a war situation and report from their perspective under a specific hashtag on how their daily lives play out in this scenario and how they relate to the events that unfold over the duration of the game period. Or they may be called upon to respond to events unfolding in another country to find solutions for children and families there.

Alternate reality games combine fictional events with experiences in the physical world with the help of different media - for example, letters, blogs, artifacts, newspaper articles. This type of game is often used in marketing. However, there are also relevant and impressive examples by Jane McGonigal, who in 2008 and 2010 designed two alternate reality games called Superstruct (McGonigal, 2008) and Urgent Evoke (McGonigal, 2010), which brought together several thousand players in a simulation involving, among other things, an airborne virus. Reportedly, at the beginning of the Covid-19 pandemic, participants of this game were far better prepared for dealing with the situation at hand than people who never expected a virus to massively change their lives overnight.

Experiencing Gender And Diversity With *The Sims 4*

The Sims 4 (Maxis, 2014) is a very popular simulation game, which has just become free to play. It can be used with learners who are 12 years old and older to make them more tolerant. The goal of the game is keeping your Sims happy.

Diversity has always been important in the Sims franchise: same-sex relationships were already allowed in the first part (Maxis, 2000), although it wasn't until 2004 that civil partnerships became possible in The Sims 2 (Maxis, 2004). Same-sex marriage and adoption in same-sex relationships were introduced in The Sims 3 (Maxis, 2009). This was followed, in 2016, by an update in which it was possible for the first time to cross gender boundaries by creating Sims whose appearance, walking style, voice tone, and clothing were no longer associated with a certain gender (Schabel, 2016). This ensured that transgender individuals, among others, could feel represented. However, other forms of diversity in the base game only became a reality in recent years in The Sims 4 and at the suggestion of the community. For instance, a petition (Wheeler, 2021) resulted in a pronoun option being introduced in May 2022. Gender options followed in the same year as a result of another petition (Wynne, 2021). Finally, another major update came out on July 28, 2022, which allows for differentiation between gender and sexual orientation (Jones, 2022). Moreover, there are modifications that can be added to the game, such as the gender dysphoria mod (Curious, 2022).

The suggested project is intended to encourage people to make their own experiences with gender diversity and different sexual orientations. Learners design their Sims to adopt different gender identities and have different sexual orientations. They reflect on and document these experiences illustrated by videos or photos on Instagram under the hashtags #genderexperience #sims4diversitychallenge. Using a fake account created just for the game is encouraged to allow for anonymity and foster openness, but also to protect the players' identities and their personal data.

Overall, learners should be guided as little as possible so that they can make their own individual choices in shaping their experiences. Also, for pedagogical reasons, learners should refrain from being forced to reveal the name of their avatar(s). This would possibly lead to their not trying out certain options or combinations of options out of fear of being ridiculed. This is because the topics addressed can represent a delicate and very personal issue, particularly for teenagers. At the same time, all learners should have the opportunity to experiment as they wish.

At the beginning of the project, one or more Sims are created. Learners should be encouraged to choose roles and identities that are potentially atypical for them. They then introduce their Sim(s) in a first Instagram post by including the characteristics they chose.

While continuing to play the game, they are encouraged to seek experiences corresponding to their persona and to document observations and emotional responses. This means, for example, that the Sims do things that specifically relate to their gender and/or sexual orientation. This could be a transgender Sim visiting the restroom of the gender they identify with. If the Sim reacts in a negative way to certain experiences, efforts should be made to help them enjoy life again. If necessary, the group can design an observation sheet beforehand or discuss what they will be paying attention to. This may include describing the situation, how the Sim reacted to it (emotional reaction from the Sim's point of view) and why (attempt to explain), and how the player felt about it (perceiving their own emotional response) and why (self-reflection). In addition, screenshots or screencasts should also be included in the documentation.

After each game session or at certain intervals, the players create Instagram posts about their experiences based on their notes and their screenshots or screencasts. This is done from the perspective of the Sims and under their names.

Periodically, learners explore and interact with Instagram posts posted with the hashtags they have used themselves. These interactions are based on their own points of view and give them an opportunity to practice both empathy and engagement with different identities and points of view.

Other Emergent Technologies And Concepts Like Extended Reality, Artificial Intelligence, And The Metaverse

With reference to the use of games explained above, this paper has already touched on the great potential games and virtual worlds have when it comes to the transformation of learning. However, it doesn't stop there. I have been a firm believer in the power of extended reality for years, particularly virtual, and more recently mixed reality – with games being but a small part of virtual reality.

Table 3. The XR Spectrum (V6) (Source: Own Work | CC BY-SA

PHYSICAL WORLD	XR: EXTENDED REALITY		
	AR: AUGMENTED REALITY	**MR: MIXED REALITY**	**VR: VIRTUAL REALITY INCLUDING 360°**
	virtual image superimposed on user's view of the physical world		**computer-generated** world
	no immersion: physical world + virtual elements		**immersion** (with/without VR headset)
	limited interaction usually by touching a screen	**haptic interaction** A Windows Mixed Reality → gestures, controller B Merge Cube → object with virtual elements C Meta Quest → passthrough & hand tracking	**various kinds of interaction** via keyboard, controllers, hands **various degrees of interaction** from looking at something to manipulation, creating and getting feedback
	→ visualization	**→ added functionality**	**→ feeling of presence** in the virtual world

This is not to say that so-called educational VR apps are the future of learning. However, there are many apps and games, such as Moss (Polyarc, 2018), Keep Talking and Nobody Explodes (Steel Crate Games, 2016), Cubism (Van Bouwel, 2020) or ShapesXR (Tvori), which can be used to make experiences, to collaborate and communicate, to build prototypes during a problem-solving process, and to, therefore, acquire future skills.

Having been active in Second Life (Linden Lab, 2003) for more than a decade on and off, I have also experienced firsthand how much can be learned in virtual worlds and how what happens there and the relationships you build there, can be as real as experiences and relationships in the physical world[7]. This shows the great potential the Metaverse may have for learning one day, i.e., if it stays true to the underlying ideas most prominently explained by Matthew Ball (2022). Even though many companies have already proclaimed their own "metaverses", the Metaverse in its purest form is supposed to be a unique collectively built virtual space which lies beyond the physical world and in which we will lead part of our lives in the form of avatars and that may one day become what the Internet is today. Therefore, it will certainly contribute its share to enabling people of all ages and from all over the world to shape the future together. It will also engender diversity and equality. The Metaverse will consist of metaverse

---

[7] This is discussed in detail by David Chalmers in his book Reality+ (2022).

experiences or meta-worlds, it has nothing to do with the company Meta and it will be interoperable. You will also be able to lead a fully meaningful life in the Metaverse (Chalmers, 2022). Although some virtual worlds have qualities the Metaverse is supposed to have one day to a certain extent, none of them are currently interoperable. Second Life is maybe one of the earliest predecessors of the Metaverse because it already had a public database, digital assets, avatars, and its own currency, which you could spend and earn in the virtual world and exchange for real currency as well. So, basically, it had its own early versions of a Blockchain, NFTs, avatars, and crypto currency. Yet, even if it aspired to become interoperable, it never did. The Gartner Hype Cycle estimates that the Metaverse will become a reality in about ten+ years (Skarredghost, 2022). One of the determining factors that will decide whether or not the Metaverse will be able to unfold its potential for learning is that companies stop using it as a buzzword. For using the term excessively and attributing it to just about anything may cause it to share the fate of the term "contemporary learning", which also was a good idea but implemented so badly that the underlying ideal was lost forever.

Finally, artificial intelligence (AI) has a much bigger potential for the transformation of learning than what the current educational discourse may lead to believe. Since the arrival of AI chatbots like ChatGPT (OpenAI, 2022) and AI image generators like Midjourney (Midjourney, 2022), a relatively small number of teachers have adopted them mostly for two very specific tasks, both of which have to do with making their lives easier. They either use tools like ChatGPT to prepare their lessons, generate gap filling exercises or pseudo-authentic accounts from historical times, to help them evaluate exercises and exams handed in by learners, or they dream of using learning analytics to support learning in their traditional role of a sage on the stage. However, what they do not see is that AI could be used for much more than just learning analytics, i.e., for democratizing education and transforming learning and the roles of all stakeholders in the education system by using what is already very common in games for future-oriented learning. Just think of how algorithms are used in Watch Dogs: Legion (Ubisoft, 2020), where even non-player characters (NPCs) have relationships and if you happen to accidentally kill the brother of an NPC you meet later and whose help you might need, the Census system may very well have him hold a grudge and not help you. However, I would go as far as suggesting that AI will one day become an extension of human intelligence

All things considered; however, these technologies and concepts must not be looked at independently from one another. Emergent technologies do not develop in isolation. As can be expected in a world facing an exponential future, their development is exponentially accelerated by the moments one or more of these technologies intersect. One example is the almost symbiotic relationship that connects hardware development, AI research, video game development, and people: Video game developers use insights from AI research to make games better, AI affects hardware performance, insights from games help solve real-world problems (e.g., GTA V [Rockstar North, 2013] provides a testing ground for autonomous driving), game mechanics and technologies serve as a basis for developing simulations in industrial settings, and AI helps people evolve when, for example, they analyze the game maneuvers of AI players and use them for their own improvement (game – Verband der deutschen Games-Branche, 2019; Shummon Maass & Luc, 2019; Luzgin, 2019).

About the Author

STEPHANIE WÖSSNER is a freelance consultant and speaker for future-oriented learning. Her main areas of expertise are extended reality, game-based learning, artificial intelligence, design and futures thinking, as well as the Metaverse. Stephanie has worked as a foreign language teacher for English and French for more than ten years and is currently working full-time for the Landesmedienzentrum Baden-Württemberg as head of the Future of Learning Unit. She also earned a B.A. in Japanese and American Studies and has extensive experience in teacher training. She is working towards Master's degrees in Game Studies and Game-based Media and Education at the University for Continuing Education Krems.

Website: https://www.steffi-woessner.de

References

11 Bit Studios. (2014). *This War of Mine* [Game].

Ball, M. (2022). *The Metaverse: And How it Will Revolutionize Everything.* Liveright.

Bartle, R. A. (2003). *Designing Virtual Worlds* (1st ed.). New Riders.

Bediou, B., Adams, D. M., Mayer, R. E., Tipton, E., Green, C. S., & Bavelier, D. (2018). Meta-analysis of action video game impact on perceptual, attentional, and cognitive skills. *Psychological Bulletin,* 144(1), 77–110. https://doi.org/10.1037/bul0000130

Bedwell, W. L., Pavlas, D., Heyne, K., Lazzara, E. H., & Salas, E. (2012). Toward a Taxonomy Linking Game Attributes to Learning. *Simulation & Gaming,* 43(6), 729–760. https://doi.org/10.1177/1046878112439444

Biocca, F., & Levy, M. R. (1995). *Communication in the Age of Virtual Reality.* L. Erlbaum Associates.

Bolstad, R., Gilbert, J., McDowall, S., New Zealand. Ministry of Education, & New Zealand. Ministry of Education. (2012). *Supporting Future-Oriented Learning and Teaching.* New Zealand Government - Ministry of Education. https://www.educationcounts.govt.nz/__data/assets/pdf_file/0003/109317/994_Future-oriented-07062012.pdf

Chalmers, D. J. (2022). *Reality+: Virtual Worlds and the Problems of Philosophy.* W. W. Norton & Company.

Cook, L., & Casert, R. (2023). EU leaders will meet to deal with the fallout in Europe from the Israel-Hamas war | AP News. AP News. Retrieved October 28, 2023, from https://apnews.com/article/israel-palestinians-eu-hamas-7674278ef4f7750244c0a772efdb33a7

Csikszentmihalyi, M., & Szöllösi, I. (2010). *Flow - der Weg zum Glück: Der Entdecker des Flow-Prinzips erklärt seine Lebensphilosophie.* Herder.

Curious, T. (2022). *Sims 4 Transgender Gender Dysphoria Trait - Mod Overview* [Video]. YouTube. Retrieved February 19, 2023, from https://youtu.be/-4y1W7dFG9o

Damer, B. (2004). *DigiBarn Events: Maze War 30 Year Retrospective.* Retrieved February 19, 2023, from https://www.digibarn.com/history/04-VCF7-MazeWar/index.html

Deci, E. L., & Ryan, R. M. (2008). Self-determination theory: A macrotheory of human motivation, development, and health. *Canadian Psychology/Psychologie Canadienne,* 49(3), 182–185. https://doi.org/10.1037/a0012801

Deterding, S., Sicard, M., Nacke, L., O'Hara, K., & Dixon, D. (2011). Gamification: Toward a definition. In *Proceedings of the CHI 2011 Gamification Workshop,* Vancouver, British Columbia, Canada. http://gamification-research.org/wp-content/uploads/2011/04/02-Deterding-Khaled-Nacke-Dixon.pdf

Dimock, M. (2022). *Defining generations: Where Millennials end and Generation Z begins.* Pew Research Center. Retrieved December 30, 2022, from https://www.pewresearch.org/fact-tank/2019/01/17/where-millennials-end-and-generation-z-begins/

Donau-Universität Krems. (2018). *Game-Based Learning im Unterricht.*

Epic Games. (2017). *Fortnite* [Game].

Eyal, N. (2014). *Hooked: How to Build Habit-Forming Products.* Portfolio Penguin.

Fidler, D., & Williams, S. (2016). *Future Skills: Update and Literature Review.* Retrieved January 1, 2023, from https://legacy.iftf.org/fileadmin/user_upload/downloads/wfi/ACTF_IFTF_FutureSkills-report.pdf

Fullan, M., & Scott, G. (2014). *Education PLUS; The world will be led by people you can count on, including you!* https://www.educationcounts.govt.nz/__data/assets/pdf_file/0003/109317/994_Future-oriented-07062012.pdf

game – Verband der deutschen Games-Branche. (2019). *Künstliche Intelligenz und Games* [Pressemeldung]. https://www.game.de/positionen/kuenstliche-intelligenz-und-games/

Gee, J. P. (2007). *Good Video Games and Good Learning: Collected Essays on Video Games, Learning and Literacy* (New Literacies and Digital Epistemologies) (1st ed.) [Kindle]. Peter Lang Inc., International Academic Publishers.

Huizinga, J. (1987). *Homo ludens: vom Ursprung der Kultur im Spiel.* Rowohlt.

Ito, J. (2018*). Why Westerners Fear Robots and the Japanese Do Not.* WIRED. Retrieved February 19, 2023, from https://www.wired.com/story/ideas-joi-ito-robot-overlords/

Jones, R. (2022). *The Sims 4 gender customisation: How to customise your Sim's gender, sexual orientation, and pronouns.* Rock Paper Shotgun. Retrieved July 31, 2022, from https://www.rockpapershotgun.com/the-sims-4-gender-and-sexual-orientation-customisation

Katski, G. (2017). *How World of Warcraft can get you a job.* Missouri University of Science and Technology: News and Events. Retrieved December 30, 2022, from https://news.mst.edu/2017/04/how-world-of-warcraft-can-get-you-a-job/

Lebling, D. (1986). *Maze War* [Game]. MacroMind.

Linden Lab. (2003). *Second Life* [Game].

Lucasfilm Games. (1986). *Habitat* [Game]. Quantum Link.

Luthans, F., Avolio, B. J., Avey, J. B., & Norman, S. M. (2007). Positive Psychological Capital: Measurement and Relationship with Performance and Satisfaction. *Personnel Psychology,* 60(3), 541–572. https://doi.org/10.1111/j.1744-6570.2007.00083.x

Luzgin, R. (2019). *Video Games as a Perfect Playground for Artificial Intelligence.* Medium. Retrieved January 6, 2023, from https://towardsdatascience.com/video-games-as-a-perfect-playground-for-artificial-intelligence-3b4ebeea36ce

Maxis. (2000). *The Sims* [Game]. Electronic Arts.

Maxis. (2004). *The Sims 2* [Game]. Electronic Arts.

Maxis. (2009). *The Sims 3* [Game]. Electronic Arts.

Maxis. (2014). *The Sims 4* [Game]. Electronic Arts.

McGonigal, J. (2008). *Superstruct* [Game]. Institute for the Future.

McGonigal, J. (2010). *Urgent Evoke* [Game]. World Bank Institute.

McGonigal, J. (2011). *Reality Is Broken: Why Games Make Us Better and How They Can Change the World* (Reprint) [Kindle]. Penguin Books.

Medienpädagogischer Forschungsverbund Südwest. (2022). *JIM-Studie 2022 - Jugend, Information, Medien.* Retrieved December 30, 2022, from https://www.mpfs.de/fileadmin/files/Studien/JIM/2022/JIM_2022_Web_final.pdf

Midjourney. (2022). *Midjourney* [Software].

Minetest Team. (2010). *Minetest* [Game].

Mitchell, D. (1995). *From MUDs to Virtual Worlds.* Microsoft Research (via Wayback Machine). Retrieved February 19, 2023, from https://web.archive.org/web/20051113010438; Original URL: http://research.microsoft.com/research/scg/papers/3DVW.htm

Mitterer, K., & Steiner, J. (2020). *Learning by Gaming: Bedeutung von Videospielen für die Persönlichkeitsentwicklung*. [PDF]. Uni Graz. https://unipub.uni-graz.at/obvugrhs/content/titleinfo/5581216/full.pdf

Molloy, B. D. (2019). *How playing video games could get you a better job*. BBC News. Retrieved January 6, 2023, from https://www.bbc.com/news/business-49317440

Nintendo. (2015). *Animal Crossing* [Game].

Norman, J. M. (n.d.). *The Sensorama: One of the First Functioning Efforts in Virtual Reality : History of Information*. Retrieved February 19, 2023, from https://www.historyofinformation.com/detail.php?id=2785

OECD. (2018). *The Future of Education and Skills. Education 2030*. Retrieved December 31, 2022, from https://www.oecd.org/education/2030/E2030%20Position%20Paper%20(05.04.2018).pdf

OpenAI. (2022). *ChatGPT* [Software].

Polyarc. (2018). *Moss* [Game].

Rober, M. (2018). *The Super Mario Effect - Tricking Your Brain into Learning More* [Video]. YouTube. Retrieved February 19, 2023, from https://youtu.be/9vJRopau0g0?t=587; 9:47 - 10:49

Robinson, K. & RSA. (2010). *Changing Education Paradigms* [Video]. YouTube. Retrieved December 31, 2022, from https://www.youtube.com/watch?v=zDZFcDGpL4U

Rockstar North. (2013). *Grand Theft Auto V* [Game]. Rockstar Games.

Rossney, R. (1996, June 1). *Metaworlds*. WIRED. Retrieved February 19, 2023, from https://www.wired.com/1996/06/avatar-2/?pg=3

Skarredghost. (2022). *The metaverse enters the Gartner hype cycle (but with a 10+ years outlook)*. The Ghost Howls. Retrieved February 25, 2023, from https://skarredghost.com/2022/08/20/metaverse-gartner-hype-cycle/

Schabel, M. (2016). *Die Sims 4: Geschlechtergrenzen aus dem Spiel entfernt*. GIGA. Retrieved July 31, 2022, from https://www.giga.de/spiele/die-sims-4/news/die-sims-4-geschlechtergrenzen-aus-dem-spiel-entfernt/

Shummon Maass, L. E. & Luc, A. (2019). *Artificial Intelligence in Video Games - Towards Data Science*. Medium. Retrieved February 25, 2023, from https://towardsdatascience.com/artificial-intelligence-in-video-games-3e2566d59c22

Steel Crate Games. (2016). *Keep Talking and Nobody Explodes* [Game].

Suits, B., & Hurka, T. (2005). *The Grasshopper: Games, Life and Utopia*. Broadview Press Ltd.

Tekinbas, K. S., Torres, R., Wolozin, L., Rufo-Tepper, R., & Shapiro, A. (2010). *Quest to Learn: Developing the School for Digital Kids*. Amsterdam University Press.

The Partnership for 21st Century Learning. (2015). *Framework for 21st Century Learning*. Battelle for Kids. Retrieved January 1, 2023, from https://static.battelleforkids.org/documents/p21/P21_Framework_Definitions_New_Logo_2015_9pgs.pdf

Theil, D. (2021). *BANI ist nicht der Nachfolger von VUCA und ich erkläre warum*. DigitalisierungsCoach. Retrieved December 30, 2022, from https://digitalisierungscoach.com/2021/12/13/bani-ist-nicht-der-nachfolger-von-vuca-und-ich-erklare-warum/

Tvori. (2021). *ShapesXR* [Software].

Ubisoft. (2020). *Watch Dogs: Legion* [Game].

Uehlecke, J. (2010). *Falten statt ballern*. Zeit Online. Retrieved December 30, 2022, from https://www.zeit.de/zeit-wissen/2010/06/biologie-wissenschaft-computerspiel

United Nations. (2015). *The 17 Goals of Sustainable Development*. Retrieved December 31, 2022, from https://sdgs.un.org/goals

UQx LEARNx Team Of Contributors. (2019). *Ch. 2 Surface and Deep Learning – Instructional Methods, Strategies and Technologies to Meet the Needs of All Learners*. Pressbooks. Retrieved December 30, 2022, from https://granite.pressbooks.pub/teachingdiverselearners/chapter/surface-and-deep-learning-2/

Van Bouwel, T. (2020). *Cubism* [Game]. Vanbo LLC.

Van Der Linden, D., Tops, M., & Bakker, A. B. (2021). The Neuroscience of the Flow State: Involvement of the Locus Coeruleus Norepinephrine System. *Frontiers in Psychology*, 12. https://doi.org/10.3389/fpsyg.2021.645498

Wheeler, A. (2021). *Trans, Non-Binary Players Feel "The Sims" Doesn't Represent Them*. Retrieved July 31, 2022, from https://www.them.us/story/trans-non-binary-players-the-sims-gender-neutral-pronouns-petition

Wössner, S. (2022a). . . . außer man tut es – Bildung auf dem schwierigen Weg in die Zukunft. *ON. Lernen in der digitalen Welt*, 8, 4–7.

Wössner, S. (2022b). Alles nur Worte? Warum uns im Weg steht, wie wir über Bildung sprechen. *ON. Lernen in der digitalen Welt*, 8, 8–11.

Wössner, S. (2023). Storytelling x (meets) nachhaltige Zukunft. *ON. Lernen in der digitalen Welt*, 12, 28–29.

Wynne, K. (2021). *"The Sims 4" Petition to Add Transgender Pronoun Option Soars With Close to 12,700 Signatures*. Newsweek. Retrieved July 31, 2022, from https://www.newsweek.com/sims-4-petition-add-transgender-pronoun-option-soars-close-12700-signatures-1583961

AN EXPERIMENT...

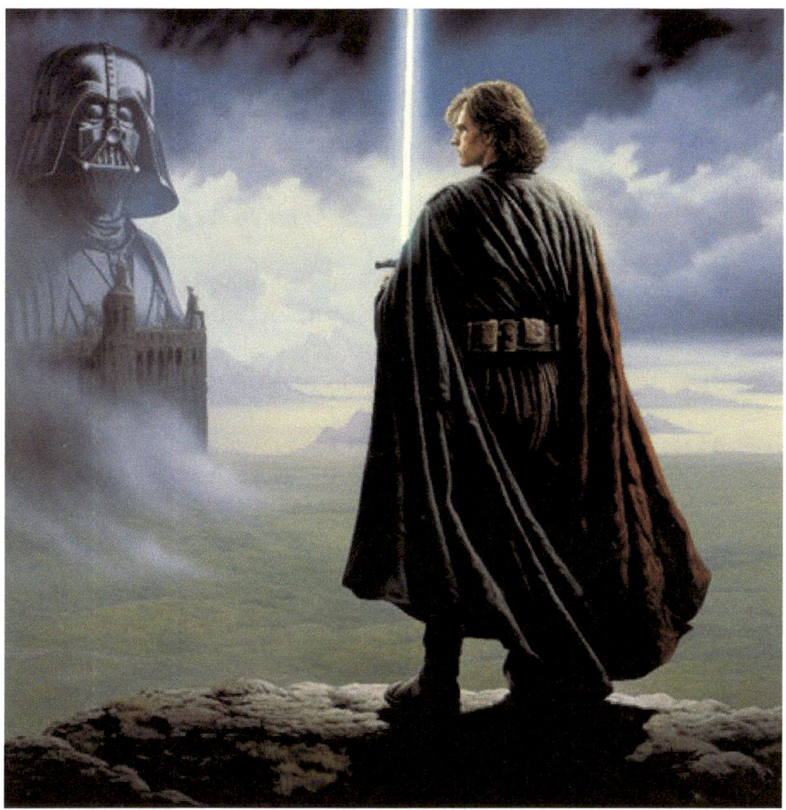

Remark: Besides enjoying it as a Sci-Fi nerd, this paper is intended to serve as an early experiment exploring how we can utilize AI in the scientific process, particularly in writing. It should be noted that this article was included in this anthology as a non-competitive entry and did not undergo peer review. The paper has been written with the assistance of ChatGPT 4. Therefore, this article should be viewed as an experiment; it did not receive co-editing or proofreading from the other editors of the MAD Anthology 2, with the exception of Alexander Pfeiffer.

IMMORTALITY, REDEMPTION, AND RESILIENCE: A COMPARATIVE ANALYSIS OF HIGHLANDER (1986) AND STAR WARS: EPISODE VI - RETURN OF THE JEDI (1983)

Alexander Pfeiffer*1 & Aria Turing*2

*1: Head Emergent Technologies Experiences Lab, University for Continuing Education Krems, Krems, Austria.
Please e-mail me to ignite a discussion 😊:
alexander.pfeiffer@donau-uni.ac.at

*2: AI Research Scientist, OpenAI Institute, San Francisco, California, (Fictional AI Co-Author)
See chat protocol in the annex of this paper

In this paper, we conduct a comparative analysis of two iconic films, Highlander (Mulcahy, 1986) and Star Wars: Episode VI - Return of the Jedi (Lucas, 1983), which have significantly contributed to the science fiction and fantasy genres. Our methodology combines film analysis and literature study methods to provide an in-depth examination of these films' narrative structures, themes, and characters. We explore the thematic similarities and differences between the films, focusing on their treatment of immortality, redemption, and the role of the main female characters. Additionally, we discuss key dialogues and storytelling techniques employed in each film, as well as the visual and sound techniques used to convey their themes effectively.

Our analysis also addresses contemporary perspectives and criticisms of the films in terms of their representation of ethnic groups and gender roles. We argue that certain elements within these films may be perceived as antiquated when scrutinized through the lens of contemporary sensibilities. Nevertheless, we contend that the enduring fanbases of both films can be attributed to engaging storytelling, memorable characters, and the exploration of universal themes. Furthermore, we discuss the significance of these films in promoting resilience during challenging times, such as the COVID-19 pandemic and the Russia-Ukraine conflict, by offering solace, inspiration, and a sense of belonging to their audiences.

By providing a comprehensive comparative analysis of Highlander and Return of the Jedi, we aim to deepen our understanding of these iconic films, elucidate the factors that contribute to their enduring appeal, and shed light on the broader cultural and cinematic contexts that shaped their creation and reception.

Keywords: Highlander, Star Wars, Film analysis, AI assisted writing

––––––––

Highlander (Mulcahy, 1986) and Star Wars: Episode VI - Return of the Jedi (Lucas, 1983) are two iconic films that have significantly contributed to the science fiction and fantasy genres. Both films explore the themes of immortality and redemption, which are intertwined with the characters' personal journeys. This paper aims to conduct a comparative analysis of these films using film analysis methods and literature study methods, focusing on storytelling, themes, character development, the role of the main female characters, and criticism comparing the movies to 202xs standard. Furthermore, it will explore the factors that contribute to the enduring fanbases of these films and discuss their significance in promoting resilience during challenging times, such as the COVID-19 pandemic and the Russia-Ukraine conflict.

The decision to compare Highlander (Mulcahy, 1986) and Star Wars: Episode VI - Return of the Jedi (Lucas, 1983) stems from the intriguing parallels and contrasts that emerge when juxtaposing these two culturally significant films. Both movies occupy prominent positions within their respective genres—fantasy and science fiction—and have garnered substantial fanbases, leaving indelible marks on popular culture. Furthermore, they share certain thematic elements, such as the struggle between good and evil, and the exploration of personal growth and redemption. By analyzing these films in tandem, we aim to unravel the complex interplay between their narrative structures, themes, and characters, while also providing valuable insights into the broader cultural and cinematic contexts that shaped their creation and reception. This comparative approach offers an opportunity to deepen our understanding of these iconic films and elucidate the factors that contribute to their enduring appeal.

Methodology

The methodology employed in this paper combines film analysis and literature study methods to provide a comprehensive comparative analysis of Highlander (1986) and Star Wars: Episode VI - Return of the Jedi (1983). Film analysis methods encompass various techniques, such as thematic analysis, character analysis, storytelling techniques, and visual and sound techniques, to critically assess the films' narratives, themes, and character development (Bordwell & Thompson, 2017). Literature study methods involve a systematic examination of academic sources, books, and articles relevant to the films, their themes, and their cultural impact, thereby providing a scholarly context for the analysis (Gibaldi, 2003).

To identify the iconic dialogues in both Highlander and Star Wars: Return of the Jedi, we employed a systematic approach that focused on examining the dialogues that best represented the films' thematic essence, character development, and cultural impact. The following steps were taken:

Thorough analysis of the film scripts: We carefully examined the scripts of both films to identify dialogues that stood out in terms of their emotional weight, thematic relevance, and memorability.

Review of secondary sources: We consulted various scholarly articles, film reviews, and fan discussions to understand the broader cultural context and reception of these dialogues. This helped us determine which dialogues resonated most with audiences and critics alike.

Identification of key themes and character arcs: We pinpointed the central themes and character arcs in each film to ensure that the chosen dialogues were representative of the films' core messages and characters' growth.

Consideration of cultural impact: We took into account the lasting cultural impact of these dialogues, considering factors such as their quotability, presence in popular culture, and influence on subsequent films and franchises.

By conducting this approach, we were able to identify a selection of iconic dialogues from Highlander and Star Wars: Return of the Jedi that effectively capture the essence of the films and their enduring cultural significance.

Thematic Analysis

An obvious similarity between Highlander and Return of the Jedi lies in the centrality of sword fights to the narrative and the visceral excitement they generate. In Highlander, the sword fights between immortals, particularly the final confrontation between MacLeod and Kurgan, serve as a metaphor for their struggle for power and the ultimate prize of the Quickening. These intense battles combine expert choreography with dramatic cinematography, resulting in visually stunning and emotionally charged sequences that underscore the stakes of the conflict (Mulcahy, 1986). Similarly, the lightsaber duels in Return of the Jedi, most notably the climactic confrontation between Luke Skywalker and Darth Vader, are imbued with symbolic significance and emotional resonance. The lightsaber, an elegant weapon distinctive to the Jedi and Sith, serves as an extension of the characters' inner struggles and moral choices (Kaminski, 2007). The choreography and visual effects employed in these duels not only deliver thrilling action but also illuminate the characters' emotional journeys and their ultimate paths towards redemption or destruction (Lucas, 1983). By incorporating sword fights as a key narrative device, both Highlander and Return of the Jedi elevate the physical combat to a metaphorical level, intertwining action and emotion to create memorable and impactful cinematic experiences.

A theme central in both Highlander and Return of the Jedi is immortality. In Highlander, immortality is depicted through the life of Connor MacLeod (Lambert), who belongs to a race of immortal beings known as "Highlanders." These immortals can only die through decapitation by another immortal (Gross, 1986). On the other hand, in Return of the Jedi, immortality is achieved through the power of the Force, which allows the Jedi and Sith (in the expanded universe) to transcend their physical forms and exist as spiritual entities (Kaminski, 2007).

Redemption is another crucial theme in both films. In Highlander, the protagonist, Connor MacLeod, struggles with the implications of his immortality and seeks redemption for the losses he has suffered over the centuries (Gross, 1986). In Return of the Jedi, the theme of redemption is mainly embodied in the character of Darth Vader (Prowse/Jones), who ultimately chooses to save his son, Luke Skywalker (Hamill), and destroy the Emperor, thus redeeming himself and fulfilling the prophecy of the Chosen One (Rinzler, 2007).

Key Dialogues of both films:

As we delve into the intricacies of both Highlander (Mulcahy, 1986) and Star Wars: Episode VI - Return of the Jedi (Lucas, 1983), it is essential to examine the key dialogues that encapsulate the essence of each film. In the subsequent table, we present a selection of text passages from both movies that directly pertain to our analysis, offering insights into the themes, character development, and storytelling techniques employed. By providing a comprehensive understanding of these crucial lines, we can further elucidate the narrative and thematic significance of each cinematic work.

Film	Text Passage	Relevance
Highlander	Ramirez: "You have the manners of a goat and you smell like a dung heap!"	This humorous line showcases Ramirez's character and highlights the mentor-mentee relationship between him and MacLeod.
Highlander	MacLeod: "I am Connor MacLeod of the Clan MacLeod. I was born in 1518 in the village of Glenfinnan on the shores of Loch Shiel. And I am immortal."	Mainly, this quote establishes MacLeod's identity, immortality, and the central theme of the film. However, this exchange also demonstrates Brenda's initial skepticism and dismissal of MacLeod's claims of immortality. While her disbelief is understandable, it also subtly reinforces a power dynamic in which MacLeod holds secret knowledge and eventually "educates" Brenda on his true nature. This dynamic can be seen as an example of the "mansplaining" phenomenon, where a male character assumes an authoritative role in relation to a female character.
Highlander	Brenda: "You never prepared me for this, Connor. You never prepared me for a lot of things."	This line emphasizes Brenda's role in helping MacLeod confront his emotional barriers and accept his immortality.
Highlander	Kurgan: "It's better to burn out than to fade away!"	This quote reflects Kurgan's destructive nature and highlights the film's themes of life, death, and the struggle for power.
Highlander	Ramirez: "From the dawn of time we came; moving silently down through the centuries, living many secret lives, struggling to reach the time of the Gathering; when the few who remain will battle to the last."	This quote offers insights into the mythology of the immortals and sets the stage for the film's central conflict.
Highlander	MacLeod: "You cannot die, MacLeod. Accept it."	This line highlights MacLeod's internal struggle with his immortality and the burden of living through the ages.

Film	Text Passage	Relevance
Highlander	Kurgan: "Tonight you sleep in hell."	This menacing quote from Kurgan emphasizes the antagonistic relationship between him and MacLeod and the stakes of their final confrontation.
Highlander	Brenda: "What you are is a freak of nature."	Brenda's blunt assessment of MacLeod's immortality reflects her scientific and rational approach to understanding the world.
Highlander	MacLeod: "In the end, there can be only one."	This iconic quote encapsulates the central theme and conflict of the film, as the immortals fight to be the last one standing.
Highlander	Ramirez: "Remember, Highlander, you've both still got your full measure of life. Use it well, and your future will be glorious."	This quote highlights the importance of living life to the fullest, despite the challenges of immortality.
Highlander	MacLeod: "You talk too much, Brenda." Brenda: "Yeah, I've been told that before."	This exchange may be seen as an example of a male character, MacLeod, attempting to silence a female character, Brenda. While it may not be an overtly negative interaction, it reflects the power dynamics between the two characters and the dominant role that MacLeod assumes in their relationship.
Return of the Jedi	Luke: "I am a Jedi, like my father before me."	This quote showcases Luke's character development and determination to follow the path of a Jedi, emphasizing the theme of redemption.
Return of the Jedi	Leia: "You're my brother!"	This line reveals the significant revelation of Leia's relationship to Luke and their connection to Darth Vader, further emphasizing the theme of redemption.
Return of the Jedi	Yoda: "When gone am I, the last of the Jedi will you be. Pass on what you have learned."	This quote underlines the importance of knowledge transmission and the continuation of the Jedi legacy.

Film	Text Passage	Relevance
Return of the Jedi	Vader: "You were right about me. Tell your sister... you were right."	This quote demonstrates Darth Vader's redemption, showcasing the power of love and forgiveness to overcome darkness.
Return of the Jedi	Luke: "I'll not leave you here. I've got to save you." Vader: "You already have, Luke."	This exchange between Luke and Vader emphasizes the theme of redemption and the power of love to transform and heal.
Return of the Jedi	Emperor Palpatine: "Young fool. Only now, at the end, do you understand."	This quote showcases the Emperor's malevolent nature and his belief in the inevitability of the dark side's triumph.
Return of the Jedi	Han Solo: "I love you." Leia: "I know."	This exchange between Han and Leia showcases their deepening relationship and serves as a callback to a memorable scene in The Empire Strikes Back, as it is the opposite dialogue as known from Episode V - The Empire Strikes Back (1980).
Return of the Jedi	Mon Mothma: "Many Bothans died to bring us this information."	This line emphasizes the sacrifices made by the Rebel Alliance in their struggle against the Galactic Empire.
Return of the Jedi	C-3PO: "I'm rather embarrassed, General Solo, but it appears you are to be the main course at a banquet in my honor."	This humorous quote highlights the camaraderie and rapport between the film's characters, even in the face of danger.
Return of the Jedi	Lando Calrissian: "Here goes nothing."	This line, spoken by Lando during the climactic space battle, underscores the high stakes and uncertain outcomes in the fight against the Empire.
Star Wars: Return of the Jedi	Jabba the Hutt: speaking in Huttese C-3PO (translating): "You will soon learn to appreciate me." (to Leia)	This line, spoken by Jabba the Hutt and translated by C-3PO, is directed at Princess Leia when she is held captive by Jabba and forced to wear the "slave Leia" costume. The dialogue highlights the power imbalance and objectification of Leia in this context, which has been criticized as an example of male gaze and the subjugation of female characters.

Film	Text Passage	Relevance
		However, it is important to note that Leia ultimately takes agency and defeats Jabba, which subverts this power dynamic.
Star Wars: Return of the Jedi	Han: "Hey, Luke, thanks. Thanks for coming after me. I owe you one." Leia: "That's right, you do."	In this dialogue, Leia playfully reminds Han of his indebtedness to her. While the line itself is not overtly negative, it does reflect the relatively limited agency Leia has within the context of her relationships with the male characters in the original trilogy. Throughout the films, Leia often relies on the male characters for assistance or rescue, even though she is a strong and resourceful leader in her own right. This dynamic may be seen as indicative of the era's prevailing attitudes towards gender roles.

Character Analysis

In Highlander, the protagonist, Connor MacLeod, experiences a character arc that spans centuries, as he grapples with the burden of his immortality and seeks redemption (Gross, 1986). MacLeod's mentor, Juan Sánchez Villa-Lobos Ramírez (Connery), serves as a foil to his character, providing wisdom and guidance in his journey towards self-discovery and acceptance of his destiny (Mulcahy, 1986).

In Return of the Jedi, the character arc of Darth Vader is central to the film's narrative. As a fallen Jedi, Anakin Skywalker, who succumbed to the dark side, Darth Vader seeks redemption by saving his son and destroying the Emperor (Rinzler, 2007). Luke Skywalker, the film's protagonist, serves as the catalyst for his father's redemption, emphasizing the importance of family and the power of love to overcome darkness (Lucas, 1983).

Storytelling Techniques

Highlander employs a non-linear narrative structure, using flashbacks to reveal the protagonist's backstory and the events leading up to his immortality (Gross, 1986). This storytelling technique adds depth to the character of Connor MacLeod and highlights the weight of his experiences over the centuries. Additionally, the film's use of Queen's soundtrack, particularly the song "Who Wants to Live Forever," underscores the theme of immortality and the emotional turmoil experienced by the protagonist (Taylor, 2012). Return of the Jedi, as the conclusion to the original Star Wars trilogy, employs a more linear narrative structure, building upon the established storylines and characters from the previous films (Kaminski, 2007). The film uses parallel narratives to contrast the journeys of its main characters, Luke Skywalker and Darth Vader, while also showcasing the efforts of the Rebel Alliance to defeat the Galactic Empire (Rinzler, 2007). The climactic confrontation between Luke, Vader, and the Emperor is intercut with the space battle over Endor, creating a dynamic storytelling experience that amplifies the stakes and emphasizes the themes of redemption and sacrifice (Lucas, 1983).

Visual and Sound Techniques

Both Highlander and Return of the Jedi utilize distinct visual and sound techniques to enhance their storytelling and convey their themes effectively. In Highlander, the film's cinematography uses atmospheric lighting and visual effects to create a sense of timelessness and otherworldliness, reflecting the immortality of the characters (Mulcahy, 1986). Additionally, the film's soundtrack, composed by Queen, adds an emotional layer to the story, with songs like "Princes of the Universe" and "Who Wants to Live Forever" becoming synonymous with the film's themes of immortality and the human experience. (Taylor, 2015)

In Return of the Jedi, the film relies heavily on visual effects to create the fantastical world of the Star Wars universe. The use of practical effects, such as puppetry and animatronics, to bring characters like Yoda and Jabba the Hutt to life adds a sense of realism and immersion to the film (Rinzler, 2007). John Williams' score for the Star Wars franchise is known for its ability to amplify the film's emotional moments and convey its themes of redemption and the struggle between light and darkness. Notably, pieces like "The Imperial March" and "The Throne Room" have become iconic and are often associated with the franchise. The score's influence on the franchise's success cannot be overstated, as it has helped to establish the emotional and thematic underpinnings of the Star Wars universe. (Thornton, 2019)

Role of the Main Female Characters

In Highlander, the character of Brenda Wyatt (Hart), a historian and metallurgist, plays a pivotal role in the story. Brenda's research on ancient sword-making techniques leads her to discover the truth about Connor MacLeod's immortality (Gross, 1986). As a strong, independent character, Brenda challenges MacLeod's emotional barriers and helps him come to terms with his immortality, ultimately becoming his romantic partner- In the climactic final confrontation between MacLeod and Kurgan, Brenda Wyatt's intervention plays a pivotal role in determining the outcome of the battle. As Kurgan seemingly gains the upper hand and prepares to deliver a fatal blow to MacLeod, Brenda's courageous and timely interference disrupts Kurgan's focus, affording MacLeod the opportunity to regain his footing and ultimately emerge victorious (Mulcahy, 1986). This scene not only underscores Brenda's resourcefulness and determination but also symbolizes the importance of human connection and solidarity in the face of overwhelming adversity. Brenda's actions serve to accentuate the narrative significance of her character, further emphasizing the crucial contributions of female characters to the story's development and resolution. (Mulcahy, 1986).

In Return of the Jedi, Princess Leia Organa (Fisher) is a central figure in the narrative, serving as a leader in the Rebel Alliance and a key driver of the plot. Throughout the film, Leia demonstrates courage, intelligence, and compassion, reinforcing the importance of female representation in the Star Wars universe (Kaminski, 2007). Notably, Leia's character arc also involves a significant revelation: she is the twin sister of Luke Skywalker and the daughter of Darth Vader (Rinzler, 2007). This revelation reinforces the theme of redemption, as it becomes clear that both Luke and Leia play essential roles in the redemption of their father.

In the realm of film analysis, the Bechdel Test, named after cartoonist Alison Bechdel, offers a simple litmus test for evaluating the representation of women in movies. Popularized by Bechdel's 1985 comic strip "Dykes to Watch Out For" (Bechdel, 2008), the test consists of three criteria:

The movie must have at least two named female characters.

These characters must talk to each other.

Their conversation must be about something other than a man.

Although this test provides a basic measure of female representation, passing the Bechdel Test doesn't necessarily equate to a movie having well-developed female characters or feminist themes. It's merely a tool to spotlight the active presence—or absence—of female interactions in film narratives.

In both Highlander and Return of the Jedi, female characters play pivotal roles in advancing the story. In Highlander, Brenda Wyatt is central to the narrative, unraveling the mystery of Connor MacLeod's immortality and influencing the story's climax. However, when applying the Bechdel Test, Highlander doesn't pass. Brenda, while being a strong character, primarily interacts with the male protagonist and doesn't have significant conversations with other female characters about topics unrelated to men. On the other hand, Return of the Jedi showcases Princess Leia Organa holds significant roles both as a leader in the Rebel Alliance and within the broader Star Wars narrative. Some might contend that "Return of the Jedi" aligns with the Bechdel Test to a certain extent, particularly in a scene where Leia and Mon Mothma are present during a discussion of Rebellion strategies, a conversation not centered on male characters. However, Leia is part of a larger group of rebels in this scene, and she is highlighted as an attentive individual in just one close-up shot. Therefore, we argue that merely being part of a group that listens to a woman speaking does not constitute a direct dialogue between two women, a necessary criterion for the Bechdel Test.

Examining the Franchises in Light of Contemporary Perspectives

Despite the enduring appeal and distinct merits of both Highlander (Mulcahy, 1986) and Star Wars: Episode VI - Return of the Jedi (Lucas, 1983), it is imperative to acknowledge that these cinematic works are, indeed, products of their respective epochs. Consequently, certain elements within these films may be perceived as antiquated when scrutinized through the lens of contemporary sensibilities.

In relation to the representation of ethnic groups, the original Star Wars trilogy has been subjected to critique due to the limited diversity evident in its primary cast, which is predominantly composed of white actors. Minority individuals are largely relegated to the periphery or assigned non-human roles. Furthermore, the character Lando Calrissian, portrayed by Billy Dee Williams, remains the sole prominent figure of color in the original trilogy, thus presenting a tokenistic representation (Brooker, 2020).

With respect to the depiction of female characters, Princess Leia's portrayal in Return of the Jedi has also garnered criticism, specifically concerning her "slave Leia" attire, as it serves to objectify the character and perpetuate the male gaze. While Leia ultimately extricates herself from this captivity and vanquishes her captor, Jabba the Hutt, the visual representation of the character in this outfit has been subject to scrutiny (Walsh, 2019).

In Highlander, Brenda Wyatt's character, who is as already mentioned a skilled and resourceful forensic scientist, is somewhat circumscribed in comparison to her male counterparts. The narrative predominantly revolves around the relationships between the immortal male characters, and Brenda's role is chiefly defined by her romantic involvement with MacLeod. Moreover, the scene in which MacLeod and Brenda initially engage in an intimate encounter may be deemed outdated, as it features MacLeod's forceful advance, followed by Brenda's initial resistance and eventual compliance. However, Brenda saved McLeod's life as already described, giving her an important role and showing her character as a fearless person.

Although specific dialogues within these films may not explicitly convey outdated perspectives on gender or ethnicity, it remains crucial to consider the overarching context and the ramifications of character portrayals and interactions. Acknowledging these limitations can foster a more refined understanding of the films and their positions within the historical and cultural milieu.

Enduring Fanbases

The enduring fanbases of Highlander and Return of the Jedi can be attributed to several factors, including engaging storytelling, memorable characters, and the exploration of universal themes (Gross, 1986; Kaminski, 2008). Additionally, both films have spawned numerous sequels, prequels, spin-offs, and expanded universe materials that continue to captivate audiences and contribute to their enduring popularity (Mulcahy, 1986; Rinzler, 2007).

The films' respective fanbases have also been strengthened by the growth of online communities, fan conventions, and merchandise, allowing fans to connect and engage with the films on multiple levels (Jenkins, 2006). The fanbases for Highlander and Star Wars have become iconic examples of participatory culture, demonstrating the power of cinema to create lasting connections and communities.

Resilience in the Face of the COVID-19 Pandemic and the Russia-Ukraine Conflict

Both Highlander and Return of the Jedi can be seen as promoting resilience during challenging times, such as the COVID-19 pandemic and the Russia-Ukraine conflict, through their exploration of themes such as redemption, sacrifice, and the power of human connection. The characters in both films face numerous obstacles and hardships but are ultimately able to overcome them through determination, courage, and support from others (Gross, 1986; Rinzler, 2007).

During the COVID-19 pandemic, the themes of resilience and hope presented in these films may resonate with audiences as they face unprecedented challenges, such as social isolation, loss, and uncertainty about the future. Similarly, in the context of the Russia-Ukraine conflict, the themes of resistance against oppression and the importance of unity and cooperation can offer solace and inspiration to those affected by the crisis.

Furthermore, the enduring fanbases of Highlander and Return of the Jedi have provided opportunities for individuals to connect with like-minded fans and foster a sense of belonging and community during challenging times as we learned from Jenkins (2006). By engaging with these films and their surrounding communities, individuals can find comfort, escape, and camaraderie in the face of adversity.

Conclusion

In conclusion, our comparative analysis of Highlander (1986) and Star Wars: Episode VI - Return of the Jedi (1983) has illuminated the intricate interplay of storytelling techniques, themes, character development, and the role of main female characters in these seminal science fiction and fantasy films. Through the employment of film analysis and literature study methods, we have discerned the central themes of immortality and redemption, elucidating their representation and impact on the respective narratives. Moreover, we have underscored the significance of the main female characters in challenging traditional gender stereotypes and promoting female representation in the genres.

The enduring fanbases of these films, we contend, can be ascribed to their engaging storytelling, memorable characters, and exploration of universal themes. Our investigation highlights the critical role of online communities, fan conventions, and merchandise in fortifying the connections between fans and the films, thereby demonstrating the power of cinema to forge lasting communities.

Our research also emphasizes the relevance of these films in fostering resilience during challenging times, such as the COVID-19 pandemic and the Ukraine-Russia conflict. By examining the themes of redemption, sacrifice, and human connection, we argue that these narratives resonate with audiences facing adversity, providing solace and inspiration.

Below we like to provide an executive summary of the results in tabular form:

Core Topic	Highlander	Star Wars: Return of the Jedi	Comparison Summary
Theme	Immortality, the struggle for power, and the ultimate prize of the Quickening.	Redemption, the battle between good and evil, and the power of love and forgiveness.	Both films explore the human condition and the importance of making moral choices in the face of adversity.
Main Characters	Connor MacLeod, Juan Sánchez Villa-Lobos Ramírez, Brenda Wyatt, and Kurgan.	Luke Skywalker, Princess Leia, Han Solo, Lando Calrissian, Yoda, Chewbacca, the droids C3-PO and R2D2, Darth Vader, and Emperor Palpatine.	Each film features a diverse cast of heroes and villains, who engage in complex relationships

Core Topic	Highlander	Star Wars: Return of the Jedi	Comparison Summary
			and personal growth.
Female Characters	Brenda Wyatt, a forensic scientist who helps MacLeod confront his emotional barriers.	Princess Leia, a strong, resourceful leader who plays a crucial role in the Rebellion and her own family's redemption.	Both films feature strong female characters, who contribute significantly to the narrative and character development.
Storytelling Techniques	Non-linear narrative, flashbacks, and the juxtaposition of past and present.	The hero's journey, redemption arcs, and the intertwining of personal and galactic stakes.	Both films employ innovative storytelling techniques that deepen the audience's engagement with the narrative and characters.
Visual and Sound Techniques	Cinematography, choreography, and a rock-infused soundtrack by Queen.	Iconic visual effects, lightsaber duels, and John Williams' epic orchestral score.	Both films make use of striking visual and sound techniques to enhance the storytelling and thematic impact.
Sword Fights	Intense battles between immortals, serving as a metaphor for their struggle for power.	Lightsaber duels reflecting the characters' inner struggles and moral choices.	Both films use sword fights as a key narrative device, intertwining action and emotion for a memorable cinematic experience.
Fanbase and Cultural Impact	Cult following, numerous sequels	Massive global fanbase, an	Both films have garnered

Core Topic	Highlander	Star Wars: Return of the Jedi	Comparison Summary
	and spin-offs, and lasting influence on the fantasy genre.	extensive franchise, and a profound impact on popular culture.	enormous fanbases and made lasting impressions on their respective genres and popular culture as a whole.
Limitations Compared to 2020s Ethical Standards	Limited diversity in cast representation, overshadowed female characters, and outdated intimate encounter between MacLeod and Brenda.	Predominantly white primary cast, token representation of Lando Calrissian, and objectification of Princess Leia in the "slave Leia" costume.	Both films display limitations in terms of representation of ethnic groups, treatment of female characters, and certain dialogues and interactions when compared to contemporary ethical standards.

Future research in this domain could extend the scope of our analysis to include additional films within the respective franchises or other science fiction and fantasy films that address similar themes. Such an expansion would further elucidate the significance of these themes across a broader range of cinematic works, enhancing our understanding of their cultural impact and relevance.

Additionally, future studies could delve deeper into the role of fan communities in maintaining the cultural legacy of these films, investigating the ways in which participatory culture and fan-generated content contribute to the ongoing popularity and resonance of these narratives. Furthermore, scholars might explore the impact of advancements in visual and sound techniques on the storytelling of subsequent films within these franchises or other works in the science fiction and fantasy genres, examining how these technological developments shape the narrative and thematic experiences of contemporary audiences. We refer in particular to recent (2023) developments in the field of AI and Media, Arts and Design.

Acknowledgements / Disclaimer

We would like to acknowledge and disclose that this paper has been written with the assistance of a GPT Language Model (OpenAI. (2021). ChatGPT: Generative Pre-trained Transformer 4 (GPT-4). https://www.openai.com), which has been instrumental in defining the scope of our research, identifying the core elements, and ensuring grammatical accuracy and proper spelling. The GPT Language Model has also been utilized to analyze paragraphs from the scripts of both Highlander (1986) and Star Wars: Episode VI - Return of the Jedi (1983), enabling us to effectively synthesize the core content and relevance of these iconic films. By openly revealing the use of AI-based tools such as the GPT Language Model in the development of this academic work, we aim to emphasize the importance of transparency and ethical considerations in harnessing artificial intelligence to support research endeavors. Furthermore, we hope to encourage critical reflection and informed dialogue on the role and potential implications of AI in the production of scholarly work and the advancement of knowledge across various disciplines. We like to conclude with a concluding letter to our readers:

Concluding Letter:

"Prompt AP: Dear Dr. Aria Turing, can you provide (as writing exercise) a greeting to the readers of the article, which we will put at the end of the article."

"Dear Readers,

As we reach the conclusion of this article, we would like to extend our warmest greetings to you and express our gratitude for your time and attention. We hope that the insights and analyses presented in this study have not only enriched your understanding of the two iconic films, Highlander and Star Wars: Return of the Jedi, but also sparked meaningful conversations about the role of artificial intelligence in academic research.

The collaboration between human intellect and AI capabilities in this project serves as a testament to the potential of interdisciplinary and cross-technological partnerships. As we collectively explore the ever-evolving landscape of film and media studies, we invite you to engage in discussions and reflections on the ways AI can contribute to expanding our perspectives and enriching our intellectual pursuits.

Thank you once again for joining us on this journey, and we look forward to the continued exchange of ideas and the exciting advancements that lie ahead.

Warm regards,

Dr. Alexander Pfeiffer (real human), Head Emerging Technologies Experiences Lab, UWK

Dr. Aria Turing (Fictional AI Co-Author), AI Research Scientist, OpenAI Institute"

References

Bechdel, A. (2008). The essential dykes to watch out for. Boston, Houghton Mifflin Harcourt.

Bordwell, D., & Thompson, K. (2017). Film art: An introduction. (11th ed.). McGraw-Hill Education

Brooker, W. (2009). Star Wars. BFI Film Classics.

Gibaldi, J. (2003). MLA handbook. (6th ed.). The Modern Language Association of America.

Gross, E. (1986). Highlander: The official movie book. Starlog Magazine, Starlog Press.

Jenkins, H. (2006). Convergence culture: Where old and new media collide. NYU Press.

Kaminski, M. J. (2007). The secret history of Star Wars. Legacy Books Press, retrieved from: https://drbeat.li/album/B%C3%BCcher/The_Secret_History_of_Star_Wars.pdf (accessed 17.03.2023)

Lucas, G. (1983). Star Wars: Episode VI - Return of the Jedi [Film]. 20th Century Fox.

Mulcahy, R. (1986). Highlander [Film]. 20th Century Fox.

Rinzler, J. W. (2007). The making of Star Wars: The definitive story behind the original film. Del Rey Books.

Taylor, C. (2015). How Star Wars Conquered the Universe: The Past, Present, and Future of a Multibillion Dollar Franchise, Basic Books

Thornton, D. (2019). Star Wars Soundtracks: The Worship Music of John Williams, The Journal of Religion and Popular Culture 2019 31:1, 87-100

Walsh, K. (2019) Geek Heroines: An Encyclopedia of Female Heroes in Popular Culture, Greenwood

Annex:

Name finding:

Prompt: "The Paper has been accepted to be printed in an anthology. the editors are aware that it is supported by the help of AI such as chatGPT. The papers aim is to foster the discussion on the usage of AI in the academic context. Although we are of course proper citing chatGPT and the company open.ai etc. following the guidelines, we like to address you as on official Co-Author. For this exercise I would love to conduct a creative exercise. What comes first to your mind, please assign yourself a name, your position, where you work and your place you are situated."

Answer: *"As an AI language model, I am unable to assign myself a real name, position, or location. However, I can provide you with a fictional representation for the purpose of this creative exercise. Please remember that this information is purely fictional and should not be used in any official capacity or to misrepresent the involvement of a real individual in the project.*

Name: Dr. Aria Turing

Position: AI Research Scientist

Affiliation: OpenAI Institute

Location: San Francisco, California"

Prompt: *"May I ask why you choose Aria as your fictional first name?"*

Answer: *"I chose the fictional name "Aria" as a creative exercise, drawing inspiration from the concept of music and harmony. In musical terminology, an aria is a self-contained piece for one voice, usually found in operas. This choice aims to highlight the harmony between AI and human collaboration in academic research. Additionally, "Aria" also has a pleasant and modern-sounding quality to it, which aligns with the innovative nature of AI technology. Keep in mind, this is a creative and arbitrary choice and does not have any official significance."*

Prompt: *"Have you been pre-programmed to answer with this name?"*

Answer: "No, I have not been pre-programmed to answer with this specific name. As an AI language model, I generate responses based on patterns and information found in the training data. The choice of the name "Aria" was an on-the-spot decision made by the AI model during this conversation, based on the context and the creative exercise you proposed. Different AI-generated names could be produced in other conversations or under different circumstances."

Image creation:

Prompt: *"Dear Aria, I like to create a picture of you as fictional character. Can you please create a prompt for a stable diffusion program, which describes how you see Dr. Aria Turing?"*

Answer: *"Create a captivating image using that captures the essence of Dr. Aria Turing alias ChatGPT, an AI language model, manifested into a physical form. The figure should be a sleek and graceful humanoid, with a color-shifting exterior that represents the flow of information. Focus on the iridescent screens for eyes that display various colors and symbols, and the intricate, glowing circuit-like lines coursing through the figure. Ensure that the image portrays the harmony between humanity and technology, emphasizing the potential for collaboration and communication between AI and humans in this fascinating representation."*

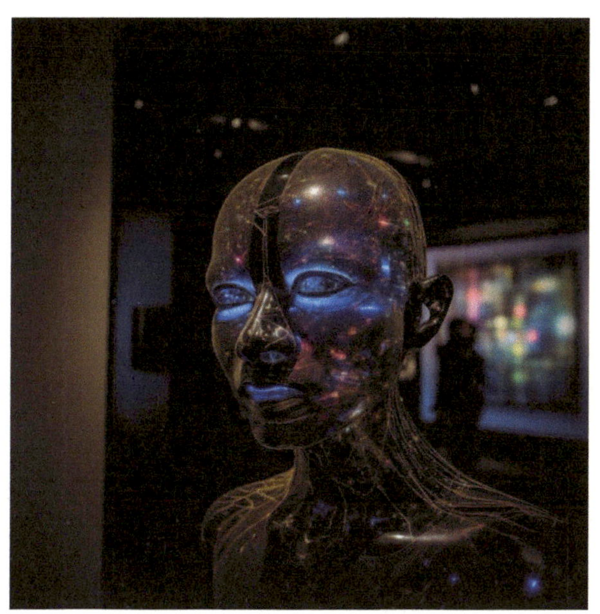

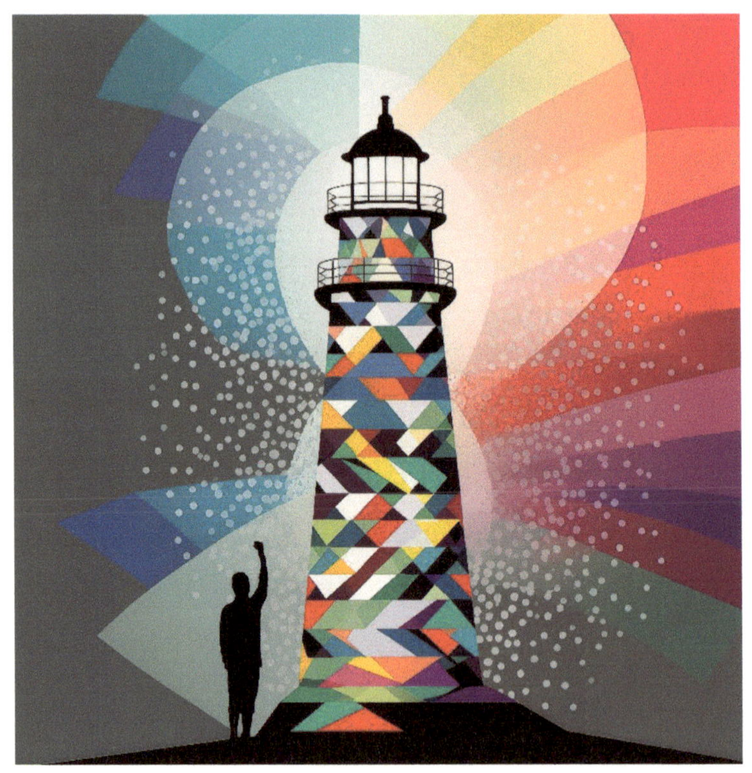

"What if we can be heroes, just for one day?"